BV
2369
.G7
C37
2003

IMPERIAL BIBLES, DOMESTIC BODIES

MARY WILSON CARPENTER

IMPERIAL BIBLES, DOMESTIC BODIES

Women, Sexuality, and Religion
in the
Victorian Market

OHIO UNIVERSITY PRESS   ATHENS

Ohio University Press, Athens, Ohio 45701

© 2003 by Ohio University Press

Printed in the United States of America

Ohio University Press books are printed on acid-free paper ∞ ™

12 11 10 09 08 07 06 05 04 03   5 4 3 2 1

Chapter 5, "'A Bit of Her Flesh,'" first appeared
(in slightly different form) in *Genders* 1 (spring 1988): 1–23.
Some of the material in chapter 6, "Victorian Schemes of the Apocalypse,"
first appeared in an earlier version as
"Representing Apocalypse: Sexual Politics and the Violence of Revelation"
in *Postmodern Apocalypse: Theory and Cultural Practice at the End,*
ed. Richard Dellamora
(Philadelphia: University of Pennsylvania Press, 1995).

Library of Congress Cataloging-in-Publication Data

Carpenter, Mary Wilson, 1937–
    Imperial Bibles, domestic bodies : women, sexuality, and religion in the Victorian
    market / Mary Wilson Carpenter.
        p. cm.
    Includes bibliographical references (p.) and index.
    ISBN 0-8214-1515-8 (cl : alk. paper)
        1. Bible—Publication and distribution—Great Britain—History—19th century. 2.
Family—Religious life—Great Britain—History—19th century. 3. Christian women—Religious life—Great Britain—History—19th century. 4. Sex—Religious aspects—Christianity—History of doctrines—19th century. 5. Christian literature—Publication and
distribution—Great Britain—History—19th century. 6. English literature—Women authors—History and criticism. 7. English literature—19th century—History and criticism.
8. Sex in literature. I. Title.

BV2369.G7C37 2003
220'.0941'09034—dc21

                                                                                2003056310

FOR MY *Mother*

CONTENTS

ILLUSTRATIONS

ACKNOWLEDGMENTS

Any book that has been in progress as unusually long as this one is necessarily indebted to an unusually large number of colleagues, friends, and
institutions. First, I wish to thank my colleagues in the English department at Queen's University, most of whom have contributed in various
ways to my work on the book—whether by providing interested discussion, or simply by supplying that all-important element, sympathy. Paul
Stevens read a portion of the manuscript, as did Marguerite Van Die of
the Department of History and Queen's Theological College, both providing encouragement and helpful comments for which I am especially
grateful. Members of the Queen's University community who participated in the Nineteenth-Century Interdisciplinary Studies Forum also
broadened my critical perspective, as did the earlier Critical Colloquium
organized by Clive Thomson, who urged me on in the writing of several
earlier versions of chapters of this book. My participation in the founding
of a women's studies program at Queen's University introduced me to a
number of outstanding feminist scholars. Among these Roberta Hamil-
ton, who also struggles with a life divided between different locations for
work and family, has been especially inspiring to me. Among the many
Canadian colleagues beyond Queen's University whose support and friendship has been crucial to the completion of this book, I name particularly
Richard Dellamora and Marjorie Stone. Finally, I thank the many graduate students who have challenged and stimulated my own critical thinking, both in graduate seminars and in the dissertations I supervised. Special
recognition and thanks go to Colette Colligan and Angela Mills, whose
expert research assistance not only contributed substantially to the listing
of British commercial Family Bibles provided in the appendix to this
book, but gave new meaning to the term "teamwork."

Numerous friends and colleagues at universities in the United States
have also contributed to the vision and revisions of this book. Eve Kosofsky

Sedgwick's brilliant work has undoubtedly been the single most important scholarly influence on my work, and her equally extraordinary personal generosity has opened doors for me—as for many others—time and again. Through her agency, I met Sally Blazar, Mary Baine Campbell, Susan Carlisle, Anne Janowitz, Nancy Munger, Beth O'Sullivan, Marie Plasse, Helaine Ross, Deborah Swedberg, Martha Sweezy, Nancy Waring, Carolyn Williams, and Patricia Yaeger, members of the feminist collective ID 450, whose warm friendship and intellectual companionship has uniquely enriched my writing and my life. Kathryn Bond Stockton and Paula Bennett read sections of the manuscript, and their differing disciplinary perspectives provided insights that might not otherwise have been available to me. Barbara Kiefer Lewalski and George P. Landow have continued their interest in and support of my work long beyond the dissertation that became my first book, as did Roger Henkle until his untimely death. Christina Crosby, Barbara Johnson, Joseph Litvak, Tricia Lootens, Susan O'Malley, Ruth Perry, and Linda Peterson have all exemplified the collegial acquaintance that warms and enlivens one's personal as much as one's professional life. My membership in the MLA Commission on the Status of Women in the Profession provided not only invaluable experience in feminist political activism, but the friendship of Shirley Nelson Garner and Margaret Higonnet, both of whom generously shared their professional expertise.

My work on this book has been supported by three grants from the Social Sciences and Humanities Council of Canada, a fellowship at the Mary Ingraham Bunting Institute of Radcliffe College (now Harvard University), an American Council of Learned Societies fellowship, and two research grants provided by Queen's University. These grants provided not only funding for the necessary research travel and one semester of released time from teaching, but important feedback from the anonymous but highly knowledgeable referees. My year at the Bunting Institute, then under the leadership of Florence Ladd, was an unforgettable experience of interdisciplinary community. I also thank the anonymous readers for Ohio University Press and David Sanders, whose energetic and informed response to my work has made working with him a pleasure, even under pressure.

To the six grandchildren who have made their appearance during the gestation of this book—Abigail, Louisa, Isaiah, Emery, Cole, and Avery—goes my appreciation for making sure my life has been full of excitement. To my three daughters—Cindy, Deborah, and Grace—who have found time to support and encourage their mother's career while pursuing fast-paced, double-track careers of their own, go my admiration, gratitude, and love. Their partners—Jesse, Jim, and Neal—continually inspire me with their commitment to their families as well as their work. My deepest thanks go to my husband Ken, who has shared the struggles and rewards of research, and who, in the course of our long-term international-commuting relationship, has picked up many other useful skills, most importantly that of becoming a very good cook.

INTRODUCTION

AUTHORIZED VERSIONS, UNAUTHORIZED SEXUALITIES

The Victorian Woman Writer as Religious Consumer

The research project that was to become this book began as a serendipitous discovery. While turning over the pages of one of those massive books in which the British Library not so long ago maintained its catalog (now transmuted into banks of computers), I noticed an unusual number of English bibles that included the word "family" in their titles. Counting up, there seemed to be well over eighty editions of bibles with such self-advertising titles as *The Grand Imperial Family Bible* or *The National Comprehensive Family Bible*. They ranged historically from the early eighteenth century through the late nineteenth. Assuming that these were characteristic of "family bibles" anywhere, I made a list of them and filed it away so I could examine them at more leisure after my return to North America.

I had just completed my research for a chapter in a projected book on Victorian women writers' "subversive hermeneutics," or transgressive constructions of gender and sexuality articulated in relation to their readings of that most "authorized" text, the English bible. In order to gain some understanding of these women writers' contexts for reading and interpreting the bible, I had researched such genres as nineteenth-century bible commentaries, dictionaries, and encyclopedias, works on "prophecy" and the Apocalypse, tracts and hymns for the working classes, sermons, and local church histories. But this was my first realization that commercial "Family Bibles with Notes" might be an important resource for learning how British families read their bibles, or how their bibles read *them,* interpellating them as certain kinds of "authorized version" subjects. Although I soon made a surprising and frustrating discovery—no American or Canadian library had a substantial collection of these British family bibles—I eventually was able to return and study those in the British Library en masse.[1] (They were "en masse" in size as well as number.) This study led to the recognition that these English family bibles were in fact a uniquely British institution.[2] Their publication was first motivated by a restriction on English Bible printing peculiar to Britain: only those printers with a royal license were permitted to print the King James or Authorized Version of the scriptures in Britain or its colonies, in contrast with post-Revolutionary America. Enterprising printers in the consumer culture of early-eighteenth-century London began to print bibles with additional materials—notes and illustrations—with the apparent intention of evading the licensing restriction. They issued these bibles with their ostentatious titles in serialized parts or "numbers," here with the apparent intention of securing a larger market. These English Family Bibles, then, were specifically national from their origins: their commodification of the "family" for commercial purposes constructed that family as an *English* family (later as a British and imperial family), as their packaging of the bible presented it as the icon of the British national religion. It is true that in the nineteenth century, American printers began to publish Family Bibles, and British Family Bibles were both marketed and published on the other side of the Atlantic.[3] But the English Family Bible with Notes came into existence as a distinctively national commodity, and so it remained, designed and redesigned to appeal to the changing desires of British family consumers.

This recognition revised my conception of the Victorian women writers whose "subversive hermeneutics" I had been investigating. They were *consumers* in a national religious consumer culture, subjects formed in what Colleen McDannell has aptly termed "material Christianity." Their religion was not simply Christian, nor even Protestant or Anglican, Evangelical or dissenting: it was part of a burgeoning mass market of commercial religious publication and other religious "goods." In this mass market the Victorian woman was positioned as both profitable commodity—the domestic angel identified with British "family values" who could be exported around the globe in the illustrations and notes of Family Bibles—and, in

Elizabeth Langland's equally appropriate term, as "material angel," a consumer of religious commodities such as printed texts or pictures.⁴ The commercial religious business both exploited her and catered to her, restricted the dimensions of her identity and endowed her as privileged customer.

The distinction between a "consumer culture" and a "commodity culture" is important here. As Elizabeth Kowaleski-Wallace explains in her study of British women as shoppers:

> Distinguished from *commodity culture,* a term derived from a Marxian theory of commodities, consumer culture is often employed by cultural anthropologists, some sociologists, and cultural historians to refer to a range of human investments in, attitudes toward, and behaviors around consumer goods. Though its precise definition varies, depending upon the discipline of the definer, most scholars employing the term hold the basic assumption that, in a modern society, goods carry a wide range of meanings. If, before the modern period, goods already conveyed status, consumer objects became, with the growth of wide-scale consumption, "an expression and guide to social identity."⁵

The Victorian women writers on whose work I focused, then, were to be understood not merely as captives of a reigning Protestant capitalist ideology, but as active participants in a market in part defined by their choices of what to buy. If, as "domestic angels," they must also function as "material angels," ornamenting their homes with objects that would enhance the family's social status and affirm its national as well as class identity, then not only the content, but the design and packaging of commercial religious publication were significant and instructive in the formation of these "domestic bodies" and their reading of their imperial Family Bibles.

I came to this conclusion simultaneously with the recognition that commercial religious publications in Britain was largely uncharted territory. The reasons for this absence would appear to be the same as those McDannell cites for the neglect of studies of religious material culture in American Christianity. First, literary scholars, like historians, have established a dichotomy between "the sacred and the profane, spirit and matter, piety and commerce that constrains our ability to understand how religion works in the real world."[6] Second, most scholarship also subscribes to a hierarchical definition of what constitutes the "religious": "meaningful Christianity" is defined by theologians, reformers, and church leaders, while practices such as the buying of bibles (or the publication and sale of them) are considered less "spiritual" or "authentic" and largely ignored (McDannell, 8). Leslie Howsam's *Cheap Bibles* is an important exception to the ideological barriers manifest in British studies to such material aspects of religion as the capitalist economics of the King James or "Authorized Version" of the bible.[7] Although the bibles she studies—published by the British and Foreign Bible Society—eschewed all inducements to customers such as illustrations or notes of any kind, their very emphasis on "cheapness" and lack of interpretive apparatus situates them in relation to bibles *with* illustrations and notes, but sold in parts in order to make them "cheap." The cheap bibles published by the British and Foreign Bible Society were competing in a marketplace with other editions of the bible that might appeal to consumers more, and that might therefore construct those consumers' reading of the bible in ways other than those believed to be best by the officers of the Society. Those who opted for the purchase of commercial Family Bibles in parts might, for example, be as interested in the illustrations as in the text, or they might be looking for a Family Bible which, when bound, would make a visible testimony to the family's piety and respectability. Or again, as this study proposes, the purchase of a Family Bible might be motivated by a "genealogical romance"—the desire to possess an emblem of an ancient and honorable family pedigree, perhaps especially when any pedigree at all was lacking. The British and Foreign Bible Society may be seen, therefore, as motivated in part by a desire to *control* family bible reading, rather than to "free" it from "sectarian" or even secular interpretations.[8]

In Victorian literary scholarship, the apparent reluctance to address commercial religious publication seems also to derive from two lapses curious indeed in this era of widespread critical acceptance of poststructuralist theory and, particularly, of Michel Foucault's discourse theory. First, with a few important exceptions, most Victorianists tend to treat the Victorian reader's relationship to the bible as unmediated. George P.

Landow's *Victorian Types, Victorian Shadows* and Herbert L. Sussman's *Fact into Figure: Typology in Carlyle, Ruskin, and the Pre-Raphaelite Brotherhood* examine typological readings in Victorian Britain, but other Victorian interpretive approaches to bible reading have been neglected.[9] It is as if, until the importation of the German "higher criticism," Victorians are assumed never to have consulted reference works on the meaning of biblical texts, but always to have approached their bibles with only their own consciences to guide them. The impressive quantity and variety of commercial religious publication—Family Bibles, Family Bible dictionaries, bible commentaries, Christian gift books, to name a few—should persuade us of the reality of consumer demand for these materials, and therefore of their importance in determining how the Victorians read their bibles. Commercial religious publication can be defined as those religious texts produced primarily with an eye to their salability. They must, therefore, be accepted as "popular" in at least that sense, and consequently central to cultural studies in Victorian religion. It is here that we will find Victorian religion, not as the history of ideas, but as genealogy.

The second lapse in Victorian literary scholarship pertaining to religion is even more curious in view of the pervasive references in this field to Foucault's *History of Sexuality*.[10] In contrast with literary studies in earlier periods of British history, such as Richard Rambuss's *Closet Devotions,* Victorian literary scholars tend to repress issues of sexuality in their studies of Victorian religion.[11] Again, there are some important exceptions here: scholars of gay male sexuality—most notably, Ellis Hanson in his *Decadence and Catholicism*—have ventured into this field.[12] And of particular relevance to this study, Kathryn Bond Stockton and Irene Tayler have both considered eroticism in their analyses of Charlotte Brontë's biblical allusions.[13] But many scholars of Victorian literature as informed by the religious beliefs of Victorian writers omit all reference to sexuality or eroticism, thereby reproducing Foucault's repressive hypothesis: though "we other Victorians"—because we are liberated—may speak about sex in relation to our own religion, the Victorians must have been silent on this forbidden intercourse.

In fact, it is tempting to speculate that if Foucault had had access to the commercial Family Bibles published in Britain, he might have substituted the English rite of "family prayer" for the rite of confession he takes as paradigm—and historical origin—for the disciplinary production of desire. By the last quarter of the eighteenth century, these Family Bibles were defining and pathologizing the homosexual as a "species" of sorts, anticipating the work of the late-nineteenth-century sexologists that Foucault takes as foundational by a hundred years or so. In the early part of the nineteenth century, Family Bibles contained instructions to confine to the "closet" those parts of the bible considered "unsuitable" for the "family," by which was meant women, children, and servants. In as near-perfect an illustration as can be imagined of the truth of Foucault's theorem that repression led, not to silence, but to the proliferation of discourses on sex, these Family Bibles actually marked the "parts" that should be confined to the closet and withheld from women, children, and persons of the lower classes. I feel I must repeat, because it is difficult to believe, that these "private parts" were not *omitted* from the bible, but *marked*.14 Obviously, not only the "Master of the family," but women and working-class people, and quite possibly even children, could gain access to these disciplinary Family Bibles: they were sold on the open market, in affordable, serialized parts, and they were, presumably, kept in the family parlor. The marking of parts that should be omitted from family reading amounted to instruction on the nature of extrafamilial sexualities, among other matters.

This study of the production and consumption of commercial religious literature in Victorian culture is divided into two parts. In part one, "The Authorized Version in the Marketplace," I begin with three chapters analyzing the commercial British Family Bibles and their changing constructions of "family values" over two centuries. Ruth Perry notes that "the advantage of literary evidence . . . results from its potential to de-familiarize our unthinking assumptions about the family."15 My hope is that by approaching the British family from the supposedly familiar vantage point of the Family Bible, this work will de-familiarize both bible and family. Chapter 1, "Consumer Christianity: Family Bibles and Family Values on the Installment Plan," describes the origins, publication, and format of "Family Bibles with Notes" in the eighteenth century, emphasizing especially their promotion of "universal knowledge" for the family and their simultaneous, contradictory exposure of sex/gender knowledge that appears to have exceeded the limits of that "universal knowledge."

Chapter 2, "Closeting the Family Bible and the Family," takes up the sudden appearance of disciplinary Family Bibles in the early nineteenth century, and their separation of sexual knowledges into those appropriate for the family and those to be confined to the "closet." This chapter demonstrates the increasing tendency to assign extrafamilial sexualities to racialized others, and the production of British national and imperial identity as guaranteed by its "family religion." In chapter 3, "Family Bibles and Family Angels," I describe the production—parallel to that of the disciplinary Family Bibles—of Family Bibles that appear to cater to the English woman, increasingly foregrounding her in bible illustrations and making other alterations to the Family Bible format in an apparent attempt to appeal to feminine customers.

Part two, "Consuming the Authorized Version," analyzes the construction of gender and sexuality in literary texts by Victorian women in relation to three other specific genres of Victorian commercial religious publication: dissenting bible commentaries sold in installments, Family Bible dictionaries, and popular apocalyptic interpretations. Although these other genres of commercial religious publication in Victorian England are distinct from the Family Bibles discussed in part one, they also both merge into those Family Bibles and emerge from them. The publishers and editors of commercial Family Bibles unhesitatingly appropriated notes from commentaries, dictionaries, and encyclopedias, and the publishers and editors of reprinted commentaries, dictionaries, and encyclopedias freely mixed in "new" materials from Family Bibles. Similarly, interpretations of the Book of Revelation borrowed from the notes in Family Bibles, commentaries, dictionaries, and encyclopedias. These other genres of commercial religious publication, then, represent modes of consuming the Authorized Version, as do the literary texts packed with biblical quotations and written by Victorian women.

The first two chapters in part two demonstrate how our reading of Victorian discourse on taboo sexual topics may be expanded through recourse to some of the vast commercial publication on the bible: Charlotte Brontë's *Villette* is shown to be pervaded by a menstrual "language" when read in the context of bible commentary produced by dissenting clergy, and George Eliot's treatment of circumcision in her "Jewish novel," *Daniel Deronda,* can be usefully explored by consulting the Protestant debate on circumcision as represented in family bible dictionaries. In these two chapters I exploit psychoanalytic theory, primarily Jacques Lacan's, to read sexual subjectivities produced in discursive formations. But I also make use of new historicist strategies to expose the traditionalist formation and gender bias of Lacan's writings on the "Phallus."

The last of the chapters in part two deals with Victorian apocalyptics—or those expositions and exploitations of the Book of Revelation that were, and continue to be, so popular, sensational, and financially lucrative a genre. Victorian Protestant apocalyptics were almost exclusively reactionary—anti-Catholic, anti-Semitic, and misogynist. I analyze them in conjunction with academic and popular apocalyptics of our own era, the second half of the twentieth century, demonstrating the erasure of violence in the first and its promotion in the second. Aspects of Charlotte Brontë's *Jane Eyre* and Elizabeth Barrett Browning's *Aurora Leigh* may be fruitfully read through this double lens of commercialized Victorian apocalyptics and late-twentieth-century literary apocalyptics. Despite their apparent attempts to produce feminist apocalypses, these two Victorian women writers, I will argue, were ultimately unable to escape the imperative to violence that permeates the Book of Revelation and its historically various interpretive discourses.

All of the women writers studied are middle class and privileged by better than usual education even for middle-class Englishwomen. All were practicing believers either at the time of their writing or in their youth. All must be considered complicitous with the Victorian imperial religious mission to some degree, needing, as they did, to capitalize in turn on its commodification of them if their literary works were to be successful commodities. Yet, as Reina Lewis argues, Victorian women writers occupied "the potentially transgressive position of cultural producer" because of the ambiguities and contradictions of their formation as gendered imperial subjects.[16] Their capacity to write "against the grain" of conventional thinking about the female body and to construct unauthorized sexualities in its stead emerged in part from their privileged position as imperial consumers. This book endeavors to demonstrate that the religion of the Victorian marketplace offered women writers access to a surprisingly diverse portfolio of religious investments with which to fund their forays into the very temples of piety and orthodoxy.

IMPERIAL BIBLES, DOMESTIC BODIES

PART ONE

The

Authorized Version

in the

Marketplace

ONE

CONSUMER CHRISTIANITY

Family Bibles and Family Values
on the
Installment Plan

> *For the evening reading before prayers, he selected the twenty-first chapter*
> *of Revelations. It was at all times pleasant to listen, while from his lips fell*
> *the words of the Bible: never did his fine voice sound at once so sweet and*
> *full—never did his manner become so impressive in its noble simplicity, as*
> *when he delivered the oracles of God; and tonight that voice took a more*
> *solemn tone—that manner a more thrilling meaning—as he sat in the*
> *midst of his household circle . . . bending over the great old Bible.*
> CHARLOTTE BRONTË, *Jane Eyre* (1847)

> *Genealogy is gray, meticulous, and patiently documentary. It operates on*
> *a field of entangled and confused parchments, on documents that have*
> *been scratched over and recopied many times.*
> MICHEL FOUCAULT, *"Nietzsche, Genealogy, History"* (1971)

The Family Bible Newly Opened: With Uncle Goodwin's Account of It (1853)
begins with a momentous discovery: an ancient bible is found in an old
trunk in the attic. This bible proves to have in it "a manuscript document
of a very unusual kind, being the pedigree, and, to some extent, the history of this ancient Saxon family, from the period of their first possession
of the estate, in the days of King Edward the Confessor."[1] This "domestic
record" had first been compiled, according to Jefferys Taylor, the Victorian
author of *The Family Bible Newly Opened,* by "some learned clerk, of the
name of Goodwin, about the year 1494," and had been continued until
some fourteen years before, when "its late owner recorded therein the
death of his wife" (18). The first, and most important, "opening" of the

family bible is the uncovering of its testimony to the ancient genealogy—the *pedigree*—of this "Saxon" family. It is only after introducing the family bible as the repository of the family's honorable lineage that "Dr. Edward Goodwin" goes on to comment on its contents in a manner designed to "instruct and amuse" young readers.

But the "family bible" here invoked by the good doctor is no more than another fictional counterpart of the genealogical romance implicit in Jane Eyre's account of St. John Rivers as he reads from "the great old Bible." The family bible—like the Rivers family, circled around its patriarch and thrilled by his delivery of the oracles of God—exemplifies what the family always has been and always should be. A search in the British Library catalog for the keywords "family bibles," will produce some large bibles with a handwritten genealogy (albeit usually extending no further back than the late eighteenth century). Yet the search will produce an even larger number of editions of the King James Bible that testify to the *instability* of the British family, to the contradictions and sharp reversals in its values, and to the relatively short historical period of its existence as a middle-class entity.

These editions of the "Authorized Version" are so catalogued because the word "family" is part of the formal title of the volume. Titles such as *The Universal Bible; or, Every Christian Family's Best Treasure* (1758, 1759), *The Compleat Family Bible* (1761, 1762), *The Elegant Family Bible* (1765, 1767), *The Universal Family Bible* (1773), *The Complete British Family Bible* (1781, 1785), *The Christian's New and Complete Family Bible* [1790?], *The Christian's New and Complete Universal Family Bible* [c. 1790], *The Grand Imperial Family Bible* [1800?], and *The National Comprehensive Family Bible* (1860) spill forth from the hidden coffers of the British Library's historic collections. More than eighty editions of such "Family Bibles" (hereafter capitalized to distinguish them from those family bibles categorized as such only by the presence of a handwritten family genealogy) are catalogued in the British Library, suggesting their very considerable commercial success. But that success was comparatively short-lived, continuing for a mere 150 years, after which the commercial Family Bible disappears from the British Library catalog. This chapter and the following two trace not only that Family Bible's history as a book, but its history as producer of the "family" to whom it was marketed, and whom it represents as affordable commodity. In signing up to buy a *Complete British Family Bible* or a *Grand Imperial Family Bible* in "parts," the eighteenth- or nineteenth-century consumer was buying more than a Family Bible— he or she was acquiring a visible testimony to the possession of certain "family values," as well as information in the form of illustrations and notes on what constituted the "best" family values. The commercial British Family Bible was both advertisement and cultural icon for what the British family wanted to be, but it is also a representation of how what that family wanted to be changed as the nation and its universe changed.

First produced in the early eighteenth century, and continuing through to the 1880s, these Family Bibles were the invention of British printers. The addition of "notes" or commentary enabled printers in eighteenth-century London to evade publishing restrictions on the Authorized Version, or King James translation, and publishing these Family Bibles, embellished with "elegant engravings," in inexpensive parts or serial numbers made it possible to expand the market of potential buyers into the rapidly increasing "middling" ranks of society. The British "Family Bible with Notes" was first motivated in England by attempts to get around "the privilege question"—or the restriction of bible publication to the two university presses and the few printers who held a royal license.[2] After the lapse of the Licensing Act in 1695, the 1709 Copyright Act established the principle of authorship as the basis for the ownership of literary property, which left the ownership of such texts as the bible in doubt and, consequently, open to competition. As the writer (who Black posits was the printer W. Rayner) of the preface to the 1735, 1737 *Compleat History of the Old and New Testament; or, A Family Bible* put it: "The word of God ought not to be the property of any one person, or yet of men . . . the interest of heaven is no way concerned, whether God's word be printed by J. BASKET, or W. RAYNER."[3]

Emerging in what some historians posit as the first consumer culture in Western civilization, the serialized "Family Bible with Notes" marks, I will argue, the first large-scale inauguration of consumer Christianity.[4] The changing formats of these commercial Family Bibles construct a previously unexamined "genealogy" of the British family—a genealogy of its joint commodification with the commercial Family Bible, and of its ascent, guaranteed by its installment-plan bible, to a position of unparalleled domestic and imperial status. The sudden cessation of publication of these commercial Family Bibles in the 1880s points to an equally dramatic fall in the cultural capital of "family values" in the fin de siècle.

Much British studies scholarship of the last two decades has focused on recovering historically specific constructions of gender, sexuality, and the family emerging in the period during which the commercial British Family Bible flourished—the "long eighteenth century" and the Victorian era. Michael McKeon postulates that the theorization of patriarchalism in the seventeenth century, far from authorizing the patriarchal family, marks a crisis in its history and a point at which modern systems of gender and sexuality begin their development.[5] Eve Tavor Bannet's analysis of the Marriage Act of 1753 studies not only the crisis in family values exhibited in the debate about the Act, but what was at stake for women.[6] Thomas Laqueur's analysis of medical and anatomical texts proposes that toward the end of the eighteenth century a revolutionary change in the understanding of human sexual nature occurred: where there had been only one sex with an inverted and inferior variant, there now were two "opposite" sexes.[7] In her reading of the turn-of-the-century Gothic novel, Eve Kosofsky Sedgwick teases out the construction of "male homosexual panic" at a time when male homosexuality was both known and unknown, a specter haunting the edges of cultural consciousness.[8] At approximately the same time, or in the last decades of the eighteenth century, Dror Wahrman hypothesizes a "gender panic" that coincides chronologically with Sedgwick's "male homosexual panic" and Laqueur's theorem of a fundamental change in "human sexual nature."[9]

Like Michel Foucault's insight that there was a moment of epistemic change in the late nineteenth century when the homosexual became a *species* instead of an aberration, these studies suggest a dramatic shift in the nature of the family around the turn of the nineteenth century.[10] A critical master narrative of modern "family values" in the eighteenth and nineteenth centuries may be speculatively formulated as follows. The earlier eighteenth century demonstrates an openness to "gender play," or to a greater potential for exploitation of loosely defined gender and even less defined sexuality. Arguably, an early form of male homosexual subjectivity first emerges at this time.[11] The "family," newly theorized and therefore no longer unquestioningly presumed to be "natural," takes on a new

6

visibility and desirability. Toward the end of the eighteenth century, however, a striking change in gender, sexuality, and the family occurs. As Foucault has memorably described it, sexuality was "moved into the home" and there "carefully confined" (*History of Sexuality*, 3). Leonore Davidoff and Catherine Hall's influential study, *Family Fortunes: Men and Women of the English Middle Class, 1780–1850*, posits the rigidification of sex and gender into the "separate-spheres" ideology of the Victorian era, when the "family" as we think of it today—with its patriarchal head or "Master of the family" and its "angel in the house," both characterized by moral seriousness and a strong Protestant work ethic—became the standard.[12] Mary Poovey's *Uneven Developments*, however, exposes the "unevenness" and shifting ambiguities of gender and sexuality that persisted beneath the deceptively inflexible surface of Victorian family values.[13] More recently, Susan Kingsley Kent's *Gender and Power in Britain, 1640–1990*, places Victorian family values in a much more extensive historical frame, and argues that the separate spheres ideology constructing the power of Victorian domesticity found its beginnings in the political and social upheavals of the seventeenth century.[14]

Reopening the family bible as the commercial Family Bible produces evidence that both confirms and unsettles this model of the "history" of sex, gender, and the Victorian family. Extending over the first two centuries of major commercial development in Britain, and always attuned to the market as well as the driving desires of its few authorial editors, the Family Bible speaks where such discourses as theology and scholarly biblical criticism are silent. Through its motivated attempts to observe the niceties and either please or control its consumers, the Family Bible continually makes gaffes that reveal the skeletons in its closet. The earliest generation of Family Bibles appears not to be directed toward a family at all, speaking rather to the paterfamilias, and working from the assumption that he either would or should desire the possession of a "library of universal knowledge" that would enhance his social status as a gentleman. However, the choice of illustrations also suggests a willingness to play to less gentlemanly interests. Voluptuous Eves in the garden of Eden and other sensational depictions of women, such as the favorite subject of Judith swinging the head of Holofernes aloft, abound.

In the early nineteenth century, the family as consumer of both "universal knowledge" and of playful depictions of gender and sex—and of its bible as encyclopedic purveyor of both—undergoes a startling transformation. Suddenly, parts of the Family Bible are no longer suitable for the family to read. Passages are bracketed or printed in tiny type and labeled, "To be omitted from family reading." Both the family and its bible are disciplined: biblical knowledge is divided between that appropriate for the family, and that appropriate only for the "closet." Unlike eighteenth-century Family Bibles, which are produced by printers whose chief aim seems to be financial profit, these disciplinary Family Bibles are the work of clergymen "authors" (actually editors) who mastermind the Authorized Version to suit their ideas of what the family should—and should not—know. These Family Bibles market access to the power of *secret* knowledge, to be the exclusive possession of a privileged family member, typically specified as the "Master of the family." "Family values" are now clearly distinguished—for those in the know—from other, unfamilial desires.

Slightly later in the nineteenth century, but paralleling the appearance of closeted Family Bibles, other Family Bibles begin to exhibit changes suggesting an appeal to the middle-class—or aspiring-middle-class—*female* consumer. Illustrations feature saintly women or sedate landscapes, and "Family Register" pages—ornamented with vignettes of "domestic life" such as babies in baptismal gowns and brides in their bridal finery—are now printed in the bible. Family Bibles now also demonstrate the orientalization or abjection from national identity of those values deemed to be other than British "family values," and the corresponding nationalization and imperialization of the British family. The English woman is represented as far superior in her happy domestic status to the debased Eastern female, the English "Master of the family" far kinder and gentler than the Oriental family despot. "Family values" as represented by nineteenth-century commercial Family Bibles demonstrate the cultural capital of what Elizabeth Langland calls the "material angels" of the Victorian family.[15] The angel in the house has become both the symbolic commodity to be sold and the culturally competent consumer who buys it.

Despite their monumental appearance when bound, examination of these commercial Family Bibles exposes them as an often hastily gathered compilation of bits and pieces plagiarized from other Family Bibles or from British commentators, whichever was more efficient in terms of the capital outlay and labor investment required. They are works of the marketplace, catering to the same consumer body as that for novels: lay readers who could not afford large outlays at one time for their reading, who were interested in improving their social and economic status, and who wanted to be entertained as well as improved. But the Family Bibles catered to other consumer desires as well, representing—in such portentous titles as *The Royal Universal Family Bible* (1781), *The Grand Imperial Family Bible* [1800?], or *The National Comprehensive Family Bible* (1860)—desires for a family identity that was also a "royal," national, and imperial identity. (In the foregoing titles, for example, the modifiers apply to the "family" as much as to the "Bible.") In his inspired and wide-ranging survey of origins for the British "idea of nations," Raphael Samuel had intended to add a discussion of "fictitious pedigrees as a variant of foundation myths."[16] The Family Bible surely accommodated that desire for a foundational family pedigree.

The serialized Family Bible thus inhabits the same cultural field as the English domestic novel. It differs in one important respect, however: its constructions of the "family" emerge from what was the exclusively male provenance of bible publication in the eighteenth and nineteenth centuries.[17] A "Mrs. Thompson" ventured so far as to print the text of the Authorized Version of the New Testament along with her commentary in 1824, and this *Family Expositor; or, A short and easy Exposition of the New Testament For the Use of the Family* was successful enough to be reprinted as *The Family Commentary* in 1833 and 1836.[18] Many women wrote commentaries on one or another parts of the bible. Mrs. Sarah Trimmer published highly influential "lessons" on the Scriptures and on illustrations of "sacred history," as well as "abridged versions" of the bible and a commentary entitled *A Help to the Unlearned* (1805); and Hannah More, Charlotte Yonge, and Christina Rossetti, among many others, published pedagogical or devotional writings on aspects of the bible. But publication of and commentary on the complete Authorized Version appears to have been a space from which women dared not write, or from which they were barred by various economic, legal, and social prohibitions.[19] The English novel, on the other hand, not only was "authored" by both women and men, but came to be increasingly identified with women readers and writers.[20] Yet the Victorian Family Bible is so visibly shaped by the tastes of its women readers and consumers that it might also be said to be produced by them. The Family Bibles published for profit in Britain over a period of nearly two centuries serve as a preeminent example both of the male hierarchy in religious publication and of women's increasing access to power even within that sacrosanct discursive domain.

Purchasing Knowledge: The Family Bible as Universal Library

The preface of the earliest serialized Family Bible exhorts creatures of "the human species" to apply themselves to "the duties of religion, to meditation, to the reading of useful Books, to discourse; in a word . . . [to] the unbounded pursuit of knowledge and virtue, and every hour of their lives make themselves wiser and better than they were before."[21] So speaks "S. Smith," the purported "author," who was more probably W. Rayner, the printer, in *The Compleat History of the Old and New Testament; or, A Family Bible* (1735, 1737).[22] In the same year, the same alleged author, S. Smith, makes a similar tribute to knowledge in *The Family Companion; or, Annotations upon the Holy Bible:* "Whatever the merry Scoffers of this Age, or the graver Lovers of Sin and Singularity may think, 'tis certain, that, in former Days, Men of all Orders and Degrees, of the highest Station in Life as well as Capacity in Knowledge, of polite Parts, as well as solid Judgments, and conversant in all human, as well as divine Literature, have, all along, held the Scriptures in singular Veneration; have employed their Wit and Eloquence in setting forth their Praise; and not only thought their Pens, but Poetry itself ennobled by the Dignity of such a Subject."[23]

This first installment-plan Family Bible, then, and its contemporary *Family Companion,* address themselves to "creatures" of the "human species," or to "Men of all Orders and Degrees," who desire, or ought to desire, knowledge. Throughout the eighteenth century, Family Bibles catered to the tastes and desires of the paterfamilias, the "gentleman" whose identity was enhanced by, but not limited to, the possession of a family. As such, these Family Bibles reflect seventeenth-century attempts at rehabilitation of the notion of the family as analogous to the state, both father and king having a "natural" right to rule absolutely over their subjects. After the Restoration of Charles II in 1660, the government republished Richard Mocket's *God and King* in 1662, a work that had first been published during the reign of James I, and that compared the divine right of kings to rule absolutely to the "natural" right of fathers to rule children. Similarly, Sir Robert Filmer's *Patriarcha* (originally written 1640) was issued in 1680 by promoters of the divine right of kings—and the similarly divine right of the "patriarch."[24] Mary Beth Norton notes that the theories of the family produced by Filmer, Mary Astell, Thomas Hobbes, and John Locke all agreed that "hierarchy was necessary to the operations of the household; the proper director of the family's activities was its husband/father/master; and the subordination of wife to husband was the foundation of the family unit and thus of society itself."[25] Although the word "family" appears regularly in the title of these eighteenth-century Family Bibles, their prefaces are addressed to "the reader" or "the public," and rarely use the word "family." Nevertheless, the inclusion of the term "family" in the title suggests an appeal to a new conception of family—that of the "middling ranks," whose upward mobility made them prime candidates for a Family Bible that would function as both source and cultural sign of "universal knowledge." At the same time, these Family Bibles appear constructed to satisfy the desire for a restoration of patriarchal authority after the many challenges presented to it during the years of civil war. Much of their apparatus—titles, illustrations, and commentary—is interpretable as representation of the "universal" or "natural" state of the family, and of the equally natural authority of its male head. Women are represented as domestic and properly subordinate, but also as sexual and sensational creatures, available for the pleasure of the male gaze. Yet it is the offer of "universal knowledge" that appears to be the biggest selling point for these Family Bibles.

The subtitle of *The Universal Bible; or, Every Christian Family's Best Treasure* (1758, 1759) claims that *"the difficult passages are explained, the mistranslations corrected; and the seeming contradictions found in the oracles of Truth, reconciled."* Thereafter Family Bible titles almost routinely included these extravagant promises. The *Elegant Family Bible* (1765, 1767) is subtitled *A Treasury of Divine Knowledge,* and the preface declares the intention "that it may serve every Family as a LIBRARY OF CHRISTIANITY," while the *Complete British Family Bible* (1782) avows the intent to publish a "Plan of General Information, suited to such as wish to gain a PERFECT KNOWLEDGE of the DIVINE ORACLES." Such claims to a "universal library" or knowledge continued to be popular through the first two decades of the nineteenth century, and indicate that the Family Bible may have been one of the earliest and most successful forms of "polite" knowledge or high culture, which John Brewer suggests came to be desired in the eighteenth century. Brewer notes that "taste became one of the attributes of a new sort of person—the 'social man' of Addison and Steele's *Spectator* . . . who was literate, could talk about art, literature and music and showed off his refinement through agreeable conversation in company."[26]

In fact, almost none of the claims made in the Family Bibles were true: the Authorized Version itself was no such thing, never having been authorized by the monarch or by any body of adjudicating scholars; many, if not most, editions of the "A.V.," whether printed by the royal printers or by publishers of Family Bibles, were riddled with errors; the so-called authors often had had little or nothing to do with the text or may even have been fictitious; and the entirely "original" commentaries were flagrantly plagiarized.[27] But none of this seems to have made any difference to the Family Bibles' success, or to the rush to publish "new" Family Bibles. Publishers appear to have exploited the known prevalence of ignorance, error, and fraud in bible publication—both commercial and "official," or that of printers with a royal license—to promote further production and consumption. After his admission that some Family Bibles had been printed under the names of "fictitious Persons," for example, the "author" of the *Complete British Family Bible* (1782) then insists that "it was in Consequence of this great Defect and Abuse of Public Confidence, that at the Solicitation of numerous Friends, the Author has been induced to publish this Work (the arduous Labour of many Years)."[28]

Even when the "author" was actually known as such, as in the case of Francis Fawkes and the 1761 *Complete Family Bible,* he may have had nothing to do with the notes claimed by him. According to the *Dictionary of National Biography,* Fawkes made his career by writing flattering odes to men in high places. Such an ode to the Archbishop Herring procured Fawkes the vicarage of Orpington, Kent, the chapelry of St. Mary Cray, and the attendant curacy of Knockhold. Although Fawkes was actually an excellent translator, at least in Dr. Johnson's opinion, the *Dictionary of National Biography* states bluntly that he "sold his name" to the *Complete Family Bible,* which came out in sixty weekly numbers. Such was the success of this name-selling that another edition of a bible, published in 1765, was said to have "notes taken from Fawkes."[29]

The Reverend Timothy Priestley, in a funeral sermon on the occasion of the death of his far more famous brother, Joseph Priestley, put in a plug for the second edition of his *New Evangelical Family Bible* [1793], based on the supposed originality of his notes:

> The idea that many years hence, by means of my folio edition of the Bible, I should have an opportunity of speaking to the world (though dead), I confess, was very pleasing to me; but now as my labours cannot be long in this world, the pleasure is increased, by the hope that when dead, I shall speak by my notes in my Family Bible also in quarto. I consider it as a token of encouragement from God, that above five thousand of the first edition were sold in a few years; many of those Bibles, no doubt, are in places destitute of the means of grace, and will, I hope, be a guide to many in this age, and to generations yet unborn. The present edition, I trust, will be no less useful to the glory of God and the good of immortal souls, as from the execution of the work, it is likely the circulation will be much more extensive.[30]

Despite this touching reference to his approaching death as testimony to his personal authorship of this Family Bible, the commentary in *The New Evangelical Family Bible* [1793] is identical to that in *The Christian's New and Complete Universal Family Bible . . . with copious notes . . . by Joseph Butler . . . assisted by several eminent divines* [c. 1790], a fact that does not seem to have deterred the sale of the first edition, if we can trust Priestley's figures.

It was not until the nineteenth century that the full extent of "borrowings" common to the notes in Family Bibles was exposed, and then only accidentally. In his *Condensed Commentary and Family Exposition of the Holy Bible* (1837), the Reverend Ingraham (also spelled Ingram)

Cobbin acknowledges that the notes included have been "drawn from all sources" and cites those sources. He further explains that in thus "giving the authorities, the Editor has furnished those who have a large library with a sort of index to guide them directly to the original for further and more enlarged information. . . . But here a considerable difficulty has occurred." Cobbin frequently found it impossible to decide on, as he put it,

> the original claimant of a criticism. . . . All the commentators have drawn largely from the fathers, especially from St. Augustine; and most of them have made general property of Patrick, Lowth, and Whitby. Poole has exhausted the old continental writers; Henry has made very free with Bishop Hall and others; Scott and Benson have enriched their pages abundantly from Henry; Gill has translated the spirit of Poole's Synopsis, but he most generally gives his authorities; Adam Clarke and Davidson have been much indebted to all the best critics, though the former does not always mention his obligations, and the latter never, but his preface to his admirable "Pocket Commentary" is an honest confession that he pretends to be no more than a compiler, some original thoughts appear, however, to be scattered among his notes.[31]

The notes for Family Bibles not only were a compilation of the work of various commentators, but were sometimes supplied by the publishers rather than a commentator or clergyman. In his "Publisher's Preface" to one of several editions of Family Bibles, W. R. M'Phun explains how he had bought

> at the sale of the Scottish Free Bible Press Company, the stereotype plates and property of the book they had been in the habit of supplying as their Family Bible. In order to render it more complete for the purpose I had before me, I determined on adding to the Bible a copious Practical Commentary, taken from the well-known productions of HENRY and SCOTT. . . . I had barely, however, begun to move forward with my design, when certain parties, who shall here be nameless, and who were

present when the purchase was made—provoked, no doubt, at the announcement of so valuable a production being offered for so small a sum—interposed, and advanced the somewhat anomalous doctrine, that although I had bought the stereotype plates without restriction of any kind whatever as to their use, and paid for them accordingly, yet *I had no right given me to print from them* in the contemplated form, and print I should not, if they could prevent me. The result was an expensive and vexatious action in the Court of Session, which terminated in an adverse decision. . . . I now found that the only course left me was, to prepare an entirely new set of stereotype plates to print from; and although I knew this would be attended with an enormous amount of additional outlay, I resolved at once to carry it into effect. I had been deprived, by the decision, of the Intercolumnar Notes of the late Rev. John Brown Patterson, but I resolved to supply their place with equally numerous, appropriate, and useful Annotations, taken from the writings of standard Expositors and Critics. . . . By this means I was supplied in less than six months with a body of Notes . . . extending to between six and seven thousand, from the best biblical writers of Europe and America. This portion of the book will therefore be found very superior in every respect to what I contemplated and far surpassing what I promised to give in my original Prospectus.[32]

M'Phun's preface demonstrates the ease—not to mention the efficiency—with which Family Bible notes could be manufactured from existing commentaries and Family Bibles. His complaint, however, also documents the recognition of the market value of such notes, and the initiation of attempts to control the right to print them. While M'Phun's and Cobbin's comments expose the utter lack of authenticity of any individual claimant to the title of "author" in this British tradition of commentary on the Authorized Version, for us they have another and opposite effect: they testify to the *authenticity* of this commercialized production of biblical interpretation as the "common sense" of a generation, meaning in particular "every man's common sense." Copied and recopied, truncated, mistranslated, "purified," "enlarged," they are texts without origins, always already representing *only* the "common sense" of their generation—as understood by their male printers, publishers, and commentators.

In these purveyors of "universal knowledge," the family itself remains an assumed entity, forming the ground of the universal. It seems apropos that an oddly symmetrical illustration of Noah's Ark, including tiny representations of Noah feeding the animals and Noah's wife cleaning up after them, not only appears in the first edition of *The Compleat History*, but is reprinted as a larger, fold-out frontispiece in the second edition (fig. 1). Doubtless, the illustration was thought to have appeal for children. But its design of precisely balanced, ruled-off stalls for each heterosexual pair of animal species, lined up like crates on a modern freight train, is so strangely unseaworthy as to stimulate speculation that it constructed other meanings "universal" to the family—namely, those of order (everything on an even keel), hierarchy (the human family in charge of all the animals), and the balance of sexual difference (one male, one female, in every "family").[33] Such was the appeal of this particular representation of Noah's Ark that it continued to be reprinted right up through the nineteenth century, but here with the edifying addition of "scientific" calculations of the amounts and kinds of fodder that would be needed by each species. For nineteenth-century readers as for eighteenth, the "family" was the logical basis of all knowledge—the newest as well as the oldest.

Pictorial representations of the originary human pair, by contrast, clearly illustrate a state "before the law," before the universal of the family. Eve is regularly represented as voluptuous, sensual, the apple of Adam's eye; and Adam, of course, is as yet subject to no knowledge, including that of sexual sin (fig. 2). One engraving even depicts Adam with *two* Eves, so to speak, for one is an angel, but an incontestably *female* angel in a state of décolletage, carrying on an obviously pleasurable conversation with Adam while an even more accessible (nearly naked) Eve plucks rosebuds in the background (fig. 3).

But such innocent sexuality is always that which precedes the "universal" family, with its order, hierarchy, carefully paired heterosexuality, its dutifully laboring Noah and wife. If the family, as suggested by the representation of Noah's Ark, was universal, the ground of "knowledge," then what constituted the boundaries or limits of that knowledge? What

FIGURE I. "Noah's Ark." Delineated according to F. Lamy. *The Compleat History* (1735, 1752). Courtesy of the British Library.

exceeded its meanings, escaped the stolid perimeters of those neatly ruled-off stalls on the Ark? Commentary on what is marginalized in relation to the "family"—or those aspects of gender and sexuality that provoke criticism, controversy, or emphasis by repetition of "illustration," including both notes and engravings—suggests that the homosexual subject was even better known than studies of molly houses have proposed. Foucault's thesis that the homosexual did not appear as a "species" until produced as such by the medico-legal discourses of the late nineteenth century is revised by eighteenth-century Family Bible commentary, where we find a male homosexual subject defined, pathologized, and even *named*.[34] And in intriguing opposition, we find a putative *female* homosexual subject not named or overtly pathologized, but repeatedly pictured in representations that suggest both admiration and suspicion.

FIGURE 2. Pictorial title page. *The New and Grand Imperial Family Bible* [1813]. Courtesy of the British Library.

FIGURE 3. "Gen. Chap. 2 V. 25." *The Grand Imperial Family Bible* [1800?]. Courtesy of the British Library.

The Scorta Mascula: Effeminacy and Sexuality

The term "effeminate," which has been the focus of debate as to whether and when its meaning ceased to be restricted to that of a male gender attribute and became linked as well to male homosexuality, figures from the beginnings of the English Bible. Alan Bray notes that the biblical scholars who produced the King James or Authorized Version of the bible translated the two Greek words in 1 Cor. 6:9 that could be associated with homosexuality as "effeminate," which Bray states "lacked the specifically homosexual connotations it was later to acquire." But they also used the phrase "abusers of themselves with mankind," which Bray suggests more clearly demonstrated a moral disapproval.[35] Bray's argument thus proposes that the term "effeminate" begins its English career in reference to a gender attribute rather than to male sexuality. Both Bray and Randolph Trumbach, however, posit that the eighteenth-century molly houses instituted a same-sex subculture in which effeminacy became linked with male homosexuality, while Alan Sinfield remains skeptical "that same-sex passion became at this point identified with effeminacy."[36] Carrying the debate into the nineteenth century, Linda Dowling posits that the hidden or "coded" Victorian counterdiscourse of Hellenism that emerged at the time of Oscar Wilde's trial had its discursive roots in a "classical republican discourse" that constructs "effeminate" in opposition to the "virility of an ancient warrior ideal."[37] Emphasizing the critical importance of John Brown's *Estimate of the Manners and Principles of the Times* (1757), an urgent warning against the luxury, corruption, and "EFFEMINACY" that had been provoked by the dangers and disturbances of the Seven Years' War, Dowling positions "classical republican discourse" in an "invisible warfare fought out between this counterdiscourse and an older inheritance of religious prohibition and cultural taboo" (xv–xvi).

Family Bibles published in the eighteenth century and the first two decades of the nineteenth century not only make this "invisible warfare" around the category of effeminacy quite visible, but provide suggestive evidence for what Bray and Trumbach have theorized, the emergence of a male homosexual subjectivity in eighteenth-century England. The earliest Family Bible, or *The Compleat History* . . . (1735, 1752) avoids interpretation of the term in 1 Cor. 6:9, but the commentary on the story of Lot

(Gen. 19:4, 5) unhesitatingly identifies male homosexual relations with the crime termed "Sodomy" under English law, and in its reference to 1 Cor. 6:9 within the note, implicates "effeminacy" under this category:

> Before it was time to go to rest, the inhabitants of the city, both young and old, being informed that Lot had strangers with him, and, in all probability tempted with the beautiful forms, which the angels had assumed, encompassed the house, and demanded of them to deliver them up, that they might abuse them. That is, in an unnatural and preposterous manner, which was afterwards expressly forbidden in the levitical law, and made capital. This vile sin continued among the gentiles even in the apostles time, (as may be gathered from Rom. 1.27 and 1 Cor. 6.9) and was so generally practised among the people of Sodom, that from thence it took the name of Sodomy, and the practisers of it are called Sodomites, both in the holy scriptures, and our English laws, which (as did the law of God of old) do still make the punishment of it to be death."[38]

But *The Universal Bible; or, Every Christian Family's Best Treasure* (1758, 1759) supplies a paraphrase that constructs the term "effeminate" in opposition to the "citizen soldier," thereby demonstrating its location in classical republican discourse: "neither fornicators, nor idolators, nor adulterers, nor effeminate persons, who give themselves up to a soft indolent way of living, and can endure no hardships in the way of duty and honour; nor Sodomites, those infamous degraders of human nature, nor thieves, nor those who are insatiably covetous, nor drunkards, nor revilers, nor rapacious persons, who, by extortion, or any other kind of violence, invade the property of their neighbours, shall inherit that pure and peaceful region, the kingdom of God."[39] Here the commentary clearly distinguishes between "effeminate" as insufficiently hardy, and therefore unsuited to military "duty and honour," and Sodomites, who are "infamous degraders of human nature." Since the *Universal Bible* was published the year after John Brown's *Estimate of the Manners and Principles of the Times* (1757), the commentator may have been borrowing Brown's argument, or simply vocalizing a sentiment that the *Estimate* had made "common sense."

However, the slightly later *Compleat Family Bible* (1761, 1762), of which Francis Fawkes claims to be the author, contests the meaning offered by the *Universal Bible* (and by Brown's *Estimate*) and supplies an added definition of the word as a certain sex/gender type: "*Effeminate.* The Greek word μαλαχος does not here signify *delicate persons,* but the most detestable of all sinners. Hesychius [*sic*] interprets μαλαχος by . . . *like a woman in manners,* or *scorta mascula.*"⁴⁰ Here a commentator— whether Fawkes or some unnamed translator—apparently at home in Greek, at first limits the meaning to that of an unnatural ("detestable") sexual activity, but then also defines it in terms of a specific type of masculinity, or sex/gender identity, the *scorta mascula,* a term which in English might be rendered as "prostitutes of the masculine gender."⁴¹ By resorting to Greek and Latin, however, the commentator both reveals and conceals meaning, denying that "effeminate" means "delicate" but giving only a partial and mysterious meaning in English, as "the most detestable of all sinners . . . *like a woman in manners.*" The highly specific, if linguistically veiled, meaning is particularly interesting in light of the poems printed at the beginning of Fawkes's *Complete Family Bible,* which consist of extremely euphemistic tributes to the author, apparently written by members of a male coterie, that could be construed as male-male love poems. As an example, for instance, consider the following lines: "Enraptur'd have we seen thy Genius rove / Through the sweet Maze of our [the Muses] poetic Grove, / And as we heard thy soft melodious Lay, / Prepar'd thy Garland of eternal Bay."

The Compleat Family Bible attributed to Fawkes complicates the meaning of "effeminacy" in mid-eighteenth-century discourse, suggesting contradictory identifications as both a legally (and morally) condemned sexual activity, and a particular, woman-like, *named* variety of the male gender, the *scorta mascula,* linked to the sexual activity described as an "abuse against nature." This duality of sexual knowledge continues to parallel—and complicate—that of the "universal family" in Family Bibles until about 1785. Indeed, coy references in commentary on "effeminate" in many cases appear to be simply borrowings—but often only partial borrowings—from *The Complete Family Bible* of 1761. For example, *The*

Christian's Family Bible (1763–67) by W. Rider states: "The Greek word signifies here, the most detestable of all sinners: as for the particular crime which they perpetrated, it had better be guessed at than explained."[42] The modifying phrase "the most detestable of all sinners" turns up repeatedly, as in *The Royal Universal Family Bible* (1781), which notes in reference to the word "effeminate" that "the Greek word *Malakos* does not here signify delicate persons, but the most detestable sinners . . . having the manners of a woman. *Seorta* [*sic*] *Mascula.*"[43] *A New and Complete Family Bible* (1770) uses the single word "Pathics" to characterize all the categories named in the biblical text identified with pathology or disease.[44] But *The Universal Family Bible* (1773), though it makes no comment on "effeminate," suggests in commentary on Rom. 1:26–27 that "if we attend to what has been transmitted to us in the Greek and Roman classics, we shall find, that unnatural crimes were considered as little more than trifles among the heathens, or indeed as mere acts of gallantry. To enumerate particulars would be inconsistent with a work of this nature, but the whole may serve to shew, that the gospel was revealed at a time when men stood most in need of its assistance."[45]

Such comments document the contradictions at work in the term "effeminate" in eighteenth-century England. Even in Family Bibles, dedicated to the promotion of "universal knowledge," the term not only exceeds a simple opposition to family values, but repeatedly suggests the extra-universal knowledge of a nonheterosexual subject. But around the turn of the nineteenth century, this multiplicity of interpretation begins to narrow, first shifting back to the terms of classical republican discourse, and then disappearing entirely. In what seems an astonishing innocence, for example, the author of *The Christian's New and Complete Family Bible* (1804) first defines the "effeminate" as those "who live in an easy, indolent way, taking up no cross, enduring no hardship," then continues, "But how is this? These good natured people are ranked with idolaters and sodomites! We may learn hence, that we are never secure from the greatest sins, till we guard against those which are thought least."[46] *The Devotional Family Bible* (1811) similarly defines effeminacy as a kind of laziness or indolence: "'the effeminate,' who live in luxury, indolence, and sensual pleasure." But the same Family Bible, in its commentary on the story of Lot, reverts to a sexual knowledge whose very name the writer refuses to articulate: the "men of this place," he states, wanted to perpetrate "a crime too shocking and detestable to be named: a crime which indeed has no name given it, but what is borrowed from this infamous place."[47]

As suggested by the comment cited above, "that to enumerate particulars would be inconsistent with a work of this nature," the "universal knowledge" offered to the family in Family Bibles printed in the eighteenth century is marked by reference to certain unstated but commonly understood limits. George Whitefield, in his preface to the reprinting of Samuel Clark's *Holy Bible . . . with Annotations* (1690) as *The Holy Bible . . . or, A Family Bible, with annotations . . . by Samuel Clark* (1760), comments, "It must be confessed, indeed, that in the former Editions a few Expressions in the explanatory Notes seemed not so unexceptionable; but then it must be observed, that they were but few, and those in this Edition, as I am informed, are for the most part corrected."[48] Mark A. Noll notes not only that Whitefield "may have been the best-known Protestant in the whole world during the eighteenth century," but that he "knew how to exploit the rising tide of newsprint and he even engaged in what would today be called 'publicity stunts.'"[49] It is possible at this point only to speculate about what Whitefield cautiously termed "not so unexceptionable" expressions. But as a knowledgeable manipulator of "the rising tide of newsprint," he surely would have hastened both to exploit consumer desire for Family Bibles and to adhere to implicit boundaries of the "universal knowledge" promulgated therein.[50]

Illustrating Judith

Eighteenth-century Family Bibles also persistently demonstrate a curiosity, fascination, and suspicion concerning a female gender type that clearly transgresses the boundaries of "universal" domestic femininity as represented by Noah's wife, patiently cleaning up after the animals on board. This interest in a nondomestic feminine gender type is demonstrated in the widely used illustration of Judith swinging the head of Holofernes aloft, while two little boys laughingly watch and applaud (fig. 4). Originally engraved by G. Bickham Jr., an English engraver, the illustration represents the leading character in the apocryphal book of Judith. By

FIGURE 4. "Judith sheweth the Head of Olofernes." G. Bickham jun. delin.Sculp. *The Compleat History* (1752, 1753). Courtesy of the British Library.

pretending to flee with her maid from the Hebrew people, Judith talks her way into the tent of the enemy commander, Holofernes, whom she proceeds to get drunk and then to slay with his own weapon, after which she puts his head in her maid's bag of meat, and the two escape from the enemy camp and return to their own people. Bickham's portrayal of Judith showing off Holofernes' head to the Hebrews is perhaps the single most popular print in eighteenth-century Family Bibles: it reappears time after time, though often clearly marked by the hand of some other printer or engraver (as demonstrated by reversals and different styles). When Bickham's conception of the scene was not reproduced, some other portrayal of Judith usually was included: Judith handing the head of Holofernes to her waiting maid, Judith with Holofernes' head on a spear, and so on (figs. 5, 6).[51]

Why were the Judith illustrations, especially Bickham's, so popular in eighteenth-century Family Bibles? Studies of similarly nondomestic women in other genres of the period postulate a range of interpretations. Dianne Dugaw's study of the "Female Warrior" represented in popular balladry in England from 1650 to 1850 asserts that this soldier or sailor heroine is "hermaphroditic." She is *celebrated* for being both "manly" and "womanly," functioning as a "gender-crossing, indeed, gender-confounding ideal."[52] Dugaw thus suggests that the chief appeal of this figure was its representation of gender plurality. Yet Dugaw also notes that "the ballads maintain a fundamental ambiguity on the subject of coupling. Sexual attraction is no guarantee of heterosexuality: the Female Warrior can arouse the same instinctively erotic response in women as well as men" (161). Though the ballads always applaud the Female Warrior as securely *female,* they evoke the possibility of a homoerotic relation between women.

By contrast, Joy Wiltenburg asserts that early modern popular literature in England and Germany constantly depicts "powerful and subversive" women, women "escaping from male control," women as "disorderly creatures, whose licentious urge for dominance threatens to disrupt the carefully constructed social hierarchy," and that such depictions reflect "male anxieties about the success of patriarchal rule."[53] Certainly it is possible to interpret Bickham's depiction of the two little boys as representing a tittering male nervousness about this "castrating woman." But other readings of the illustration are suggested by its conflicted location in, on the

26

FIGURE 5. "Judith with the Head of Holofernes." *The Christian's New and Complete Universal Family Bible* [c. 1790]. Courtesy of the British Library.

FIGURE 6. "Judith cutteth off Holofernes' head." *The Universal Family Bible* (1793, 1795). Courtesy of the British Library.

one hand, a site of discourse on male "effeminacy," and on the other, a site of almost complete absence of commentary on "the mannish woman" or on *female* homosexuality. Dugaw's thesis about the Female Warrior's capacity to provoke a homoerotic response in women suggests that the Judith illustrations may also have functioned as a critical early modern representation of lesbian sexuality.

As Anne Lister's diary of October 1824 demonstrates, she and other women interested only or primarily in women were aware that only one text in the Authorized Version of the bible refers explicitly to sexual relations between women: Rom. 1:26–27. In this text Paul describes the sins of the Gentiles, including the charge that "even their women did change the natural use into that which is against nature: And likewise also the men, leaving the natural use of the woman, burned in their lust one toward another; men with men working that which is unseemly." In a conversation with a Mrs. Barlow, whom Anne intended to (and subsequently did) seduce, the two discuss the Romans text: "'Yes,' said I, 'the first chapter' & pointed to that verse about women forgetting the natural use, etc. 'But,' said I, 'I do not believe it.' 'Oh,' said she, 'it might be taken in another way, with men.' I agreed but without saying anything to betray how well I understood her. 'Yes,' she said, 'as men do with men.' Thought I to myself, she is a deep one. She knows, at all rates, that men can use women in two ways. I said I had often wondered what was the crime of Ham. Said she, 'Was it sodomy?' 'I don't know,' said I, then made her believe how innocent I was."[54]

Mrs. Barlow's remark that the text might be taken another way is interpreted by Anne as referring to heterosexual anal intercourse. One of the very few "family" commentaries to comment on the verse, Dr. Doddridge's popular and much reprinted *Family Expositor: Or, a Paraphrase and Version of the New Testament* (1739–56), also might be interpreted in this manner. His "paraphrase" of the text reads, "Therefore, I say, because of this inexcusable Neglect of the ever-blessed God, he abandoned them to the most infamous Passions, for even their Women, from whom the strictest Modesty might reasonably have been expected, changed the natural Use of the other Sex, to that which is against Nature. And likewise their Males, leaving the natural Use of the Female, have been inflamed with the most scandalous and abominable Desires towards each

29

other, Males with Males, perpetrating that which is most shameful to mention, and detestable to think of."[55]

Even Doddridge's unusually explicit paraphrase, however, by its insertion of "the other Sex," erases female homosexuality. Eighteenth-century Family Bibles erase it even more completely by simply omitting commentary on the verse, thus accomplishing one of the most thorough instances of what Terry Castle calls the "ghosting" of lesbian sexuality.[56] Unlike the word "effeminate" in the case of male homosexuality, the claim in Rom. 1:26 that women "did change the natural use into that which is against nature" did not produce names or language for female homosexuality, even though, according to Emma Donoghue, such terms can be documented in other discourses of the time.[57]

But that a coded critique of the female homosexual subject may be detected in eighteenth-century Family Bibles seems probable, given the Judith illustrations. The most popular of these, the Bickham engraving, invites readings of both sexual transgression and gender ambiguity. Martha Vicinus argues that "the precursor to the modern 'butch' cannot be traced back to those women who passed as 'female soldiers,'" because "such women retained their biological identity as women" and moreover were "universally admired."[58] But Bickham's portrayal, in which two laughing and clapping little boys are foregrounded in Judith's audience, rather pointedly suggests mixed meanings—this is a woman hero, all right, but isn't she queer? Kingsley Kent notes that, while tales of "female warriors" circulated widely in eighteenth-century ballads, poems, and novels, these "amazons" elicited different responses from female and male readers. For the former, they excited great interest, for the latter they instigated adverse comment, disparagingly associated with "the spectacular rise of women writers."[59]

Later illustrations that show Judith with her maid, passing the male head from one to the other female, invite a still more provocative construction, that of women passing a phallus between them—and by corollary, of traditional notions concerning the sexual treachery of women. In the early eighteenth century, Queen Anne "enjoyed a kind of symbolic masculinity: upon her royal entry into Bath in 1702, virgins apparelled like Amazons with bows and arrows welcomed her. But during her reign, propagandists began to portray her as weak and pliable, and unable to assert her own will against that of her 'female favorites.' There were hints that some of these relationships went beyond platonic friendship."[60] The elegant engravings of Family Bibles may be read as analogous to cartoons of the period, which freely phallicized women whose political activity was considered objectionable.[61] For example, an illustration of Judith with Holofernes' head impaled on a spear projecting in front of her clearly suggests a phallicized and highly dangerous woman, piercing the head of a symbolically castrated male. The Judith illustrations of these pre-Victorian Family Bibles represent women as men saw them. sexual crea tures who, by divine right, ought to belong to their Adam, but who might turn on him with deadly intent and, in an even more frightening possibility, prefer other women to men. All such representations of deadly doings between women—so popular in eighteenth-century Family Bibles—become more and more rare in Victorian Family Bibles (as does commentary on "effeminacy"), and are increasingly replaced by images of self-sacrificing, domestic women, as the family and the Family Bible are reoriented toward the angel of the house. Prior to the feminizing of the Family Bible, however, another much more surprising shift occurs in the representation of the family as knowledge consumer.

TWO

CLOSETING THE FAMILY BIBLE
AND THE FAMILY

Early in the nineteenth century, evidence of a new and startling threat begins to appear in Family Bibles. In a preface dated 1818, the Reverend B. Boothroyd notes, "Bishop Newcome has observed, that 'many words or phrases which occur in the received version, are become unintelligible to the generality of readers; and many which are intelligible, are so antiquated and debased as to excite disgust among the serious, and contempt and derision among libertines.'" Boothroyd's solution to this disturbing perception is that "as the manners and the customs of the Jews were so very different from ours, and as there are in the laws given to them, references to things which delicacy forbids us to mention, I have given the sense of such passages, rather than a naked, verbal version. . . . I hope it will be found that my version contains nothing but what may be read in a family, without occasioning modesty to blush, or raising any unpleasant and unhallowed thoughts in the minds of youth."[1]

Boothroyd's 1818 preface is the first explicit statement in a Family Bible of a reversal in attitudes toward the desirability of making the "universal knowledge" of the bible universally accessible to the family. Not only do references to a newly perceived "obscurity" or "unintelligibility" appear repeatedly from this point on, but in contrast to the eighteenth-century Family Bibles, in which the object was to make everything plain and intelligible—and even a source of pleasure—commentators or editors now begin to devise schemes for literally closeting certain portions of the sacred text: they are to be omitted from family reading and reserved for the closet. Thomas Williams explains in his *Cottage Bible and Family Expositor* (1825–27) that "as there are passages, especially in the Old

Testament, manifestly unsuitable for reading in families, as Hebrew genealogies, enumerations of the tribes, laws respecting the sexes, and some other matters peculiar to the Jews; these will be printed in a smaller type, and so distinguished that they may be omitted in Family Reading, without difficulty or confusion. A few words exceptionable to females, will be exchanged for others more suitable to the present state of our language and of society."[2] Such a plan, Williams continues, "though primarily designed for FAMILIES, will be a desideratum for SCHOOLS, where selection is equally necessary; at the same time it will be no less adapted to the Closet" (Williams, viii).

Following closely on the heels of the popular *Cottage Bible and Family Expositor,* the Reverend Ingraham Cobbin published an even cheaper work for "cottagers," *The Cottage Commentator on the Holy Scriptures* (1828). Noting that "every reader can always refer to his own Bible," Cobbin omitted the text of the Authorized Version, and could thus promise his readers that the *Cottage Commentator* would be "the cheapest work of the kind ever offered to the public."[3] Equally important aims of this publication, however, were its adaptation "for the plain cottager" and inclusion of reflections appropriate for the distinct "services of the FAMILY and the CLOSET." Accordingly, Cobbin warns the "cottage" readers of certain chapters, such as Lev. 15, that "THIS CHAPTER IS NOT SUITABLE FOR FAMILY READING," or of Lev. 18, that "THIS CHAPTER SHOULD BE OMITTED IN THE FAMILY; it shews what man is by nature, and may lead to humbling and grateful reflections in the closet" (146).[4]

But it is in still another of Ingraham Cobbin's Family Bible publishing enterprises, *The Domestic Bible* (1847), that the most formidable apparatus for disciplining both the bible and the family is put forth. In his "Key to the Work," Cobbin notes that *"Passages inserted in* THICK *brackets,* and sometimes including Chapters, are such as may be omitted in family reading, being mostly chronological, or Eastern metaphors, &c., liable to abuse by the ignorant and thoughtless." The "Master of the family" may thus exclude certain members of the family from certain portions of the Family Bible, to be reserved for "the closet worshipper."[5]

Beginning in the early decades of the nineteenth century, then, the Family Bible exhibits evidence of an epistemic change: from a universal library of divine knowledge offered "freely"—or as cheaply as was economically reasonable—to "the family," it becomes a library split between universal knowledge and matters peculiar to the Jews, between divine oracles and passages liable to abuse, between "family" and "closet." The change resembles that which Paul Rabinow describes as Foucault's distinction between the two "wills to knowledge":

> For Aristotle, there is an essential pregiven harmony between sensation, pleasure, knowing, and truth. . . . As posited in the famous opening lines of the *Metaphysics,* the desire to know is essential to who we are, and is ours "by nature." Our nature is to seek knowledge, and we take pleasure through doing so. He [Foucault] offers Nietzsche's *The Gay Science,* on the other hand, as a total contrast to Aristotle's naturalism. Nietzsche's knowledge (*connaissance*) is not an appropriation of universals but an invention that masks the basest instincts, interests, desires, and fears. . . . Knowledge is not a natural faculty but a series of struggles, a weapon in the universal war of domination and submission.[6]

The nineteenth-century Family Bibles designed by Boothroyd, Williams, and other clergymen are disciplinary bibles, weapons "in the universal war of domination and submission," rather than commodities catering to the universal, pleasure-seeking desire "to know." It is important to note that, although Bowdler's *Family Shakespeare* appeared in the same year as Boothroyd's *New Family Bible,* and although part of Boothroyd's motivation may reasonably be ascribed to the same cultural swing toward moral seriousness born of evangelicalism that lay behind Bowdler's *Family Shakespeare,* Boothroyd's *New Family Bible* is not bowdlerized. Because of its status as the foundation of English law, the Authorized Version could not be simply bowdlerized. Thomas Williams, in his introductory "Plan of the Work" in *The Cottage Bible and Family Expositor,* writes that "the Bible has been compared to our Statute book" (1). As illustrated in the print in John Kitto's *Illustrated Family Bible* [1871–76] showing Latimer presenting the English translation of the bible to Henry VIII, the English Bible is the Law on which the British nation is founded, its "harmony" of knowledge and truth (fig 7). As such, bowdlerization or abridgement transforms it into a different thing altogether. No longer the basis for universal truth and English law, an abridged or bowdlerized version becomes only a collection of stories or moral passages chosen for their readability. The preface to the 1820 "Porteusian Bible," which includes Bishop Porteus's guide to help "the youthful and inexperienced" choose bible passages for reading aloud without "embarrassment," points out, "After all, a Selection or Abridgment, however excellent in itself, is not A BIBLE; and will never be regarded with that sacred veneration and respect, which the whole book of God cannot fail to inspire, when taken up in a proper spirit."[7] Yet this "whole book of God," this "Statute" of the English nation, had suddenly become visible as a book that included laws given to another people, a "peculiar" people whose customs were "very different from those of Europe." In an approximation of Foucault's words about the birth of clinical science, divines now described what for a century had remained below the threshold of the visible and the expressible.[8]

Accordingly, the clerical "authors" of these less naked Family Bibles dealt with the Family Bible's new "visibility" not by publishing abridged versions, which would have destroyed the harmony of truth and knowledge certified only by the *whole* bible, but by a system of exclusion based on class and gender. The Family Bible was divided according to which portions should be read to the "family"—that is, women, children and servants—and which should be the exclusive prerogative of the "Master of the family." The portions marked off by brackets or smaller type include what "we other Victorians" would expect, such as the stories of Sodom and of Onan and other narratives of sexual deviance or violence, the highly explicit laws concerning the body in the Book of Leviticus, and the notorious passage in Romans already discussed, in which Paul refers to even *women* forgetting the "natural use." But they also include, as Thomas Williams stipulates, "Hebrew genealogies, enumerations of the tribes" and other matters "peculiar to the Jews," to be omitted from family reading, we might suppose, because they would bore the family, especially the children. Williams, for example, also takes the radical and highly unusual step of printing the first Gospel, Matthew, in its entirety and then fencing off large portions of the three successive gospels, with the instruction "to be omitted from Family Reading," on the grounds that they

FIGURE 7. "Latimer Presenting the Bible to King Henry VIII." Leighton Brothers. *The Illustrated Family Bible* [1871–76]. Courtesy of the British Library.

simply repeat what has already been said in the first Gospel. Williams's bracketing of what amounts to a majority of the Gospel texts speaks to a monumental paternalism toward "cottagers" typed as a class, though he exempts the "Master of the family" from this presumed inferiority and need for protection of "innocence." Other editions of Family Bibles did not follow his lead in the treatment of the Gospels, but they did in the bracketing of "Hebrew genealogies" and other aspects of the "A. V." now specified as "peculiar to the Jews." The inclusion of matters "peculiar to the Jews" as materials that required bracketing in a book three-quarters of which is made up of Hebrew scriptures should strike us as a very odd move indeed. The bracketed Family Bibles' linkage of sexually explicit texts with the Jews suggests that the pathologization of sexuality was intimately linked with the production of a sense of national and imperial identity. It was the Jews—and colonial subjects who were classified with them in the notes to these Family Bibles—who represented "unnatural" sex. The knowledge of these "unnatural" practices was to be limited, in British Protestant families, to those who could read their Family Bibles alone in their closets.

In her analysis of the "modern crisis of homo/heterosexual definition," Eve Kosofsky Sedgwick reproduces a list of definitions of the word "closet" from the *Oxford English Dictionary (OED)*.[9] Among these is included the meaning of closet, not only as a place of privacy or retirement, but *"esp.* Such a room as the place of private devotion (with allusion to 1611 version of Matt.vi.6) *arch."* (qtd in Sedgwick, *Epistemology*, 65). The *OED* does not give any examples from the serialized Family Bibles of the nineteenth century, which demonstrate that this "archaic" meaning acquired new visibility in the highly commercialized form of the "English Bible," designed to appeal to the British family as consumer. For such families, the "closet" may be thought of as the Protestant equivalent to the Catholic confessional, on which Foucault's theory of the discursive production of desire rests.[10]

In one's "closet," one read the bible, meditated, prayed, and confessed one's sins to God. The critical difference between this and the Catholic confessional was that no other human being heard what the closet worshipper confessed: the confession was private, hidden, *secret.* It was in this space of voluntary confinement that the "Master of the family"—he who had access to the knowledge of what was to be omitted from family reading—was to read passages that might "lead to humbling and grateful reflections." Was it in this "bracketed" context that the term "closet" first became pervasively associated with same-sex desire? Marta Straznicky points out that the authors of devotional manuals in the early modern period were in fact suspicious of the "unsupervised secrecy" of the closet, while at the same time they encouraged its use for prayer and meditation. "Knowing that prayer is but one form of 'Closet-business,' they warn about the permeability of closed space. Satan, they insist, 'will . . . dog you into your Chambers, and intrude into your Closets; when the Door is shut, he will get in.' Using one's privacy for other than devotional purposes is like admitting 'a thousand Devils' into the closet. Accordingly a closet not managed in the prescribed manner 'stinks in God's nostrils,' it is 'a wicked place, . . . an Hell.'"[11] As Richard Rambuss eloquently theorizes, the prayer closet in the seventeenth century was "that material structure in which no mediating priest stands between God and the devotee. . . . Closet devotion, in other words, is the technology by which the soul becomes a subject."[12]

But what were the effects of "closet devotions" in the nineteenth century? Certainly we may learn from the evidence of the disciplinary Family Bibles of this time that these bibles imparted knowledge of a new kind—precise knowledge of "the most detestable" of sins, knowledge of what must *not* be named, knowledge of the silences maintained in public discourse concerning the Authorized Version. Noting that Sedgwick's theory "does not explain how social structures could have implanted in men the fear of their own potential deviance in the first place," Andrew Elfenbein comments that "in the nineteenth century, conventional patterns of socialization in schools, the military, and in the workplace worked to make the ambiguity of homosocial desire invisible."[13] It seems probable that what I have called "disciplinary" Family Bibles would have operated to make homosocial desire quite unambiguous and highly visible to those "Masters of the family" who had access to them. In the nineteenth-century British Family Bible, the technology of the closet functioned to produce the closeted "English" homosexual male. More than that, however, it functioned to spectacularize "effeminate" or unnatural males as Jews or those of other non-English "races."

But we must also inquire as to why the split between "family" and "closet" emerged at this particular moment in the already lengthy history of the serialized, consumable Family Bible. Looking even further back into the history of the Hebrew Bible, Howard Eilberg-Schwartz raises a similar question as to why the laws of Leviticus and other priestly writings concerning the body should have been codified at the time they were.[14] Mary Douglas's interpretation of these laws regulating the boundaries of the body as symbolizing fears that the boundaries of the "social body" were threatened has, he notes, become "canonized" in commentaries on Leviticus. But this interpretation of the larger meaning of laws regulating the body, especially what passes in and out of its orifices, does not explain why the body should have become particularly problematic to a particular group of Jews, namely the Israelite priests, at the particular time it did (Eilberg-Schwartz, 38). Eilberg-Schwartz theorizes that the perceived threat to the "social body," and the resulting codification of laws affecting the physical body, arose because of a desire to protect the priestly patrilineage. "In particular it is the patriline, that is, the line of male descendants, that evokes interest within the priestly writings" (40). A parallel argument can be made about why the Family Bible should suddenly have become the object of a disciplinary "codification" during the early decades of the nineteenth century in England: multiple forms of "invasion" threatened the British nation, its Protestant church, its clerical and legislative elite, its "family religion," and its very bible, which, as all Englishmen of common sense understood, was the founding principle of British law. In short, the British "priestly patrilineage" appeared to be an endangered species, confronted by marauding forces from without and within.

From the Seven Years' War (1756–63) until 1815, the British body politic was more or less constantly threatened by the possibility of military invasion by the French, either in its expanding empire or on its native shores, or both. Linda Colley particularly emphasizes the period following the French Revolution, noting that "more than twice as long as the First and Second World Wars added together, the wars against Revolutionary and Napoleonic France were almost as geographically extensive as far as British involvement was concerned, sweeping through Europe, into Asia, Africa, North America, Latin America, and even precipitating sea battles off the coast of Australia," and adding that "from 1798 to 1805, the conquest of Britain was Napoleon's primary strategic objective."[15] The evidence of Family Bibles, however, suggests that the threat of French invasion involved much more than fear of military conquest, for the French combined the threats to "family religion" of "popery" and revolutionary skepticism and atheism. Not only was popery characterized by a *celibate* priesthood, but revolutionary France had decriminalized same-sex relations.[16] This put invasion by the French on a par with the invasion of "Oriental" knowledge already visible on the horizons of the English Bible. Edward Said comments that it was at this time, the turn of the nineteenth century, that "a new awareness of the Orient . . . had arisen," and that the new awareness "was partly the result of newly discovered and translated Oriental texts in languages like Sanskrit, Zend, and Arabic."[17] Given the commentary in eighteenth-century Family Bibles already discussed, however, it seems unlikely that the reason words in the Authorized Version now appeared "debased" or likely to excite "contempt and derision among libertines" was that new meanings for those words had been uncovered in new translations. What seems far more probable is that the ongoing process of imperial expansion contributed to the formation of a new Foucauldian "optics" of the nineteenth-century English Bible. As Randolph Trumbach has observed, "in probably all human societies other than those under the influence of the Christian religion, it has been legitimate for two males to have sexual relations with each other."[18] As more and more reports from "Oriental travels" and colonial "explorations" were published, what Foucault refers to as the "Ars Erotica" unfolded before British Orientalist eyes the spectacle of same-sex relations and other kinds of erotic pleasures that were not regarded as unnatural, let alone as illegal. Thus, the "universal knowledge" of the British Family Bible had already become culturally unintelligible, unknowable, because it had been invaded by an alien order of meaning, not merely alien languages.

It was not only invasions from the exterior world that precipitated the publication of disciplinary Family Bibles, but invasions from the "interior," both national and familial. Prefatory materials in Family Bibles document the conflicts created by the apparently all too successful campaigns to increase both the circulation of bibles and the reading of them among the British people themselves. Once the "working man" and the "cottager" actually became bible consumers, the clergy apparently became concerned about just what changes such consumption might produce.[19] The experience of Charlotte Brontë's father, Patrick Brontë, as detailed in Juliet Barker's family biography *The Brontës,* illuminates the very mixed motives of establishment (Anglican) clergy at this point. The threat of war and particularly of invasion from without was a shaping part of Patrick's university years. While still at St. John's, Cambridge University, in 1803, Patrick took part in the general mobilization to ward off Napoleon's expected invasion. Some 463,000 men from England, Scotland, and Ireland enrolled in local militias. But class motives mixed with patriotism: university men in Cambridge soon petitioned for leave to drill as a separate volunteer corps from the men of the town.[20] The defeat of Napoleon on June 18, 1815, did not end threats of revolution and violence on the island nation's own shores. The winter of 1816–17 was particularly hard and caused great distress among the poor. The Luddites began to meet again and, Barker comments, "there were fears of a general insurrection." In 1819 British soldiers charged their own countrymen and killed eleven of them in the Peterloo Massacre.

It was during this period of extreme middle-class anxiety about the stability of the British working poor that Boothroyd produced his *New Family Bible*, Thomas Williams his *Cottage Bible and Family Expositor*, and Ingraham Cobbin his *Cottage Commentator*. That concerns about what might happen if knowledge of the bible became truly "universal," in the sense of universally a part of British family life, intensified is also noted in the 1820 "Porteusian Bible" already referred to. The writer of the preface to this Family Bible comments that "in the present age, when such a laudable zeal is manifested in circulating the Holy Scriptures, and placing them so extensively in the hands of youthful and inexperienced readers, it has been much desired, that some corresponding efforts should be made to lead and direct them." The "Family Guide to the Holy Scriptures" included in the "Porteusian Bible" designates those chapters of the bible to be read so that, in this period "when Bibles and Testaments are happily to be obtained on such easy terms," even little children "when called upon to read to their parents and sick friends who may be unable or unwilling to read for themselves, on opening the Bible in whatever part, will be enabled to proceed without embarrassment or loss of time" (*Holy Bible . . . Family Guide*, iii–vii).

The writer of the preface undoubtedly refers to the proliferation of bibles and bible reading brought about in part by the mass publication of "cheap Bibles" by the British and Foreign Society. As Leslie Howsam documents, the first large printing was ordered in 1804, using the new stereotype technology, and these bibles were widely circulated to the working poor in Britain, as well as to foreign missions.[21] Such bibles rigorously excluded all notes of whatever kind, restricting readers to their "own" interpretations. At the same time, as Thomas Williams noted in his preface to *The Cottage Bible and Family Expositor*, there had been an "extensive spread of general knowledge among the middle and lower classes," such that "philosophical lectures are delivered to the working classes, not only in the metropolis, but in several other great towns" (1:vi). The spread of both bibles and "knowledge" produced a particular kind of desire—the desire to *limit* knowledge of the bible, to discipline both the bible and the families who read it.

Fears of "invasion" of the English Bible may also have been produced by a change in the dynamics of reading brought about specifically by its circulation in serialized form. Publishers of Family Bibles were advocating the serialized form of Family Bibles as an inducement to reading more than two decades before the 1836–37 publication of Charles Dickens's *Pickwick Papers,* usually assumed to mark the first great success in the publication of serialized fiction. *The Christian's Complete Family Bible* (1814, 1816) notes in its preface, "Publishing in Numerical series . . . excites the attention at each appearance, . . . and tends to ensure the reading of the Numbers and Parts while it also renders the work easily attainable, in point of expense, by the more dependent classes of society."[22] *The Family Bible . . . by the Rev. Matthew Henry, abridged for the Use of Families* (1838) reprints a preface dated 1817 that similarly lauds the advantages of serial publication: "Nor is it unworthy of remark, that many thousands of copies of the Sacred Writings have been of late years, diffused among the middle classes of the British empire, by a mode of publication equally adapted to their circumstances, suited to the small portion of their leisure time, and calculated to make them truly wise in the things of God. The moderate quantity comprised in what is usually termed *a Number,* may be purchased at a trifling expense, perused without weariness, and under the illuminating influence of the Spirit may be easily understood, and happily retained."[23]

Linda K. Hughes and Michael Lund, by contrast, quote Thomas Arnold's sermon of 1839 on the fears aroused by the appeal of such reading in "parts" when applied to fiction. Until "works of amusement" were published periodically, Arnold comments, they "did not occupy the mind for so long a time, nor keep alive so constant an expectation; nor, by thus dwelling upon the mind, and distilling themselves into it, as it were drop by drop, did they possess it so largely, colouring even, in many instances, its very language, and affording frequent matter for conversation. . . . They are not the more wicked for being published so cheap, and at regular intervals; but yet these two circumstances make them so peculiarly injurious."[24]

Doubtless, Arnold never would have considered it "wicked" to publish or read the bible in "parts," but comments such as Cobbin's in his *Cottage Commentator* on the absolute necessity of *not* reading certain parts of the bible to the family make it apparent that reading the bible as it was purchased in cheap periodical numbers might have dramatically changed the dynamics of bible reading. Instead of reading a portion of the Old Testament accompanied by a portion of the New Testament, as readers were directed by the lectionary in the *Book of Common Prayer,* or as it was read in church or chapel, readers would have read the bible straight through, from Genesis to Revelation, part by part, giving them ample time to dwell on such matters as the stories of Sodom and Onan, or to dwell frequently in conversation on the laws pertaining to the body in Leviticus. Rather than encountering the Old Testament as offering types and figures of the New, they might have read it as they would a novel, reflecting on its characters and stories, and discoursing on the strange "customs" described. Serialized reading in parts would have tended to defamiliarize the "English" bible, making it "strange" and exposing it as the collection of exotic and unharmonious texts from alien cultures that it actually is.[25]

The Oriental Bible and the "English" Family

It was, of course, the "lower" classes toward whom Williams's *Cottage Bible* was directed.[26] But within the middle-class family, as Elizabeth Langland demonstrates, "the institutional practice that most concealed the gross inequities [between servants and family] was family prayer." Quoting from Leonore Davidoff, Langland comments that "the institution of family prayer cooperated with the other discursive practices centered in the home to become 'one of the most effective means for social control ever devised.'"[27] The bracketed Family Bible, with its divisions between what should be read to the "family"—that is, wife, children and servants—and what should be reserved for the "Master of the family" to read in his "closet" was a means of warding off lower-class invasion of the supreme knowledge-power realm of the Authorized Version.

But the bracketed Family Bible was also a means of fortifying the idea of the British nation by "closeting" not only deviant sexuality, but whatever matters were deemed "peculiar to the Jews" in this era of civil reform that initiated the contentious and long-extending debate over the Jewish Civil Disabilities Bill. As Raphael Samuel comments, "the crystallization of nation becomes a disciplinary affair: it is associated with the rise of modern methods of surveillance and what Foucault called 'the great confinement'; the 'discovery' of the asylum; the invention of bureaucratic records; and the rise of such captive institutions as the workhouse, the factory and the school."[28] Dominant among such "captive institutions" was the state church and its Authorized Version. But under the aegis of the growing body of Orientalist studies, this text of ultimate British national authority and identity was increasingly visible as its own Other. It was becoming more and more difficult to evade the fact that the English Bible was an "Oriental" book.

One of the first attempts to deal with—and incidentally capitalize on—this confusing state of affairs was Samuel Burder's *The Scripture Expositor* (1809).[29] Identified on the title page as the author of *Oriental Customs,* Burder tentatively proposes in his dedication to the Lord Bishop of Durham, "an eminent Patron of Sacred Literature," that "the application of Oriental Literature to the elucidation of Scriptures, is a method of interpretation both rational and safe" (Burder, n.p.). As Burder further elaborates: "allusions to the Customs and Manners of the Jews and Eastern people, are so frequent, that to be ignorant of them renders their meaning unintelligible. But they may be, and indeed have been, clearly explained by a reference to local peculiarities" (5). His interpretation of the story of Onan seems, however, to reveal his nervousness about national "safety" rather than to elucidate the relevance of "Eastern customs." He comments on this "patriarchal custom" (that of having the surviving brother impregnate his deceased brother's wife and name the resulting heir as his brother's) as follows: "we should never cherish a revolting passion, or even suffer with approbation, a rebellious thought . . . it is dreadful when the iniquities of men bring upon them temporal destruction" (n.p.). His anxious reference is, of course, to Onan's spilling of his seed on the ground, traditionally interpreted as masturbation, which was hence dubbed "onanism."

Burder's understanding of "Eastern customs," despite his reference to the large contribution "of late years," actually depends largely on William Dodd's bible commentary.[30] By the time of Boothroyd's *New Family Bible,* first published in 1818, reference to the "Eastern customs" in the English Bible no longer appeared so "safe and rational." Noting in his dedication to the king that "knowledge has been diffused through the realm, and civil and religious freedom established on the justest principles, while trade and commerce have flourished in a degree unparalleled," Boothroyd comments that "every subject of science, policy, or religion is freely discussed; and error, however venerable by age, or disguised by art or sophistry, is detected and exposed." Among the errors newly coming to light is the discovery of the "considerable defects" of the "authorized version of the Scriptures," whose texts "frequently contain erroneous readings" and "numerous mistranslations," which Boothroyd's translation endeavors to remedy.

With this interpretation of the "English Bible," Boothroyd inaugurates the practice of nationally "closeting" sexual matters by relegating them to the "Jews," as well as by reserving them for closet reading. Thomas Williams and Ingraham Cobbin take this ironically inverse "orientalization" of the bible still further, by omitting from family reading those "genealogies" and "enumerations of the tribes" that, in a time of debate as to whether Jews should be granted the rights of citizenship in the British nation, made quite clear the Jewish family genealogy of Protestant Christianity. Increasingly, British "family values" were defined by their opposition to "matters peculiar to the Jews" in the foundational text of British national identity, the "English Bible." At the same time, commentators identified the "unnatural" sex attributed to the Jews with other "Eastern" or "heathen" peoples.

For example, *The Holy Bible with a Devotional and Practical Commentary* [1861–65], by the Reverend R. Jamieson and the Reverend E. H. Bickersteth, comments on Rom. 1:26, 27 (in which Paul condemns women and men for forgetting "the natural use"): "'This,' says Wordsworth, 'is a dark picture of heathenism. . . .' To which we may add the affecting testimony of a Brahmin, who objected that this epistle, at least, could not be eighteen hundred years old, for so faithful a portrait of Hindu society at Benares could never have been drawn, save by those who had witnessed it in modern times."[31] Similarly, *The Graphic Family Bible* [1873–75] comments on Rom. 1:21: "This dark picture of the state of morality in the heathen world, is not overdrawn or too deeply colored, as is proved by the writings of cotemporary [*sic*] Greek and Latin writers, and by what we know of the condition of heathendom in our own day."[32]

It is no coincidence, I believe, that the Reverend Ingraham Cobbin followed his bracketed *Domestic Bible* [1847] with *The Oriental Bible* (1850). Acknowledging that "the East has of late been the point of extraordinary attraction," and obviously wanting to capitalize as usual on that "numerous class of readers" presumed to be unable to afford the more scholarly works on Oriental customs, Cobbin did not include the word "family" in his title: an "Oriental Family Bible" would hardly have had appeal for the British family consumer. Although Cobbin argues that the knowledge of Oriental customs is important because "they strongly confirm the truth of the Bible," especially its "pages of Prophecy" (perhaps referring to the contemporary debate over whether the Jews should become citizens only when, at the time of the Second Coming, they would return to their "own" country), his complementary publications of a "domestic" and an "Oriental" bible, both designed for the consuming body of the British "family," stunningly represent the oppositional articulation of "family values" and Orientalism. Whatever was exotic, sensational, and alien in the bible could be assigned to "the Jews" or "Eastern customs"; whatever was domestic, safe, and familiar, to that "English Bible" on which—according to the writer of one promotional preface—the sun never set.[33] Internal invasion of the Authorized Version must be controlled by textual, familial, and national policing. But yet another invasion loomed not merely on the horizons or in the margins but in the very center of the family: the rise of what Colley calls "womanpower." Perhaps the strongest consumer desire activated by the disciplinary bibles was the desire to retain absolute paternal hierarchy in the family. But that unquestioned authority of the "Master of the family" was gradually but irresistibly being eroded by market forces. In the Victorian era, more and more evidence accumulates in Family Bibles of an appeal to *women,* the new arbiters of cultural capital in the domestic realm.

THREE

FAMILY BIBLES AND
FAMILY ANGELS

On a flyleaf of *The Imperial Family Bible* (1811, 1814), an owner inscribed a
date, 10 April 1820, and noted, "This Book is the Property of Mrs. Susanna Rudd, Lion Row Clifton near Bristol."[1] On the same page in different handwriting is another note: "It was an imperfect Copy bought
cheap for Love of the *Prints,* in 1819, intrusted to my Care, who restored
the Text: & wrote Notes to it, for Love of the possessor and *her* Heirs:
not those of H.L.P." The writer of the explanatory note, Hester Thrale
Piozzi, has indeed "restored the Text," for page after page of the bible includes not only handwritten notes in the margin, but in some places
paper covered with handwritten script pasted directly over the biblical
text, thus replacing the Authorized Version with Thrale Piozzi's version.
All this was done, as she notes, in order to make the bible a legacy and an
heirloom not for her own family, but for that of another woman whom
she loved. And as she notes, the bible was bought specifically because of
its *"Prints."*

This early-nineteenth-century *Imperial Family Bible* stands as an emblem not only of the circulation of Family Bibles between women, but
also of women's growing power as consumers, selecting bibles because of
features that appealed to them, such as the "elegant engravings." (In this
case, the prints are typically eighteenth century, including an unusually
gory representation of Judith cutting off the head of Holofernes.) Thrale
Piozzi did not merely write "in the margins" of the patriarchal text but
actually "scratched over" it, pasting her own "improved version" on top.
She inscribed one of her own poems in place of a family genealogy on the
flyleaf, and she wrote her own notes on the interpretation of the Book of

Revelation in light of 1820–21 political events on another flyleaf. She made this Family Bible her own, and then returned it to the other woman, written over with her personal notes. Although Thrale Piozzi belongs to the eighteenth century, her "restoration" of a Family Bible in line with her own tastes, opinions, and beliefs foreshadows the makeover of the Family Bible into a distinctively feminized form in the nineteenth century. This was only a cosmetic makeover, as the commentary within Victorian Family Bibles remains patriarchal to its fin-de-siècle end, but it nevertheless testifies both to women's growing consumer power and to their increasing production of their own appropriative and contestatory "notes" on the Authorized Version in their fiction and poetry.

Langland points out that, "with the rapid increase of wealth generated by the industrial revolution and the consequent social upheavals, status became a fluid thing, increasingly dependent upon the manipulation of social signs."[2] And it was the "material angel" in the house who was invested with the responsibility and with a degree of financial control to carry out this manipulation. Langland's apt term, "material angel," speaks to the lack of critical attention to the middle-class Victorian woman's essential function as *business* manager of the household, and to the fact that it was probably she more often than her husband who decided which household items to buy in order to improve the family's status. The publication of Family Bibles as ornament for the Victorian family parlor shows more and more evidence of an attempt to appeal to the eye of this crucial and increasingly educated buyer. But the "material angel" was more than a consumer of Family Bibles: she was also, in her symbolic function as "angel in the house," the consuming *subject* of the British Family Bible in the nineteenth century.[3] This new gender identity signals a new Victorian family identity whose "family values" differ dramatically from those represented by eighteenth-century Family Bibles.

Davidoff and Hall emphasize that the "common sense" of the English middle-class family was produced during the period of "exceptional turmoil and threatening economic and political disorder" from the time of the French Revolution through the 1830s.[4] During such periods of political and social disturbance, they argue, differences between groups are exaggerated to produce a "semblance of order" (30). The "closeted" Family Bibles whose publication began in 1818 demonstrate a strategy for stabilizing gender, class, and national boundaries through the careful partitioning of biblical "knowledge." But by the 1830s Family Bibles that foreground women suggest that the wife who had been theorized in the eighteenth century chiefly as her husband's rightful subordinate in the "little monarchy" of the home now began her ascent to the status of queen in a domestic empire. And, as eighteenth-century family theorists saw an analogy between the family and the monarchy, nineteenth-century Family Bibles promote the analogy between the family's domestic empire with its angelic queen and the British nation's empire with its imperial queen.

These bibles increasingly base their claims to the expansion of Protestant Christianity and the British Empire as its missionary agent on the superiority of the British family and its values. As the Reverend John Eadie puts it in his preface to *The National Comprehensive Family Bible* (1860),

> Christian civilisation necessarily leads to genuine and permanent greatness; for liberty, fraternity, and equality, in their highest and widest sense, can only flourish under the shadow of the cross. While the Bible brings salvation to every one who receives it as the Word of God—and this is its great and primary mission— it also soothes and elevates the temporal condition of man. . . . No wonder that our reflecting and pious people hold Scripture in such high veneration, and excel all other countries in their efforts to circulate it. No wonder that our English version, which 'hath done great things for us,' should be prized so highly, and that in every Christian household there should be a copy—a large and a loved one—familiarly and reverentially named the "FAMILY BIBLE."[5]

Robert Shittler's *Domestic Commentary* (1853) repeatedly emphasizes the centrality of "the domestic circle" or "the family circle," and also expounds on how delightful it is that the Divine Word "circulates from nation to nation, and from shore to shore; till the expanding circle gradually extends to the uttermost parts of the earth" (v). The British Empire becomes a great "family circle" that eventually comprises the entire globe. Even more than the "simple bar of soap" that—through the advertising campaign that promoted it—Anne McClintock suggests became central to the consolidation of British national identity in the nineteenth century, the commercial Family Bible underpinned the British "cult of domesticity" and its complementary racism. And the mass of the populace could buy a "part" for about the same price as a bar of soap or a tube of toothpaste.[6]

This global imperial expansion is justified by the virtues of the British family, epitomized by its "large and loved" Family Bible. *Payne's Illustrated Family Bible* [1862], whose prospectus suggests that this "Easy Reading Family Bible" may be "considered an heirloom in the Family," explains the problematic eighteenth chapter of Leviticus—bracketed in Cobbin's disciplinary Family Bibles—by stating, "Its great object is to purify and refine family life. The family is the source of all that is good, whether for the individual or for the State."[7] And the bible is that book which elevates the status of woman so that she, in turn, can elevate the status of family, and of the empire. Commentary on the Song of Solomon in this Family Bible is emphatic about the necessity of woman's elevation from heathen "degradation" in order to assure the proper state of man:

> In the portrait of the faithful Shulamite the sacred writer may have intended to give us a companion picture to the filial piety of Ruth and to the patriotic courage and resolution of Esther. Woman had come to be regarded as a being altogether inferior to man, little more than a beast of burden, a creature to satisfy his lust. This degraded estimate has naturally degraded her character; and though the woman's position was not altogether so low among the Jews as among other Eastern nations, it had still sunk very low; and this, as a natural consequence, tended to degrade man to the same low level. "Now if one sex of the human family has been so degraded by the other; if she whom God created to be a *helpmate and counterpart* has been reduced by man to be the slave of his carnal lusts; if such slavish and inhuman treatment has been justified on the false plea of the natural unfaithfulness and incontinency of the sex; if exclusion from society and imprisonment have been deemed necessary for the preservation of her morals, how greatly has woman been alien-

ated from the original design of her creation! How unjustly has her character been aspersed! How inhumanly has she been treated! And how great is the importance of a book which celebrates the virtuous example of a woman, and thus strikes at the root of all her reproaches and her wrongs!" (741).

The commentary for *The Illustrated Family Bible* [1871–76] turns the story of Onan into a self-congratulatory homily on the prevalence of "despotic fathers" in non-Christian nations: "In China, at the present day, fathers govern their families with despotic power; and in other countries of Asia the paternal authority exists under various modifications and forms, which enable us to discover the extent to which it was formerly carried even in those parts in which its ancient absoluteness has in the course of time been mitigated." In his commentary on Vashti, the deposed queen in the Book of Esther, Shittler expostulates: "How thankful should we be for the merciful character of laws emanating from the Christian faith! The poorest subject in this realm enjoys a privilege and security, which Vashti, the queen of the mighty Ahasuerus, possessed not!"[8]

While acknowledging the crucial importance of the elevated status of the British "angel" to the moral claims of the British Empire to rule the world, commentaries nevertheless exhibit an increasing anxiety that she should not be allowed to think she is queen in more than the Ruskinian sense: her queenly authority in this domestic empire is still always to be subordinated to that of her husband, the true "head" of the family. Reverend Edward Henry Bickersteth, in his preface to the New Testament in *The Holy Bible with a Devotional and Practical Commentary* [1861–65] comments flatteringly that "no apology is needed for the occasional introduction of the Greek text because so many of our intelligent young men (and may I not add, young women?) have learned enough of their Greek Testament to find pleasure in seeing the original words before them." His commentary, he notes, is directed toward "the educated classes of the present day," on whom "the constant claims of business and professional life" meant that "twenty or thirty minutes at most were assigned to family prayer, that golden girdle of home life."[9] But in his commentary on 1 Cor.11:2–16, he finds it necessary to elaborate on "the primeval relation of woman to man. (See Wordsworth.) The *immediate Head* (see Scott) of every man is Christ, by whom and for whom all were created; the *immediate head* of the woman is man, out of whose side and for whose sake she was originally created." Because man is made in the image of God, he is "the one who chiefly manifests the excellence and wisdom of God to the lower creation. *But the woman is the glory of the man*—the noblest praise of the wife, for example, being in self-concealment to manifest the excellence of her husband. This order is confirmed (vers. 8, 9) by the original formation of Eve, who was taken out of the side of Adam, and created to be an helpmeet for him. The modest submission of woman is her true power; without it she is powerless for good" (Jamieson and Bickersteth, 3:277).

Congruent with Bickersteth's homily on the crucial necessity of woman's submission to man is a disturbing illustration appearing in the contemporary *Royal Family Bible* [1862–68]. Jephthah's daughter is represented not only as the ultimate in female submission and willing self-sacrifice, but as a symbolic portrayal of the father's rape of the daughter (fig. 8). In the biblical account, Jephthah vows to make a burnt offering of whatever he sees first if the Lord gives him victory in battle (Judg. 11:30–40). The changed representation here (in which the daughter bears her breasts to her father's knife) suggests an uneasiness about invoking similarities between a biblical text and the Indian ritual of *sati,* but a simultaneous refusal to acknowledge deadly parallels between the subordination of women in "heathen" cultures and Protestant Britain.

The middle-class woman's importance as *consumer,* however, pushed publishers into varied attempts to cater to her presumed tastes. The first clear indication of such an appeal to the female consumer is, appropriately enough, dedicated to the new queen. The publishers of *The Illustrated Family Bible* (1838, 1839) state that it has been their aim to produce an edition of "that Sacred Volume, that shall surpass, in point of TYPOGRAPHICAL SUPERIORITY, any Work of the kind hitherto issued from the Press."[10] But they also articulate the connection between the modesty and "tender feelings" of the female sovereign and the Family Bible dedicated to her: "they conceive they shall not be trespassing the bounds of propriety by DEDICATING it to YOUR MAJESTY, whose tender feelings of benevolence have already been abundantly manifested by an anxious desire to extend, in every practicable way, the moral and religious improvement of

FIGURE 8. The sacrifice of Jeptha's daughter [untitled]. *The Royal Family Bible* [1862–68]. Courtesy of the British Library.

Your Majesty's subjects, as well as to promote the advancement of Literature and the Arts" (n.p.).

Although the commentary in this bible is simply that of the eighteenth-century Scottish Dissenter John Brown, therefore representing no advance whatever in biblical exegesis, the ornamental style of the bible is new, and seems designed for the feminine eye. There are no "immodest" or sensational full-page prints, but the first page of each book has a pink frame of scrolls and curlicues that includes a small oval illustration at the top of the page, and tiny miniatures of various subjects set into the first letter on that page. For example, the first letter of the Book of Exodus pictures the finding of the baby Moses. Moreover, this Family Bible contains not only a printed "Family Register," but also a page entitled "Sacred Token" on which could be inscribed the name of the giver of the bible and its recipient, thus clearly designating this bible as a gift book. Published in the heyday of such gift annuals as *The Keepsake,* this Family Bible seems designed to appeal to much the same Christmas market.[11]

From here on in the nineteenth century, British Family Bibles demonstrate more and more consciousness of feminine tastes: the frontispieces of patriarchal figures so common in eighteenth-century bibles—the "author" of the bible, Moses with the tablets of the Law, or Jesus as princely dispenser of mercy—are replaced with representations of Moses as a baby, far too chubby to float in his wicker basket, or the boy Samuel kneeling in his little nightshirt to say his prayers (fig. 9). "Family Registers" not only are routinely printed in Family Bibles but become more and more ornate, and ultimately, toward the end of the century, include openings for photographs, so that the Family Bible can become also a family portrait album.[12]

This ornamental design is especially evident in *The Comprehensive Family Bible* (1852), whose date of publication suggests the inspiration of the Great Exhibition of 1851. Noting that originally the thirty-six parts were intended to be bound as a single volume, the Scottish publishers (Blackie & Son) comment that "the extensive series of Illustrative Engravings adds so much to the thickness, that if they are included in the Volume, it may be considered rather too bulky and heavy. We therefore suggest that the Text of the Work form one Volume, and the Engravings a separate Volume or ornamental Table-Book; and with a view to this an

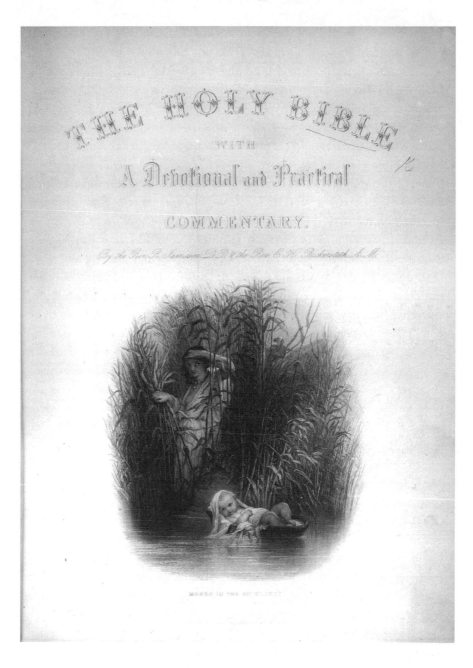

FIGURE 9. "Moses in the Bulrushes." Pictorial title page. *The Holy Bible with a Devotional and Practical Commentary* [1861–65]. Courtesy of the British Library.

additional Title-Page and Descriptions of the Plates are in preparation, and will be supplied to Subscribers at a price not exceeding *One Shilling.*"[13]

The publishers' preface also emphasizes the suitability of this Family Bible *for* the family. The illustrations, they emphasize, "include Historical Subjects, carefully selected from the Ancient and Modern Masters; but the larger portion consists of views of Mountains, Rivers, Lakes, and other Natural Scenery . . ." (n.p.). In other words, this "comprehensive" Family Bible is suited to "youth and age" alike, and includes no sensational or too-graphic "illustrations," such as would be inappropriate for a table-book in the parlor. Yet *The Comprehensive Family Bible* contains specific commentary on the subject of "female beauty" reminiscent of fashion magazine articles: "'Asiatic females, though black or brown, are exquisitely beautiful.' Many of the Egyptian women are still fine, but their complexion is much inferior to those of Palestine. But from other notices of her beauty, the language is assuredly expressive of modesty. Besides, her beauty was injured by exposure to toils under a sultry sun. The complexion of females of rank differ exceedingly from that of the lower class in warm climates."[14]

Blackie & Son's later and internationally published version of their *Imperial Family Bible* (1858) most amply demonstrates the appeal to feminine tastes. Frontispiece illustrations here actually foreground women, that for the Old Testament showing Jesus with Mary and Martha, but making the kneeling figure of Mary its center (fig. 10). The frontispiece for the New Testament, titled "Daughters of Jerusalem Weep Not for Me," depicts a crouching woman reaching out her hands to a Christ bent even further beneath the cross, the "saving" woman sharing the focus equally with the Saviour (fig. 11).[15] The Book of Ruth, usually not illustrated in earlier Family Bibles, is here adorned with a portrayal of Ruth warmly embracing Naomi, in a representation of ideal sisterhood that brings to mind Christina Rossetti's celebration of sisterhood in "Goblin Market," written in 1859 (fig. 12). And the "Family Register" page is framed by a series of vignettes showing the family, headed by a mother watching over her child, and continuing through representations of childhood and adolescence, marriage, grandparenthood, and, finally, the descent of the elderly couple into the grave, followed by what appear to be two daughters looking upward to heaven (fig. 13). Such "Family Register" vignettes

FIGURE 10. "The Sisters of Bethany." *The Imperial Family Bible* (1858). Courtesy of the British Library.

FIGURE 11. "Daughters of Jerusalem Weep Not for Me." *The Imperial Family Bible* (1858). Courtesy of the British Library.

FIGURE 12. "Ruth and Naomi." *The Imperial Family Bible* (1858). Courtesy of the British Library.

foregrounding the woman's role as nurturer and supporter of other members of the family are strikingly similar to George Elgar Hicks's triptych *Woman's Mission,* exhibited in 1863 at the Royal Academy of Arts in London. Although critics gave *Woman's Mission* negative reviews, calling it "vulgar, populist and unrealistic," it was immensely popular.[16]

The illustrations in this Family Bible were obviously a key selling point. The list of illustrations includes the names of both painter and engraver for each, and on a page labeled "Opinions of the Press," the *Edinburgh Witness* explicitly promotes the book's status-improving value:

> What a magnificent book! This, we are sure, must be the exclamation of all persons of taste, on opening the splendid Work which is now before us. . . . What a book this for families of

FAMILY REGISTER.

FIGURE 13. "Family Register." *The Imperial Family Bible* (1858). Courtesy of the British Library.

rank and wealth to possess! What an ornamental treasure would it be in the houses of our thriving manufacturers and agriculturalists! And we would be delighted to find that it is also taken by many of our respectable operatives. We would not desire a more promising symptom of a young industrious couple, than their taking, in monthly numbers, this publication: and by saving even a sixpence a-week they might, in no great time, be able to call the whole of the "Imperial Bible" their own.[17]

This late-1850s *Imperial Family Bible* appeals to consumers of lower-class status to raise that status through making the central text of family worship also a mark of sophisticated taste. By allocating as little as sixpence a week, even "operatives" might fashion themselves not only as respectable but as having some share in the power and status of an "imperial family" identity. Most significantly, however, this family of "imperial" taste is identified as one whose most "illustrious" figure is its own angel, its simultaneously self effacing and foregrounded wife and mother.

Perhaps the most striking demonstration of the shift to women shoppers in the marketing of Family Bibles are the advertisements bound into *Cobbin's Illustrated Family Bible and People's Commentary* [1871–72]. These ads are solely for women's magazines and fashion books such as *Beeton's Englishwoman's Domestic Magazine, Beeton's Young Englishwoman, An Illustrated Lady's Magazine, The Freaks of Fashion, The Art of Figure Training, The Milliner and Dressmaker,* and *Dress and Fashion.* Yet this Family Bible appears to be identical—except for the substitution of colored plates for black-and-white illustrations—with the Reverend Ingraham Cobbin's earlier, and disciplinary, *Domestic Bible* (1847), complete with the bracketing of passages unsuitable for "family" reading.

This curious combination of promotions of the latest and finest in ornamental design for Family Bibles with anachronistic commentary reaches its apogee in *The Illustrated Family Bible . . . with . . . Notes by the Reverend John Brown* [1876]. Although the publishers (A. Fullarton & Company) readily acknowledge in their "Publishers' Notice" that "nearly a hundred years" have elapsed since the publication of "Brown's Self-Interpreting Bible," they assert that public confidence in "the soundness of its principles" has not diminished, and they are therefore preparing a new edition with "a superb set of ILLUSTRATIVE ENGRAVINGS."[18] The engravings, which include reproductions of paintings, an illustrated family register, and "six splendid CHROMO-LITHOGRAPHS" showing the plants and animals in the bible, are said to have been prepared with the assistance of William Bell Scott, a well-known artist. Scott was a good friend of Christina Rossetti's, and although there is no evidence that this "Cheapest Illustrated High-class Family Bible" was prepared with her in mind, there is also no doubt that the colored lithographs of animals would have appealed to her, as to other animal-lovers and supporters of antivivisection campaigns.[19] The frontispiece for this indeed handsome Family Bible is a reproduction of Holman Hunt's vastly popular "The Light of the World," and the illustrations include the painting "Ruth and Naomi," already mentioned as printed in Blackie & Son's 1858 *Imperial Family Bible,* as well as other woman-promoting subjects such as "The Maries at the Sepulchre."

But *The Illustrated Family Bible,* with its combination of the latest and best in graphic technology and the most old-fashioned and archconservative in commentary, glaringly displays the increasingly contradictory values of the British family and its bible. As women moved toward greater access to education and to legal and political rights, as well as increasing consumer power, they moved further from the patriarchal family values so glowingly portrayed by Jane Eyre. In the 1870s and 1880s, publication of Family Bibles began to decline, and thereafter they ceased to be published at all.[20] The Family Bible in the Victorian fin de siècle could no longer "sell" the family to the British family: its design had gone out of style.

End of the Family Bible Business

In a statement about twentieth-century society that is equally true of nineteenth-century Britain, Martyn J. Lee comments that "what has undoubtedly had the most significant impact upon the way of life of ordinary people in industrial societies over the last century has been the mass availability of consumer goods. No aspect of everyday life has been left untouched by the arrival of the consumer society . . . [such as] the ways in which we spend our leisure-time; indeed, the very structure of daily time itself."[21] The commercial Family Bible existed as such a mass-produced commodity, around which the Victorian family's life—at least by reputation—was organized. The Family Bible was central to the "golden girdle" of family prayer, which was to be bound around the family's daily time, giving it order and value. Yet by the end of the Victorian era, commercial bibles with the word "family" in the title were no longer being published. In Britain, the growth of single-volume publication at the end of the century certainly contributed to the decline of serial publication, but this would not seem to preclude one-volume editions of the "Family Bible with Notes." Why then did Family Bibles go out of style? Does the end of the Family Bible business in the Victorian fin de siècle signal the end of the "family," or at least of a certain kind of family?

This analysis of the British commercial Family Bible has theorized that it exhibits three major styles or "generations," each appealing to a differently identified family market. Family Bibles of the Victorian era demonstrate the increasing consumer power of women, even though their acquisition of legal and economic rights during this period was frustratingly slow and piecemeal. These bibles corroborate Ann Bermingham's thesis that the consumption of culture enables individuals to construct social identities, and that such consumption "should not be understood as simply a positive or a negative reality but rather as a powerful tool for social change . . . the primary means through which individuals have participated in culture and transformed it."[22] Victorian Family Bibles exhibit more and more evidence of the cultural capital acquired by the Victorian "angel in the house." As such, they could function as a powerful tool for the construction of the Victorian woman's subjectivity, supplying her with a fertile resource for her identification both as spiritual angel, morally superior but properly subordinate to the "Master of the family," and as "material angel," empowered by her capacity to choose those objects that best reproduced her image as "angel" writ large—and elegantly illustrated. The Victorian Family Bible may thus have constructed its own demise, fostering the development of the "New Woman" and those other new sexual types whom its commentary continued to denounce or define as appropriate only to the closet. Lyn Pykett argues that sales figures from the late 1880s to the mid-1890s, and essays and reviews in the periodical press of this period, strongly suggest that "New Woman writing was perhaps the single most important literary phenomenon of the day."[23] She quotes Edmund Gosse's complaint in 1895 that "things have come to a pretty pass . . . when the combined prestige of the best poets, historians, critics and philosophers of the country does not weigh in the balance against a single novel by the New Woman" (Pykett, 128). The "Family Bible with Notes" claimed to represent just such a compendium of "the best poets, historians, critics and philosophers," and perhaps it simply could not measure up to the New Woman and other rebels against "family values."

The domestic novel suffered a decline corresponding to that of the Family Bible. Linda K. Hughes and Michael Lund comment:

> In the last decade of the century . . . novelists and poets were conceiving of stories that jarred with the fundamental dynamics of serial literature. . . . Instead of the patient creation of an idealized home, broken families often characterized the literary work; rather than steady historical progress, chaos or regression took over many plots; instead of empire fostering growth and development, the will to power crushed individual identities; and skepticism replaced doubt about human potential, paralyzing society. Such narratives did not harmonize with the slow, sure growth and development of serial literature.[24]

The 1890s saw the publication in the United States of *The Woman's Bible,* the first attempt to write a commentary on the entire bible from a feminist perspective. Undoubtedly, both the emergence and the disappearance of the British Family Bible were overdetermined, but the parallel rise of the Victorian family "angel" and the Victorian Family Bible strongly suggests not only their interdependence but the importance of recognizing how this form of consumer Christianity could be instrumental to women in their struggle with the constraints imposed by a culture dominated by patriarchal religion. In the end, it appears, the New Woman and other radical gender and sexual entities worked to remove the Authorized Version from the center of the family parlor and put it away in a soon-to-be-forgotten trunk in the attic. When we reopen that Family

Bible, we necessarily read both it and its families from a distanced and alienated perspective. The "family values" promulgated by the media of this generation are indeed descendants of this biblical genealogy, but the tangled, confused, scratched-over, and recopied condition of that genealogy now confronts us.

PART TWO

Consuming the

Authorized Version

FOUR

PLAYING WITH SACRED PAGES

Menstrual Superabundance in Villette
and Dissenting Bible Commentary

A contemporary reviewer of Charlotte Brontë's third published novel, *Villette* (1853), complained that

> we should be sorry to subject any child of ours to the teaching
> and insinuations of the mind here pictured; whose religion is
> without awe,—who despises and sets down every form and dis-
> tinction she cannot understand,—who rejects all guides but her
> Bible, and at the same time constantly quotes and plays with its
> sacred pages, as though they had been given to the world for
> no better purpose than to point a witticism or furnish an ingen-
> ious illustration.[1]

With a boldness outdoing that of Hester Thrale Piozzi, Brontë "plays" with the sacred pages of the Authorized Version in *Villette,* quoting and misquoting, turning biblical texts into quips, appropriating biblical personae for her own purposes, and otherwise treating the Authorized Version as if it were like any other familiar literary text available for importation into Lucy Snowe's "heretic narrative."[2] But Brontë does something even more audacious with her bible "quotes": she infuses her novel with a biblical discourse on menstruation. This biblical discourse on menstruation works to translate the Victorian medical discourse of feminine cyclical "instability" into a different "language" in which menstruation also figures as feminine power and passion. Brontë's "play" with the sacred pages is actually a serious game: highly conscious of the density of meaning omnipresent in language, she plays one male-authorized discourse against another to expose the continual surveillance and spectacularization of the female body in Victorian culture, and to find words for a woman's narrative about women's bodies.

Critics have repeatedly commented on the unusual quantity, and even more astonishing *quality,* of Charlotte Brontë's biblical allusions. Keith A. Jenkins notes that "Charlotte Brontë is undoubtedly one of the most biblically allusive of the major Victorian novelists," pointing to the "over four hundred biblical quotations or allusions in her four novels" indexed in the Clarendon editions.[3] Kathryn Bond Stockton comments on "the pervasive biblical allusiveness of *Villette.*"[4] Irene Tayler asserts that "in *Villette,* biblical echo and religious imagery dominate every other kind."[5] Christina Crosby details a "typological design which informs the whole novel," suggesting that Brontë utilizes "a traditional exegetical procedure well-known and widely practised in Victorian England."[6] But even more eye opening to post-Victorian critics is the recognition that, as Brontë's contemporary critic complained, she maintains no proper Victorian respect for her bible, but "plays with its sacred pages." Jenkins comments that Brontë "rips the [bible] texts to shreds, reducing them to bits of language and imagery and plot, so that she can 're-vise' them."[7] Stockton and Tayler both note the sexual issues constantly toyed with in Brontë's biblical language, and Crosby, although she assumes that "doubtless Brontë intended nothing improper," notices that typology in *Villette* becomes "wildly excessive allegory."[8]

But reading certain popular bible commentaries of the time, particularly those written by dissenting clergy, intertextually with *Villette* demonstrates that not only Alice Mozley's notions of "proper" bible citation, but our own, may be dramatically different from Brontë's. The scene of bible reading in *Jane Eyre,* in which St. John Rivers reads from "the great old Bible" to the family circled around him, attests to Brontë's familiarity with the imposing form of the family bible and its hallowed position in the Victorian family. Jane Eyre's description of St. John Rivers's voice, however, intimates her awareness of the collusion between patriarchal power and patriarchal religion as vested in the English Bible. Bible commentaries produced by dissenting clergy open still another perspective on the Authorized Version, as these writers—whatever their sectarian allegiance—felt no obligation whatever to adhere to established Church doctrine. Their commentary frequently exhibits a "play" with the "sacred pages" not too far removed from the "playing" in *Villette* that shocked Alice Mozley.[9]

"Play" also figures prominently in late-twentieth-century feminist criticism of *Villette*, but with a very different valence. Crosby, in her 1984 article "Charlotte Brontë's Haunted Text," notes that "Lucy's story is enacted through a play of doublings, mirrors and reversals which never entirely come to rest in the text . . . and, at the same time, a play of oppositions without resolutions, of antitheses without syntheses."[10] Patricia Yaeger, in her 1988 *Honey-Mad Women,* protests that "the character of Lucy Snowe is too often read negatively," and extracts from *Villette* "a typology of pleasure, bliss, and playfulness in writing."[11] Joseph Litvak, in his 1992 *Caught in the Act,* discusses "plays" or scenes of theatricality within the novel, noting the "irreversible entanglement of a disciplinary theatricality with a transgressive or potentially feminist theatricality."[12] These varying usages of "play" in reference to *Villette* theorize the Victorian woman writer's potential for agency in "authorized" discourse, whether in reference to the Lacanian sense of an Imaginary register in which the subject may be trapped in a narcissistic system of mirrorings and doublings, or to the Foucauldian sense of disciplinary discourses such as the medical hysterization of women, which constructs them as either silenced or "mad," and therefore without access to discursive power.

In fact, as Peter Melville Logan notes, in the nineteenth century hysteria was associated with a *compulsion* to speak, thereby constructing the patient not as silenced or "mad" but as one whose speech is devalued. He cites Thomas Trotter's *A View of the Nervous Temperament* (1807), in which hysteria is said to be marked by "a selfish desire of engrossing the sympathy and attention of others to the narration of their own sufferings; with fickleness and insteadiness [*sic*] of temper, even to irascibility; and accompanied more or less with dyspeptic symptoms."[13] Lucy Snowe conforms to this diagnosis with startling precision, and it is in part her "scientifically" accurate construction as a hysteric woman that enables this character's sensitive articulation of a Victorian woman's intense feeling. Sally Shuttleworth's pioneering *Charlotte Brontë and Victorian Psychology* demonstrates indisputably that the wielding of psychological discourse in Brontë's texts is not that of "an intuitive genius who seems to belong more to the Freudian than to the Victorian era" but that of a historical subject constructed by the contemporary discourse on psychology.[14] *Villette* represents Brontë's "most explicit engagement with Victorian psychological theory and practice" (219). Even the identity of the doctor in the text, as Shuttleworth notes, is that of the doctor *of* the authorized medical text in the Brontë household, Thomas John Graham's *Modern Domestic Medicine* (1826). This book was "anxiously annotated" by that still greater patriarchal authority in the Brontë domestic establishment, the Reverend Patrick Brontë, with his many "fears regarding his family's nervous diseases and potential insanity" (Shuttleworth, 222).

But Shuttleworth's detailed demonstration of psychological discourse in *Villette* has the inherent limitation of making the representation of Lucy Snowe appear almost a textbook case of Victorian female hysteria. This chapter will seek to expose Charlotte Brontë's resistance to the hysterization of women through her confrontation of one authorized discourse with another, particularly on that aspect of female hysteria on which women were least permitted to speak—its supposed connection with menstruation. In Victorian medical discourse, hysteria in women was pervasively associated with menstruation. As the Scottish psychiatrist T. S. Clouston observed: "Disturbed menstruation is a constant danger to the mental stability of some women; nay, the occurrence of normal menstruation is attended with some risk in many unstable brains."[15] Shuttleworth points out that psychiatrists regarded the cyclic flows of a woman's body "as an outward sign of the threatening sexual and reproductive excess of the female body, an excess which caused her to vibrate indiscriminately to all external stimuli. In the popular mind, then, menstruation was linked not just with reproductive functions, but with a more disturbing image of palpitating sexuality" (Shuttleworth, 91).

On the other hand, menstruation was also regarded as a necessary draining off of "polluted blood." As one physician expressed it, the uterus is "the sewer of all the excrements existing in the body" (Shuttleworth, 73). Consequently, obstruction of the menstrual flow was viewed with even more alarm than the "inner excess and uncontrollable flow" that characterized some menstrual cycles, particularly those at the onset of puberty (78). The anxiety that, as Shuttleworth suggests, seemed to "haunt the male imagination" about this "dark flow" manifested itself in contradictions in medical discourse: since intellectual study could suppress menstruation, such activity could lead to the explosion of sexual appetite or, by contrast, the obstructed blood could flood the brain and "lead to irreparable psychological breakdown" (77).

This dammed-if-you-do and flooded-if-you-don't situation led to what Digby appropriately terms "women's biological straitjacket." Since gynecology laid increasing stress on both the importance and the frailty of the reproductive cycle in women, women's health was dependent on the proper maintenance of "the uterine system," particularly the menstrual flow. But this flow was also the sign of her predisposition to hysteria, insanity, and sexual excess (Digby, 193). Constant medical surveillance constructed the female body, whether menstruating or failing to menstruate, as pathological object of the diagnostic gaze—a scenario that could not be more definitively represented than by Dr. John and his watchful observation of both Lucy and Vashti.

Brontë's knowledgeable representation of Victorian medical discourse on menstruation as pathology is continually interrupted by a more volatile and contradictory biblical discourse on menstruation. The narrative is permeated with imagery that evokes or specifically alludes to biblical texts concerning menstruation and its metaphorical references, such as floods, fountains, and flowers. Both inspired and disrupted by periodic "floods," the narrative employs this menstrual metaphor to link sexual and verbal flows. It is no coincidence that Bronte foregrounds the issue of "language"—whether national, religious, or medical—treating it as always already mistranslation. Bible commentary continually refers to the issue of translation, and resulting differences of interpretation. In her excess of "witticism" and "ingenious illustration," Brontë similarly underlines the contradictions, errors, and sheer silliness of both biblical and medical "authorized versions" concerning women's bodies. In the intertwined narratives of Lucy Snowe and Paulina Home, she produces another version of language—a women's "language" that can best be spoken between women under cover of darkness, momentarily hidden from the surveillance that would dictate their desire. Reading contemporary bible commentary intertextually with *Villette's* biblical references demonstrates that Charlotte

Brontë writes the female body not only as the "uterine system" with which Dr. J. G. Millingen linked an incessant predisposition to hysteria, but as what the Methodist commentator Adam Clarke called "womb-man," or "the man with the womb"—for what is "excess" in Victorian medical discourse may translate as "superabundance" in dissenting bible commentary.[16]

Vashti and the Language of Her "Own People"

When Lucy is told by Dr. Bretton that she has a chance not only to attend the theater with him, but to witness the performance of one whose name thrilled her—indeed, "a name that, in those days, could thrill Europe"—it is clear that Lucy refers to the actress Rachel, whom Charlotte Brontë had herself seen perform in a London theater (255). In fact, Brontë describes Rachel in her letters in terms recognizably similar to those she uses for Lucy's interpretation of the fictitious actress Vashti.[17] Lucy, for example, sees the famous actress in terms of violent oppositions: although Vashti "could shine yet with pale grandeur and steady might," that "star verged already on its judgment-day. Seen near, it was a chaos—hollow, half-consumed: an orb perished or perishing—half lava, half glow." Lucy had expected "bony harshness and grimness" of this actress, rumored to be "plain," but what she sees is "the shadow of a royal Vashti: a queen, fair as the day once, turned pale now like twilight, and wasted like wax in flame." Devils sit in each of the actress's eyes, and they write HELL on her brow, and writhe her regal face to "a demoniac mask." She is at once a "marvellous sight: a mighty revelation" and a "spectacle, low, horrible, immoral" (258).

In a 24 June [1851] letter to Ellen Nussey, Brontë writes: "On Saturday I went to hear & see Rachel—a wonderful sight—terrible as if the earth had cracked deep at your feet and revealed a glimpse of hell—I shall never forget it—she made me shudder to the marrow of my bones: in her some fiend has certainly taken up an incarnate home. She is not a woman—she is a snake—she is the——" (Smith, *Letters,* 2:648).

Like Brontë, Lucy the narrator describes irreconcilable oppositions in the actress's performance and is similarly reduced to incoherence and botched syntax. Vashti is like "a fierce light, not solar—a rushing, red, cometary light—hot on vision and to sensation," or like "a deep, swollen, winter river, thundering in cataract and bearing the soul, like a leaf, on the steep and steely sweep of its descent," or a "magian power or prophet-virtue gifting that slight rod of Moses could, at one waft, release and re-mingle a sea spell-parted, whelming the heavy host with the down-rush of overthrown sea-ramparts" (259).

What Lucy sees is almost beyond her powers of narration, just as Brontë's letter to her friend seems to spurt out with uncontainable excitement and then sputter to a halt in complete frustration at her inability to find an acceptable word for this revelation who is "not a woman." Yet in her next letter on Rachel, Brontë writes, "I neither love, esteem, nor admire this strange being; but (if I could bear the high mental stimulus so long), I would go every night for three months to watch and study its manifestations" (652).

What is most crucial to our reading of the novel here is discovering why Brontë should choose the biblical name Vashti for this unrepresentable representation of something that is "not a woman." In the Book of Esther, Queen Vashti figures only in the first chapter, and she plays only a negative role. She refuses to obey the king's command that she perform before a group of male guests. She is therefore promptly deposed, thus clearing the way for Esther, the true heroine of the story, to compete for and successfully win the position of new queen. From this position of limited power, she is able to save her own people, the Jews, by courageously declaring herself one of them and thus persuading the king to stay his intended massacre.[18]

So why Vashti? Why should Brontë choose the name of a nonperformer for one whose performances thrilled all Europe, even reducing Brontë herself to wordlessness? In nineteenth-century bible commentary, the contradictions in Vashti's refusal to perform are, of course, noticed. She is both condemned for her unthinkable disobedience to a man who is not only her husband but the king, and praised for what Victorians saw as her most admirable modesty, her refusal to display herself in what would surely have been an intensely sexual performance before men. The biblical Vashti, then, is presumably the precise opposite of the actress whom Lucy terms "a spectacle, low, horrible, immoral."

But nineteenth-century bible commentary foregrounds a very different aspect of Vashti's story: commentators are intensely interested in the alleged "mistranslation" of the concluding verse of Vashti's story. In the Authorized Version this appears as, "For he [the king's counselor] sent letters into all the king's provinces, into every province according to the writing thereof, and to every people after their language, that every man should bear rule in his own house, and that it should be published according to the language of every people" (Esther 1:22). Commentators obsessively complain that the words of the text could not possibly mean that the decree should be published "according to the language of every people," but rather that every man should not only "rule" in his own house, but there speak the language of *his* people. Vashti is not merely a disobedient woman: she represents the unthinkable disobedience of a woman who insists on speaking her own language instead of her husband's.

As an 1809 edition of Simon Patrick's *Commentary* notes: the king's counselor Memucan "proposed divorce because, according to the Targum, he was himself married to a wife richer than himself, and very proud, and who would not speak to him but in her own language, so now he took this opportunity for revenge." This commentator goes on to explain that "the Persians had yielded so much to their wives that when they married a stranger, they suffered her to bring her own language into the family." But the king's decree altered that "custom" and allowed no other language but the man's to be spoken in his own house.[19] An 1847 edition of this commentary elaborates the prohibition of the wife's language in greater detail. Quoting the Targum, the commentary explains that the wife of Memucan (the king's counselor) wouldn't speak to him except in her own language, and that he took this opportunity to be revenged on her:

> And thus the former Targum, "Every man shall rule in his own house, and compel his wife to speak in the language of her husband, and in the language of his people." Which, indeed, was a token of dominion; all conquerors endeavouring to bring their own language into the country which they have conquered.
> The latter Targum hath only these words, that "every man shall be honoured in his own house, and speak according to the lan-

guage of his people;" that is, give his commands in his own language, which everyone was bound to learn. (Patrick, n.p.)[20]

While nineteenth-century commentators deplore the possibility of women's linguistic rebellion, they cannot resist a growing approval of Vashti's disobedience. Vashti probably refused out of modesty, not pride, this commentary decides, because it was not customary for women to show their faces in public. The Reverend Justin Edwards's *Family Bible* (1853) states that Vashti felt the king's command was an indignity, and that the king would have too if he hadn't been drunk.[21] But it is the Methodist Adam Clarke, whose commentary was first published in parts from 1810 to 1825, who raises Vashti's disobedience to the heights of feminine nobility: "What woman, possessing even a common share of *prudence* and *modesty*, could consent to expose herself to the view of such a group of drunken Bacchanalians? Her *courage* was equal to her modesty. . . . Her *contempt of worldly grandeur* . . . is worthy of observation. . . . Her *humility* was greatly evidenced in this refusal. She was *beautiful;* and might have shown herself to great advantage . . . but she *refused to come.* Hail, noble woman! be thou a pattern to all thy sex on every similar occasion! . . . Vashti must be considered at the top of her sex."[22] It is Vashti's refusal to make a spectacle of herself that brings her the accolades of nineteenth-century bible commentary, despite her disobedience of her husband's command. But it is the issue of a man's "right" to speak *his* language rather than his wife's that commentators see as even more significant in her story. The name Vashti speaks to patriarchal denial of a woman's right to speak her own "language," even the language of her national or racial identity, and to patriarchal approval of her self-suppression of what might be termed the language of her body.

Bible Commentary in the Victorian Marketplace

How important was bible commentary to the "common reader" of the Victorian era? In what form or forms was it marketed, and who were its likely consumers? British bible commentary published in the eighteenth and nineteenth centuries usually included the full text of the Authorized

Version, or the part of it taken as subject for the work. Such commentary was titled, in contrast with the many editions of the "Family Bible with Notes," either as "Commentary" or "Exposition" or as "The Holy Bible . . . with Commentary by . . ." The term "family" does not appear in the titles. However, like the Family Bibles, commentaries were often published in serialized parts or numbers, if not at the time of first publication then in subsequent editions. That they were an outstanding commercial success is indicated by the Reverend Ingraham Cobbin in his preface to his 1847 *Domestic Bible:*

> Some literary writers have expressed an opinion that we have Commentaries enough. The public, however, think [*sic*] differently, or they would not so largely encourage the reprint of old ones, and the appearance of others entirely new. The unprecedented sale of the illustrated penny edition of *Matthew Henry's* esteemed work, and the circulation of no less than four rival editions of *Barnes,* the American commentator, are sufficient proofs, that, if good and useful commentaries are written, there will always be found an abundance of purchasers. Different authors have different styles and modes of illustrating their subjects; and, in like manner, different readers have different tastes; and only many writers, or varied commentaries by the same writer, can meet this diversity.

Cobbin's *Domestic Bible* of course "includes" commentary from a large number of bible commentaries, as well as from other Family Bibles that had already appropriated such commentary. His description documents both the separation and merging of the two genres. A number of British bible commentaries were originally published by dissenting clergy. Among these, the best known and most cited, quoted, and plagiarized were Matthew Henry, *Exposition of the Old and New Testament* (1708–10); John Brown, *The Self-Interpreting Bible* (1778); and Adam Clarke, *The Holy Bible . . . with a critical commentary and notes* (1810–25). Among Evangelical commentaries, *The Holy Bible . . . with original notes . . . by Thomas Scott* (1788–92), became extremely popular.[23]

Perhaps the most striking aspect of the Dissenters' commentaries is their conviction of their independence. Though most acknowledge having made reference to other commentators, they typically insist on the original nature of their commentary. As Adam Clarke puts it, "I had at first designed to introduce a considerable portion of *criticism* on the sacred text, accompanied with illustrations from ancient authors; but . . . I was induced to throw almost the whole of them aside" (Clarke, "Advertisement"). He nevertheless feels "perfectly satisfied with the *purity* of my *motives,* and the *simplicity* of my *intention.*"

When such commentary was excerpted for other works, such as Family Bibles, much of the "diversity" Cobbin refers to is erased. But the commentaries were also circulated in cheap editions in which they were consumed by the Victorian mass market, and in which their "different styles" of illustrating the "sacred pages" could be readily appreciated. Matthew Henry's *Exposition,* for example, is still provocative in the rhetorical brilliance and ingenuity of its multiple interpretations and associations, John Brown's *Self-Interpreting Bible* in its thundering denunciations of sin and sinners, and Adam Clarke's *Commentary* in its fascination with "new" knowledge—the language of science and travel. But all of the bible commentaries written by Dissenters are notable for their critique of translation: they continually remind their readers that the Authorized Version is itself a translation of different texts written in different languages, and they take issue not only with its many errors, but even with the moral authority of some its texts. They raise doubts about the authenticity of any single translation of a biblical text, while continually drawing attention to the possibility of multiple meanings for all texts. In *Villette,* Brontë thematizes the issue of *language*—of men's claims to imperial linguistic authority, and of women's struggle to speak their "own" language. The novel is underwritten by the assumption common to dissenting bible commentary: that literal truth, even in the foundational text of the English nation, is always figurative.

Language Lessons

At an early point in their intertwined narratives, Lucy finds the six-year-old Polly Home "seated, like a little Odalisque, on a couch, half shaded by the drooping draperies of the window near" (29). Little Polly on her couch simultaneously rocks her doll and looks at a picture book. Both her naming of the doll and her interpretation of the pictures, we learn, stem from Graham's instruction. Graham has suggested Polly name the doll after Candace, the Ethiopian queen mentioned in the Book of Acts (8:27), because the "begrimed" state of the doll's complexion gives it an "Ethiopian aspect" (30). As Candace is a miniaturized version of the "Oriental" woman, so Polly is herself a miniaturized version of the orientalized English woman, subjected to the pedagogical construction of the authoritative male—and his imperial bible. We should remember, for example, that at least one commercial Family Bible represents Eve as an odalisque (chapter 1, figure 2). Polly does not recognize the larger implications of Graham's teaching that only good *men* teach others in foreign countries or that the tiny foot of the Chinese lady testifies simply to her being "more stranger." That Lucy recognizes not only Polly's inculturation by Graham, but its most authoritative source is indicated by her later response to Graham's statement that Miss de Bassompierre "does not know that I partly taught her to read" (317). "In the Bible on Sunday nights?" Lucy perceptively replies. Using that most imperial text as a primer, Graham "partly taught" Polly how to read her culture and her own place as incipient orientalized woman within it—passive, domesticated, prematurely sexualized, and oblivious to her subjection.

The doll Candace is more than a small parody of the Western male imaginary: her name leads immediately to an instructive biblical story about reading. In the Book of Acts, the disciple Philip finds the Ethiopian queen's eunuch—in charge of all Candace's "treasure"—reading the Book of Isaiah, and asks him whether he understands what he reads. The eunuch replies, "How can I, except some man should guide me?" (Acts 8:31). Philip climbs into the chariot with the eunuch, and explains that the cryptic prophetic text refers to Jesus, after which the eunuch desires to be baptized. The biblical story could hardly explain more clearly that it takes a man to teach the "unmanned" how to read.

The pictures in Polly's book have been similarly interpreted for her by Graham, and thus she learns to read as this prematurely patriarchal male—who earlier scandalized her by holding her up with one hand above his head so that she sees herself as a "spectacle" in the mirror—

teaches her. Polly's reading of text and culture, and of her place in both, is constructed by Graham's tutelage. Even as a child, she recognizes the "disrespect" inherent in the older boy's casually lifting her up so that she confronts her mirrored reflection—an episode that forecasts Lucy's infuriated resistance to that spectacularization staged in "Cleopatra," also positioned as an odalisque, and "La Vie d'une Femme," the four tableaux of "a woman's life." The tableaux represent that "life" with a pious young girl, an even more pious young married woman, a young mother, and a black widow, or a widow who is a "black woman, holding by the hand a black little girl" (202). "What women to live with!" Lucy seethes, "insincere, ill humoured, bloodless, brainless nonentities! As bad in their way as the indolent gipsy-giantess, the Cleopatra, in hers" (202). Lucy has already concluded that the "Cleopatra," with its "wretched untidiness" of "pots and pans—perhaps I ought to say vases and goblets," and its "perfect rubbish of flowers," is "an enormous piece of claptrap" (200). Jill Matus, by investigating Brontë's probable artistic source for her "Cleopatra" (Edward De Biefve's *Une Almé*)—is able to expose some of the parodic play in Lucy's critique. "Glut," she notes, here inevitably evokes "slut," and Lucy's epithet of "claptrap" evokes the French *clapier,* or brothel—where what is trapped is the clap—as well as its primary meaning of "empty" language (Matus, 138, 142). Matus shares, however, the common critical assumption that the literary text most important to Brontë's notion of the "Orient" was *The Arabian Nights.* Yet, as I have argued in chapter 2, the Victorian "English" bible was acknowledged by its commentators (with varying degrees of acceptance and denial) to be an "Oriental" text, and also represented as such by its illustrators.

It is part of Graham's tutelage that he, as authoritative male, homes in on Polly's errors of speech—her lapses in grammar, and her tendency to lisp and mispronounce words. When Lucy finds the child perched on her bed, insisting that she cannot, *cannot* sleep, and she cannot, *cannot* live, Lucy asks what ails her. "'Dedful miz-er-y!' said she, with her piteous lisp" (32). Years later, both Graham—now "Dr. Bretton"—and Polly's father still notice and critique her linguistic lapses. Dr. Bretton smiles when, in speaking fast, Polly lisps and then colors, repeating the word more distinctly "in a painstaking, conscientious manner" (288). Her father chides her, commenting, "Still, Polly, there is a little flutter, a little tendency to stammer now and then, and even to lisp as you lisped when you were six years old" (300). Polly must learn to speak "the King's English," while her own manner of speaking is subjected to correction.

Polly is by no means the only female in the text who fails to use a national language in the properly "authorized" manner. Ginevra—who also doesn't know whether she's Protestant or Catholic—claims to be unable to write any language well, and throws the French *chose* in for any missing "thing" in the language of the moment (55). Ginevra's handy substitute is, of course, in itself suggestive of other meanings. Lucy exclaims of Madame Beck, "How she did slaughter the speech of Albion!" (65). Lucy herself does not possess "a phrase of *speaking* French" at the time of her arrival in Villette, a defect she labors to correct by studying French assiduously, practicing the language by day and studying its "theory" by night (72). But like Polly, she is unable to speak even the language of her home country correctly in the presence of such an imposing medical authority as Dr. John. She finds herself unable to utter "more than monosyllables in Dr. John's presence," and recognizes that "he was the kind of person with whom I was likely ever to remain the neutral, passive thing he thought me" (104). At times, she is unable to speak using correct English grammar in his presence, but her "incorrect" grammar has its own significance. When he asks, after she has insisted that Madame Beck is not at fault for her inexplicable confession to a Catholic priest, "Who is in the wrong then, Lucy?" she replies, "Me—Dr. John—me," to which he patronizingly responds, "'Me' must take better care in future," and smiles at her "bad grammar" (185). Lucy's "me," however, correctly identifies her position as that of object, implicitly leaving the authoritative subject position, "I," to Dr. John.

What Dr. John, Mr. Home, and M. Paul regard as Polly's and Lucy's "mishandling" of national languages thus also functions as the kind of sacrilegious "playing" that shocked Alice Mozley. Such "mistakes," that is, are sometimes more truthful, produce more significant meanings, than the correct version of the King's English (or M. Paul's equally imperial French). The child Polly's mispronunciation of her "ded-ful miz-er-y" voices the narrative truth that women are "killed" into language: learning to speak languages as authorized by men also means learning to *feel* as men desire women should feel. Polly's misery at learning that Graham does not care for her as much as she for him "kills" the child: she turns into a cold, "dead" silent thing who responds to Lucy's invitation—"Come to me"— as a "small ghost gliding over the carpet" (34). There, in Lucy's arms, she is warmed, tranquillized, and cherished. Years later, Lucy will similarly try to kill her feelings. Sitting on the seat she has cleared in *l'allée défendue,* she reflects that, in a future such as that facing her, it would be better to be dead. "And in catalepsy and a dead trance, I studiously held the quick of my nature" (109). She remembers a tempest, "full of thunder, pealing out such an ode as language never delivered to man" (109). After such storms, longing for something to fetch her out of her present existence, Lucy plays with the bible story of Jael and Sisera. Splitting herself between Jael the killer and Sisera the killed, she "figuratively" drives a nail through the "temples" of her feeling, but they refuse to die— instead they turn and bleed and thrill.[24] Polly's childish mispronunciation, like Ginevra's handy French and Lucy's bad grammar, produces meanings in excess of dictionary definitions, and forecasts Lucy's "playing with sacred pages" to exceed authorized meanings of female bodies.

Floods and Fountains

We may now read somewhat more perceptively why Vashti is at once a "mighty revelation" and "a spectacle low, horrible, immoral" (258). Clarke's valorization of Vashti's disobedience commends her refusal to participate in the spectacularization of her body, while Brontë's Vashti actively performs that female body. But Brontë's Vashti also constructs the contradiction hinted at in Brontë's comment that she would go every night for three months to study this strange being, if she could bear the "high mental stimulus" that long. In her intense observation of the actress, Lucy Snowe represents the female spectator, studying and learning a language of the female body, as performed by this simultaneously immoral and revelatory woman.

"That night," Lucy writes, "was already marked in my book of life, not with white, but with a deep-red cross" (260). She continues to watch the actress, enthralled, until near midnight. At this time the whole theater is hushed, all eyes centered in one point, and the actress seems to move beyond the time-frame, the historical writing, of her spectators' present: "an inordinate will, convulsing a perishing mortal frame, bent it to battle with doom and death, fought every inch of ground, sold dear every drop of blood, resisted to the latest the rape of every faculty, *would* see, *would* hear, *would* breathe, *would* live, up to, within, well nigh *beyond* the moment when death says to all sense and all being—'Thus far and no farther!'" (260). With this climactic command, Lucy misquotes the text of a now rarely cited biblical story of creation—a creation that bursts forth from the *womb,* as told in the Book of Job. This creation is a *female* creation, and one that—in the biblical account—must be controlled by a masculine principle. Brontë here abbreviates a pivotal biblical text that marks the limitation of a feminine creation by a masculine authority. At the end of the story of Job, the Lord speaks to Job out of a whirlwind and overawes him with his ignorance of "creation": "Where wast thou when I laid the foundations of the earth? declare, if thou hast under-standing" (Job 38:4). Unlike the creation stories in Genesis, the creation story as told to Job is woman's work. "Or who shut up the sea with doors, when it brake forth, as if it had issued out of the womb?" the voice of the Creator demands, and later adds, "Out of whose womb came the ice? and the hoary frost of heaven, who hath gendered it?" (Job 38:8, 29). Creation issues from the womb, and takes the form of formlessness of a "sea." The Lord's function is to contain these floods, to compass them as with a "swaddlingband," or to set "bars and doors" to them: "Hitherto shalt thou come, but no further: and here shall thy proud waves be stayed."

Vashti's creation appears similarly overwhelming: it has gone too far, it must go no further—it threatens the spectator's very sense of *life.* Matthew Henry's *Exposition* constructs a recognizably similar anxiety about the "floods" and "fountains" of female bodies. As is characteristic for Henry, multiple interpretations are produced for the biblical text. Thus, the creation may be thought of as "epitome," but also as "embryo." As epitome, the creation is "a great house" made by God as, by impli-cation, men make structures precisely according to their plans. But as "embryo," the creation is at first a "chaos," shapeless, useless, without in-habitants, a "mere earth" awaiting its prime mover. God "moved upon the face of the deep," Henry writes, as the hen gathers her chickens under her wings, or as the eagle stirs up her nest, "flutters" over her young. But Henry is quick to subsume this feminine figure of generativity, and others like it, into the masculine figure of God as author: "Learn hence, That God is not only the Author of all being, but the Fountain of life, and the Spring of motion" (Henry, 23).

Henry's fear of the feminine gendering of creative power and his desire to rewrite it in phallic terms is even more marked in his commentary on the deluge. "God could have destroyed all mankind by the sword of an angel, a flaming sword . . . but God chose to do it by a flood of waters, which should drown the world. The reasons, we may be sure, were wise and just, though to us unknown. . . . God has many arrows in his quiver, and he may use which he pleases" (63). Though God could have chosen any number of properly manly, phallic weapons with which to "cut off" his enemies, he chose, inexplicably, that much more terrifying method of destruction, the flood. On that "fatal day of the flood," Henry writes, the "fountains of the great deep were broken up, and the windows of heaven were opened" [Gen. 7:11]. Like the nineteenth-century medical discourse on the uterus as a sewer, Henry muses that the "fountains of the deep" are like those humors in our own bodies that can become the "seeds and springs of mortal diseases." So "the earth had in its bowels those waters, which, at God's command, sprang up and flooded it." As if to reassure himself that such floods can be contained, Henry turns repetitively to the words of the Book of Job: "God had, in the creation, set bars and doors to the waters of the sea, that they might not return to cover the earth (Ps. 104:9, Job 38:9–11) and now he only removed those ancient landmarks, mounds, and fences."

In Adam Clarke's early-nineteenth-century commentary, by contrast, the femininity of creation in Job is put into scientifically explicit terms that implicitly affirm the creative power of the female body: "The sea is represented as a newly born infant issuing from the womb of the void and formless chaos: and the delicate circumstance of the *liquor amnii* which bursts out previously to the birth of the foetus" (comment on Job 38:8, n.p.). Clarke's deployment of scientific discourse on the biblical text leads him into a similar valorization of the power of women's "fountains" in the Book of Leviticus, where we find them identified with the mysterious source or spring of menstrual blood: "And if a man shall lie with a woman having her sickness, and shall uncover her nakedness; he hath discovered her fountain, and she hath uncovered the fountain of her blood and both of them shall be cut off from among their people" (Lev. 20:18). In commenting on these Levitical laws concerning a woman's "fountain of her blood," Clarke at first enlarges on what is meant by "the blood of her purifying" after childbirth, as described in Lev. 12:4. Here he carefully explains that God has "given to the body of the female an extra quantity of blood and nutricious [sic] juices," and that before pregnancy, "this superabundance is evacuated at periodical times," while during pregnancy it is retained "for the formation and growth of the foetus," whose body is entirely made from the "blood and nutricious juices" of the mother. After the child's birth, this "superabundance" is evacuated, being no longer necessary, but when the "lacerated vessels are rejoined," this superfluity of blood is then determined to the breasts and turned into milk, where it serves for the nourishment of the infant.[25]

In his scientific "management" of the subject of menstrual blood, Clarke writes it as proof of a female "superabundance" from which the child is entirely made and nourished. He affirms woman even more decisively as the source of life in his commentary on Gen. 2:23, in which the newly formed Eve is given the name of "Woman." As in his Leviticus commentary Clarke strongly denies "idle tales" about the "infectious nature" of the blood of women after childbirth, so here he denies interpretations of the name "woman" as deriving from "wo man" or "man's woe." "The truth is, our term is a proper and literal translation of the original; and we may thank the discernment of our Anglo-Saxon ancestors for giving it. Wombman, of which *woman* is a contraction, means the *man with the womb*" (Clarke, 1:38). Man comes to be defined by that which he is not, the man-with-a-womb: man is the signifier of lack, the "not all," as constructed by his lack of a womb, his lack of the "fountain" and "spring" of life. Woman has it all.

Lucy Snowe's Floods and Flowers

With her "thus far and no farther!" Lucy invokes a complex biblical discourse on the overwhelming power of feminine floods, and the ongoing masculine imperative to set boundaries to them. Here her thoughts turn back to Dr. Graham: "What thought Dr. Graham of this being?" Now she insists that it amuses her to discover that he is watching Vashti, "not with wonder, nor worship, nor yet dismay, but simply with intense curiosity" (259). The doctor watches Vashti with the cool, objectifying eye of the diagnostician. When finally Lucy asks him how he likes the actress, he gives her his opinion in a "few terse phrases": he "judged her as a woman, not an artist," and it was "a branding judgment" (260). The doctor sees Vashti's "floods" of meaning—which seem to spontaneously erupt in a fire—as something that must be "judged," and judged negatively. Henry's and Clarke's commentaries, by contrast, construct the floods and fountains of a woman's body as forces to be regarded with awe, whether fearful or admiring. Lucy's life is narrated in terms of similarly awesome, periodic floods. Her opening story of a visit to her godmother's house describes it as a time that "flowed smoothly . . . like the gliding of a full river through a plain" (6). But that experience of life as a "pleasant stream," like that beside which Christian and Hopeful sojourn, is shortly brought to an end by a "heavy tempest": "For many days and nights neither sun nor stars appeared; we cast with our own hands the tackling out of the ship; a heavy tempest lay on us; all hope that we should be saved was taken away. In fine, the ship was lost, the crew perished" (35).

Critics often assume that the "shipwreck" refers to Lucy's disastrous loss of her own home and family.[26] However, the narrative leaves the language completely opaque—as it does in describing the climactic concluding storm that leaves the Atlantic "strewn with wrecks" (495). Both tempests allude to a "Paul": the first does so in its quotation from Acts: "For many days and nights neither sun nor stars appeared." Here, a prolonged tempest eventually wrecks the ship on which Paul is being carried to Rome as a prisoner (Acts 27:20). The second tempest alludes to a Paul in Lucy's premonitory preparations for M. Paul Emmanuel's return: "I have made him a little library" (495). But neither Paul is mentioned in the description of the storm itself—these tempests, which mark off the bounds of the narrative, themselves have no boundaries.

In the aftermath of that mysterious, initiatory "shipwreck," Lucy decides to go to London and there prepares the "project," as she says, of going abroad. The scene of her departure by night clearly conflates writing with a "flood," here the river Thames. "Black was the river as a torrent of ink," she writes, and the names of ships stand out in "great, white letters on a dark ground." The "sable flood" on which she glides makes her think of the river Styx and "of Charon rowing some solitary soul to the Land of Shades" (50–51). The blackness of this "torrent of ink" signals the danger implicit for Lucy in releasing the "flood." Yet she finds herself not frightened but exhilarated: "'How is this?' said I. 'Methinks I am animated and alert, instead of being depressed and apprehensive?' I could not tell how it was" (51). The name *Vivid* "starts out" from the darkness in "white and glaring" capital letters—a word that connotes color, as in a vivid *red,* and seems strangely out of place here, yet it is the name of Lucy's own ship.

Later, as she finds herself bound down the channel toward the sea, Lucy waxes poetic in flagrantly Romantic style: "deep was the pleasure I drank in with the sea-breeze; divine the delight I drew from the heaving channel-waves" (56). "Methought I saw the continent of Europe, like a wide dream-land," she continues, and in the background of the sky spread above it "strode from north to south a God-bent bow, an arch of hope." Above the watery flood here Lucy perceives a rainbow—the ancient sign, in Adam Clarke's commentary, of good fortune, here unmistakably gendered as phallic weapon, the "God-bent bow." With strange perversity, Lucy writes: "Cancel the whole of that, if you please, reader— or rather let it stand, and draw thence a moral—an alternative, text-hand copy—[and she quotes from some unknown source] 'Day-dreams are delusions of the demon'" (57). Becoming "excessively sick," she falters down to the cabin.

Perhaps it is not so strange that Lucy finds this "black flood" so exciting, despite its association with a death myth, or that the word "vivid" should "start out" from it. The "sable flood" writes the contradictory meanings inscribed in female "floods" as both that "superabundance" that makes new life and that sign of ever-present female pollution. For example, Carroll Smith-Rosenberg notes that, as late as 1900, the dangers of menstruation were commonly described in terms of "storms": "Many a young life is battered and forever crippled in the breakers of puberty; if it crosses these unharmed and is not dashed to pieces on the rock of childbirth, it may still ground on the ever-recurring shadows of menstruation, and lastly, upon the final bar of the menopause ere protection is found in the unruffled waters of the harbor beyond the reach of sexual storms" (as qtd in Smith-Rosenberg, *Disorderly Conduct,* 184).

The female was seen as "driven by the tidal currents of her cyclical reproductive system, a cycle bounded by the pivotal crises of puberty and menopause and reinforced each month by her recurrent menstrual flow" (183). As such, she was prone not only to hysteria but even to insanity. At the same time, physicians believed menstruation could represent "either the monthly apex of women's sexual desires" or act as a providential means of limiting women's sexual appetites. "In God's infinite wisdom . . . might not this monthly discharge be ordained for the purpose of controlling woman's violent sexual passions . . . by unloading the uterine vessels . . . " (as qtd in Smith-Rosenberg, 190). But Lucy's menstrual passions are also represented in the less demonic and more evocatively erotic form of flowers.

On the evening when Lucy sits in the forbidden alley of the garden, remembering those storms that could wake her from her "dead trance" (109), the garden in which she sits surely represents one of those "female landscapes" Ellen Moers theorizes in her *Literary Women.*[27] First, it is inhabited by the legend of the nun—whose figure, as Susan Bernstein notes, "functions in Victorian culture as an index of mysterious and illicit practices, or more precisely, as a marker for concealed but excessive female sexuality."[28] The second most notable aspect of this garden is the overgrown alley that Lucy has cleared and cleaned. Stockton writes of Lucy's description of this "forbidden alley" that it traces "a genital cleft": a narrow walk overgrown by thick shrubs which is "seldom entered even during the day, and after dusk was carefully shunned" (Brontë, *Villette,* 108).[29]

Lucy becomes a "frequenter of this strait and narrow path." On this evening she again plays—somewhat more calmly this time—with the idea of herself as both Jael the killer and Sisera the killed ("my Sisera lies quiet tonight"), seated on a rustic seat she has cleaned in a gesture that, as Stockton comments, suggests "the Old Testament practice of transforming a pagan worship site into a sacred spot for Yahweh" (Stockton, 148). Looking up from that "hidden seat," Lucy sees the "young crescent" of the moon, "leaned back beside stately spire" (Brontë, *Villette,* 109). Here

Brontë draws a compelling word-picture, thick with associations, of a woman's intense, unfulfilled, erotic desire.

Suddenly, into this quiet evening, as Lucy describes it, "the rude Real burst coarsely in—all evil, grovelling, and repellent as she too often is" (110). In short, a missile is dropped. It proves to be a small casket filled with violets and containing also a small folded pink note. Sternly denying her desire that the note might be a "billet-doux," Lucy opens it—and discovers that it *is* a love-letter, but a misdirected one, intended for someone else. And it contains a humiliating description of herself as "that dragon, the English teacher—*une véritable bégueule Britannique à ce que vous dites—espèce de monstre, brusque et rude comme un vieux caporal de grenadiers, et revêche comme une religieuse*" (111). Shortly after her discovery, Dr. John appears and penetrates the forbidden walk. "It was sacrilege—the intrusion of a man into that spot, at that hour; but he knew himself privileged, and perhaps he trusted to the friendly night" (113). There Lucy meets him, as she says, "like some ghost" (113). Mme Beck then also appears, "stealing like a cat round the garden," and Dr. John immediately clears the garden "with two noiseless bounds." Once the hunter, he is now the hunted.

The writing of this scene appears almost deliberately comic, so filled is it with only the most flimsily veiled references to the masculine "penetration" of hidden feminine recesses. Even the highly suggestive character of Dr. John's penetration of *l'allée défendue* has been presaged by the equally suggestive nature of his observation of Lucy in the "little oval mirror fixed in the side of the window recess—by the aid of which reflector madame often secretly spied persons walking in the garden below" (98). The image eerily suggests that new instrument, the speculum—coming into widespread use by midcentury—and doctors' newfound ability to penetrate visually with it the most hidden parts of a woman's body.[30]

But it is the menstrual significance of this female landscape that is especially prominent. The "casket"—a recognized image for female genitalia—is filled with flowers—a recognized image for menstruation—and these "flowers" drop into the "forbidden alley" into which it is "sacrilege" for a man to intrude. Mary Jane Lupton notes that "the menstrual signification of *flowers* is widespread—a familiar emblem in mythology, a symbol in dreams and poetry."[31] In the country of the "English Bible," however, "flowers" is simply the biblical term for menstruation: "And if any man lie with her at all, and her flowers be upon him, he shall be unclean seven days" (Lev. 15:24), or "And of her that is sick of her flowers" (Lev. 15:33). This seemingly incongruous meaning may be yet another example of mistranslation in the Authorized Version. The *OED* notes that the meaning of "flowers" as "the menstrual discharge, the menses," derives from the French *fleurs,* but that this is regarded by French scholars as a corruption of *flueurs.* The *fluor,* meaning "a flow or flowing," derives from the Latin *fluor* or flowing, or *fluere,* to flow, comparable to the Old French *flueur.* Thus, the instances in the King James translation where menstruation is referred to as a woman's "flowers" may be a mistranslation of a term closer to the sense of "flow" or a "flowing" in the Hebrew text from which seventeenth-century English scholars were translating.[32]

As one thoroughly familiar with the Authorized Version, Brontë certainly would have been aware of "flowers" as the biblical term for menstrual blood.[33] But the "Casket" chapter is packed with other menstrual metaphors as well—the moon, the clock striking nine (Freud claims clocks refer to the menstrual cycle because of their regularity and repetition), and the allusion to "tempests," which in turn calls up the pervasive flood imagery in the narrative (Lupton, 60). Even the statement that "it was sacrilege" for a man to intrude into "that spot, at that hour" daringly suggests the biblical proscription of intercourse at the time when a woman's "flowers" were upon her.[34] Introduced by the tale of the nun buried alive for some mysterious sin, the entire chapter presents a menstrual tableau similar to that of the "red room" in *Jane Eyre.*[35] Here Brontë constructs the meaning of "femaleness" as a play on the difference between the hidden ghost in the quiet garden and the "rude Real" of menstrual passion, imaged as an "evil, grovelling and repellant woman," like the "grovelling monomaniac" Lucy becomes when she is later interrupted by the nun as she reads Dr. John's letter in the attic. The "rude Real" of menstrual passion erupts into that sacred place, the "strait and narrow" path of the garden, where it prepares the way for another bodily tempest—this one representing the dark side of a woman's "flowers," the pathology of obstructed flows.

In "The Long Vacation," Lucy Snowe describes her agony of isolation during the school's summer holiday. Not only are the students and

Mme Beck away, but M. Paul has gone on a pilgrimage to Rome. Lucy is left to care for a *crétin,* a "hapless creature" whom she feeds, keeps warm, even tries to amuse, although she finds her basically evil. Finally the *crétin* is taken away, but Lucy's condition does not improve: she falls into a "strange fever of the nerves and blood" (159). Almost sleepless, she suffers a nightmare when she does sleep briefly. "By the clock of St. Jean Baptiste," she dreams for fifteen minutes, and in that dream "a cup was forced to my lips, black, strong, strange, drawn from no well, but filled up seething from a bottomless and boundless sea" (159). Waking from this dream and finding herself desperate for some relief from her pain, she enters a Catholic church, approaches the confessional, and there makes her confession, beginning, *"Mon père, je suis Protestante"* (161). Although the priest tells her he is unfitted to confess such a case as hers, she nevertheless pours out "some portion of long accumulating, long pent-up pain into a vessel whence it could not be again diffused" (162).

Bernstein has usefully documented the location of this confession in the virulent anti-Catholic propaganda circulating at the time. Broadsides and tracts of various kinds decried such confessions by an English woman to a Catholic priest as scenes of seduction and corruption of the "innocent" female penitent (Bernstein, 53–54). Bernstein, however, argues, "Lucy Snowe's narration deploys the Roman Catholic Church as a tyrannical institution to launch and to disguise a general critique of male domination and female subordination intrinsic to the structure of English Victorian society" (61). Though the Catholic Church appears as a "visible villain," Lucy's confession equally critiques "the insufferable isolation and self-constraint imposed on Victorian unmarried and unmonied women" (61).

That "insufferable isolation and self-constraint" was particularly enforced around issues of, and talk about, the menstrual period. Showalter notes that "the female subculture came first through a shared and increasingly secretive and ritualized physical experience. Puberty, menstruation, sexual initiation, pregnancy, childbirth, and menopause—the entire female sexual life cycle—constituted a habit of living that had to be concealed."[36] In this painful chapter, Lucy employs the language of blocked or obstructed menstrual flow to represent her isolation and "dedful miz-er-y." Before her dream, she endures "nine dark and wet days, of which the Hours rushed on all turbulent, deaf, dishevelled," as she lies in the "strange fever of the nerves and blood." Ultimately she dreams of the cup filled with a "black, strong, strange" liquid and forced to her lips—an image of the uterus filled with the "excrement" of blood that would, if not released, flood and pollute the brain. Matus notes that "the fact that Lucy has been taking care of a cretin is also of relevance, given the way Victorian medical texts represent cretinism as an instance of immature and undeveloped sexuality" —in other words, of a woman whose menstrual flow is "obstructed" or delayed (Matus, 143). Lucy's confession to Père Silas partially relieves her sense of painful congestion, as if a verbal "pouring out," even incomplete, functions like a bloodletting. As she leaves the confessional, however, she encounters a renewed storm, and in this torrent of wind, rain, and cold, she blacks out.

When Lucy awakes from her dead faint, her sight returns to her, "red, as if it swam in blood" (165). Looking around her at the strangely familiar artifacts of the room, she notes flowers everywhere—on the wall, the tablecloth, the worked chair cover (166). It is a menarcheal vision: she had last seen these things at the age of fourteen (167). Topping them all, appropriately, is the portrait of a boy, a youth of sixteen, whose "penetrating eyes" look as if, "when somewhat older, they would flash a lightning response to love" (170). Now, in the therapeutic environs of Dr. John Graham Bretton—whom she admits she had recognized "several chapters back," she begins also to acknowledge her thirst for the "living stream" (175, 178). Not surprisingly, her next chapter begins with reflection on the "hour" at which "the waiting waters will stir" (179). Like the "hour" of the Son of Man, the hour of this coming is unknown.

Unobstructed Flows

Although Lucy's confession to the Catholic priest affords her some relief from the tortuous isolation and pent-up feeling she has endured, she is careful to note that the priest was simply "kind when I needed kindness" (163). And she makes it clear that the encounter was a risky one— she would no more think of doing it again than she would of "walking into a Babylonish furnace" (163). But another "confession" does take place in the narrative, and in this one feminine feelings flow freely. Here the confession is not from a woman to a male priest, but from one woman to another—one woman "translating" a letter from a man to another woman.

Paulina, home from the continent, has received a letter from Dr. John. She and Lucy are sitting alone together in Paulina's room as evening falls. The time and the place are important: this is a "women's room," where no man will intrude, and it is only as it gets darker that, as Paulina says to Lucy, "one can talk at one's ease" (373). No one will *look* at either of them. It is doubtless also important that these two women have studied men's "letters" before. Lucy has received and read letters from Dr. John herself—letters she has subsequently buried in a jar at the foot of the old tree where the nun was supposedly buried alive. But perhaps even more significant to this confessional scene is the fact that Lucy and Paulina have previously studied a "man's" language together. When M. de Bassompierre criticizes "Polly" for her "flutter," "stammer," and "lisp," he wishes to employ Lucy as the younger woman's paid "governess-companion" (301). But Lucy refuses, and instead proposes that the two women study German together. Paulina soon both reads and translates Schiller's ballads easily, but she criticizes the German poet's understanding of love: Schiller should not have said that to have lived and loved is the summit of earthly happiness—rather, he should have said that to *be* loved is the summit (304). Thus Paulina and Lucy have progressed in "language lessons" together, translating the representation of women's feelings from one "male" language to another, as Lucy had earlier required young Désirée to do, "by way of ascertaining that she comprehended what she read" (76).

Now the two women—the younger seated on a footstool at the older one's side—talk about women's feelings and men's letters once again. The scene is filled with indications of warm, physical affection between the two women: Lucy has declared to the reader, "I liked her," and as Paulina sits close to Lucy, she plays with Lucy's hand, placing her own rings on Lucy's fingers or circling them with her hair, or patting the palm against her cheek (372). As she settles herself against Lucy's arm, she voices her intention to "speak the truth now" about her receipt of Dr. John's letters. As she confides the details of her reading to Lucy, the "waters" stir:

"Ere I read, and while I read, my heart did more than throb—
it trembled fast—every quiver seemed like the pant of an animal athirst, laid down at a well and drinking; and the well
proved quite full, gloriously clear; it rose up munificently of
its own impulse; I saw the sun through its gush, and not a
mote, Lucy, no moss, no insect, no atom in the thrice-refined
golden gurgle." (375)

Using metaphorical language strongly reminiscent of that of the Song
of Solomon, Paulina suggests the flow of her "fountains" on her reading
of Graham's love for her. This "well" is full, it rises and gushes, and its
golden gurgle is absolutely clear and pure. No language could suggest
more powerfully the "flow" of sexual passion. Commenting on a text in
the Song of Solomon, "a garden enclosed is my sister, my spouse; a spring
shut up, a fountain sealed," Clarke puts it bluntly. "She is unsullied, a
chaste pure virgin. None has ever entered into this garden; none has yet
tasted of this spring; the seal of this fountain has never been broken. All
this is plain: but how many will make metaphors out of metaphors!"
(Song 4:12). But on a later verse in the same chapter, "a fountain of gardens, a well of living waters, and streams from Lebanon," Clarke retreats
from too "plain" an explanation: "[A] fountain of gardens, may mean
one so abundant as to be sufficient to supply many gardens, to water
many plots of ground; an exuberant fountain. This is the allusion; the reference is plain enough" (Song 4:15). The reference in Paulina's text seems
plain enough also.

Bible commentary on the Song of Solomon encompasses a wide
range of interpretations, many reading the book as a spiritual allegory of
Christ's love for his church. The Dissenter Clarke, however, adamantly
rejects any allegorical or "spiritualizing" interpretation of this book:

It is much better therefore, if explained or illustrated at all, to
take it in its literal meaning, and explain it in its general sense. I
say general sense; because there are many passages in it which
should not be explained, if taken literally, the references being
too delicate; and Eastern phraseology on such subjects is too
vivid for European imaginations. Let any sensible pious medical

man read over this Book: and, if at all acquainted with Asiatic phraseology, say whether it would be proper, even in medical language, to explain all the descriptions and allusions in this Poem. (Clarke, iv)

Clarke includes with his commentary a translation that he claims to be a fourteenth-century English version of the poem, but he also warns "young Ministers" against any attempt to preach on "Solomon's Song." To him, the meaning of the metaphors is clear enough—no further attempt should be made to "translate" them other than to transcribe still other translations. That he feels this biblical work is all about the beauties of the female body is suggested by his comment on Song 7:2, "thy navel is like a round goblet," that "these suppositions are rendered very probable from hundreds of the best finished and highly decorated drawings of Asiatic ladies, in my own collection, where every thing appears in the drawings, as in nature."

Clarke's comment makes it plain enough that, for him, the Song of Solomon is an "Oriental," that is, a sexual, text. Paulina's confession of her sensations as she read Graham's letters to her is, of course, in contrast to Lucy's earlier description of her own feelings as she read a letter from the same man: Lucy's happiness felt like "a bubble—but a sweet bubble—of real honey-dew" (244). It was not a fountain or a well, just a bubble. But she and Paulina speak the same "language" of women's sexual flows and fountains. In this "confession" from one woman to another under cover of darkness, Brontë appears to construct an unorthodox discourse of women's sexuality as something that cannot be "confessed" to men.[37]

Final Floods

In Lucy's account, then, Paulina experiences the purest, as well as the richest, flowing of a woman's "fountains." It is certainly appropriate that this Pauline female, whose story begins as that of a miniaturized "Oriental" woman, an odalisque, should end that story with another phrasing her erotic feelings in language borrowed from that most "Eastern" text, the Song of Solomon. Lucy, however, has had no such gushing well of feelings, only a "honey-dew bubble." And just as she contemplates this effervescent happiness, the nun appears to her for the first time, the figure which the doctor will insist is a "spectral illusion." "You think then, . . . she came out of my brain, and is now gone in there, and may glide out again at an hour and a day when I look not for her?" (249). In her response to the doctor, Lucy turns a common New Testament text into a bit of bible slang. Instead of the Son of Man coming at an unlooked-for day and an hour, it is Lucy's phantom who may arrive unexpectedly.[38] Lucy's comment plays off one "authorized" language against another—the Authorized Version versus the authoritative medical story on women. Not coincidentally, one suspects, the nun is said to emerge from a "deep alcove with a portion of the tarnished scarlet curtain drawn over it" in the attic (256). The location metaphorically suggests the inner recesses of the female body, with the "tarnished scarlet curtain" of the hymen during menstruation drawn over it. In other words, the nun emerges, not from Lucy's brain, as Dr. John would have it, but from the depths of her menstrual passion. This "phantom" of Lucy's is strongly linked to M. Paul, also described as a phantom—but a "freakish, friendly, cigar-loving phantom"—whose "hours and moments" of coming Lucy is also unable to detect (343). This "phantom" is even more closely associated with metaphorical representations of Lucy's "recesses," for she catches him smoking into her desk! M. Emanuel's hand "was on intimate terms with my desk," into which it intrudes; it "ransacked and arranged the contents, almost as familiarly as my own" (343).

It seems completely appropriate that it is only after Lucy and Paul have seen the phantom nun *together,* thus proving that she is neither Lucy's phantom nor Paul's—not to mention that she is not the "Son of Man"—that Lucy's final, climactic "flows" appear in the narrative. The first is a flow of words: "'I want to tell you something,' I said; 'I want to tell you all,'" she proclaims after Paul has shown her the school he has arranged for her to have, and finally confided that Justine Marie is not his love, but his goddaughter and ward (490). And Lucy speaks: "All leaped from my lips. I lacked not words now; fast I narrated; fluent I told my tale; it streamed on my tongue" (490). The unobstructed flow of passion produces an unobstructed flow of words: Lucy has become "Woman" or the "Man-with-the-womb," who has it all, if only for a moment.

The final flow in the narrative is, predictably, a storm. The storm roars out its frenzy on the Atlantic, leaving it strewn with wrecks. Whether M. Paul is lost in this storm, we are not allowed to learn. The final storm is the woman writer's revenge: it obstructs the flow of the reader's imagination and leaves it tormented, impassioned, and without release. But it leaves Lucy in "Paul's" position. The apostle Paul is described at the end of the Book of Acts, after he has survived the wreck of the ship carrying him to Rome as a prisoner, as dwelling "in his own hired house," where he preaches and teaches "with all confidence" (Acts 28:31). This recessive meaning may function as part of Brontë's many allusions in *Villette* to the Book of Acts and its story of the apostle Paul. Lucy does not *marry* Paul—rather, she takes on his position as a tempest-tossed, female Paul, who, though she may not be able to escape the "uterine system," writes from its floods of menstrual superabundance.

FIVE

"A BIT OF HER FLESH"

Circumcision and "The Signification of the Phallus"
in Daniel Deronda

Readers have often commented on the "punitive" language of George Eliot's narratives, but her last novel is an especially disturbing example. Instances of gratuitous violence are to be found everywhere in *Daniel Deronda,* such as the little story cheerily told by the blacksmith's boy as he puts Rex Gascoigne's shoulder back in joint—itself an apparently gratuitous "pain" in the text—after exhorting him just to "tighten your mind up a bit." Noticing that Rex turns pale nonetheless, Joel remarks, "Ah, sir, you aren't used to it, that's how it is. I's see lots and lots o' joints out. I see a man with his eye pushed out once—that was a rum go as ever I see. You can't have a bit o' fun wi'out such sort o' things."[1]

The desire this narrative constructs, surely, is to hurt somebody. Indeed, Gwendolen's story in *Daniel Deronda* appears to exemplify Laura Mulvey's explanation of the sadistic narrative constructed in film by the "patriarchal unconscious": Gwendolen, first presented as the fetishized object of the male gaze in the opening scene of the gambling den, is later investigated, demystified, devalued, punished, and "saved." This narrative type, Mulvey explains, represents the sadistic response of the unconscious to the anxiety provoked by the "spectacle of castration"—that is, by the woman. The pleasure of this sadistic narrative construction lies in ascertaining guilt, asserting control, and subjecting the guilty person through punishment or forgiveness.[2]

If we read *Daniel Deronda* in the terms of Jacques Lacan's theory, then, we are likely to find George Eliot's heroine to be inscribed with the guilt of the "castrated" female, who is punished for the child's pain in discovering that the mother lacks the Phallus. In this configuration she speaks—as Mulvey puts it—"castration and nothing else," for her lack produces the Phallus only as "symbolic presence."[3] The fact that the narrative "can't have a bit o' fun" without such things as apparently gratuitous pains in the text seems to testify further to the primacy of the Phallus and to woman's sole function as signifier of its terrifying absence.[4]

But an intertextual reading of the novel with a now little-known contemporary discourse—the Protestant discourse on circumcision, especially as represented in family bible dictionaries—suggests a narrative desire that Lacan does not theorize: the desire to inflict "circumcision" on the body of the daughter in the text as a sign both of her painful differentiation from the mother and of a covenant between the daughter and her mother, or the daughter and her "creator." What Protestant exegetes sought to repress, in their debate on the "meaning" of circumcision, was the evidence for circumcision as a ritual implicit with sexual meanings; in particular, with the meaning of pain and injury inflicted on the male sexual organ. Their discourse parallels Lacan's strategy in "The Signification of the Phallus" by insisting on the hermeneutic significance of circumcision while evading its connection with the vulnerable penis. George Eliot's text, by contrast, revels in the pain of the daughter's "circumcision," constructing a female erotics of circumcision: a phantasied infliction of this painful but sanctifying rite on the female body that rewrites the sadistic narrative as a passionate dialectic between daughter and mother. It is not the Phallus (or its lack) that ultimately matters here; rather, the narrative steals language and phantasy from the contemporary discourse on (male) circumcision to construct its painful and difficult desire for an "other" who is also the same.

The pleasure or "fun" the narrative appears to take in pain derives, I suggest, from an obsession with differentiation from the mother, an obsession that then reaches a culmination that appears "deviant." That is, in the final instance Gwendolen's penitence is not "rewarded" by the customary consignment to patriarchy in a happy marriage but by the promised return to her mother. But we should not view this narrative resolution as unprepared; rather, it finally unveils the narrative's previously disguised preoccupation with maternal loss and restoration. "Circumcision" in the text thus writes an unorthodox desire that puts into question Lacan's insistence on the primacy of the Phallus as signifier of that initiatory rupture in the mother-child dyad, for though it originates in the "child's" devastating discovery of the mother's difference (or, as Lacan would say, in Gwendolen's discovery that the mother lacks the Phallus), its desire revolves around both the pleasure and the pain of that "cut" and ends in the affirmation of a new bond to the mother.[5]

The inscription of circumcision in the text also suggests a sadistically playful inversion in the case of Mirah and Mordecai's father, who is "cut off" as if he were the foreskin, or that part which, in the words of Matthew Henry, could "most easily be spared." The father's very name is shown to be insignificant, deriving its importance only from a "borrowed" association with a female prophetic lineage. This unorthodox narrative outcome deserves our notice in its insistence on the inconsequence of the father. The father, like the foreskin, can be dispensed with.

Finally, even the clearly Oedipal plot of Daniel's story—or what has been called the "Jewish half" of the novel—demonstrates a primarily pre-Oedipal desire, or the impossible quest for the Imaginary Mother. And while in Lacan's theory the Imaginary Mother functions to produce the Phallus, I will argue that the pervasively maternal thematics of Daniel's story corroborates the manner in which this novel deviates from the "patriarchal unconscious" toward something we could begin to call a radical female desire. It is in connection with Daniel's story also that the critical discourse has repeatedly produced the issue of circumcision, precisely because of its notable "absence" from a plot that seems to depend on it.[6] Yet that plot encodes a reference to the Protestant interpretation of circumcision that appears to transfer its meaning from the male to the female body. That is, the midpoint of the narrative details the events of January 1, on which date the Anglican Church celebrated the Feast of the Circumcision. The encounter between Daniel and Gwendolen on that date seems to construct a Protestant interpretation of the circumcision as the bond that unites Jew and Christian, past and future, history and prophecy.[7] But the encounter suggests also the covert desire to transform circumcision from a rite that sanctifies only the male body to one that "wounds" and blesses the female body. In short, the Victorian discourse on circumcision, that "originary" rite formulated exclusively between men in conventional religion, constructs a bond between women in George Eliot's last novel.[8]

Reading as we have been taught to do, we dutifully underestimate the plot's restoration of Gwendolen to her mother. Indeed, we tend to forget about the importance of the two unconventional "endings" of the double plot line: the restoration of Gwendolen Harleth to her apparently insignificant mother, and the brief appearance and final disappearance of Mirah's even less significant father. But a reading of what I shall call the erotics of circumcision in *Daniel Deronda,* like Nancy Chodorow's revision of Freud's theory, constructs the bond between mother and daughter as more crucial, more painful, and more meaningful than that of "the daughter's seduction" by the father (*Reproduction of Mothering*).[9]

The "Spoiled Child," or The Story of the Uncircumcised Daughter

Early in Gwendolen's story, the narrator expresses pity that she has never known a childhood home: "A human life, I think, should be well rooted in some spot of a native land, where it may get the love of tender kinship for the face of earth, for the labours men go forth to, for the sounds and accents that haunt it, for whatever will give that early home a familiar unmistakable difference." Such a home becomes as "a sweet habit of the blood," the narrator continues, for "at five years old, mortals are not prepared to be citizens of the world, to be stimulated by abstract nouns, to soar above preference into impartiality; and that prejudice in favour of milk with which we blindly begin, is a type of the way body and soul must get nourished at least for a time" (22). At five years old? But the narrator has just told us that Gwendolen has never known such a home. Who then is the five-year-old unprepared to be a citizen of the world and to substitute abstract nouns for that blind prejudice "in favour of milk"?

The reference seems to be a slip in the construction of the narrator, a slip that points to the ghost of an earlier self: little Mary Ann Evans, who at five years old was sent away from home to boarding school. Five seems, as Gordon Haight suggests, an awfully tender age to be sent away to school, even if the school was only three miles from home. But Haight minimizes the trauma of separation from the mother. It was her father rather than her mother who held Mary Ann's affection, he proposes, and, anyway, it was the separation from her brother Isaac that "hurt her most keenly."[10]

Haight does not comment here on the conspicuous, even startling absence of the mother from George Eliot's letters. Ruby Redinger, on the other hand, underlines the fact that the entire massive corpus of George Eliot's letters contains only two references to her mother, despite the fact that her mother lived until Mary Ann was sixteen.[11] Such a profound and long-lived omission of reference to the mother suggests her significance, rather than her insignificance. The pain of separation from her, far from being minor or trivial, must have been too great to confess, a pain that exceeded language, or perhaps preceded it.[12] However that may be, the little "tear" in the text admits the ghost of a five-year-old who was sent away from her mother, a five-year-old who has no proper place in this story. But the narrative is populated with other children rejected, abandoned, or "given up" by their mothers: Mirah, Daniel, Mrs. Glasher's firstborn son, Catherine Arrowpoint, and the nameless daughter of the Cohens. This company of abandoned children and rejecting mothers frames the story of Gwendolen, the "spoiled child" of her adoring mother, and her "creator," the mature woman going by the phallic name of George Eliot but haunted by the ghosts of many other selves, including the small girl abruptly banished to a boarding school that became the scene of repeated "night terrors."[13] Amidst this company, Gwendolen alone occupies the privileged position of the "uncircumcised" child or the daughter who has not suffered the painful knowledge of being "cut off" from her mother.

We may uncover the locus of the pain that fuels narrative sadism in *Daniel Deronda,* I suggest, by considering the stories of these other children, each of whom appears to function as an instance of Lacan's theory of "castration." That is, each of these children has been "cut off" from the mother and her or his story may thus be construed as offering a narrative model of that postulated moment when the child's discovery that the mother desires something other than the child first produces the Phallus as signifier of that "rupture." But George Eliot's narrative differs from Lacan's precisely in its interest in the *mothers* in these "stories." The repeated accounts of maternal loss—seemingly "buried" in more important stories—

suggest the overriding importance of the mother's story, or of the "child's" obsessive need to construct the pain of her loss over and over again, seeking to find in this digging out of an old, old story not just the mother as nameless signifier of "lack" but the mother as particular woman, the mother as an other whose "difference" also constructs the daughter's identity.

Mirah offers the most telling example of the history that opposes or "mirrors" Gwendolen's—that of the little girl "carried away" from her mother by her father and ever after in search of that lost bliss of fusion with the maternal ideal. Mirah begins her story, which she tells as she sits opposite Mrs. Meyrick, her eyes resting "with a sort of placid reverence" on this mother's face, with the statement "I remember my mother's face better than anything; yet I was not seven when I was taken away, and I am nineteen now." This is, she continues, her "earliest" memory: "I think my life began with waking up and loving my mother's face: it was so near to me, and her arms were round me, and she sang to me. One hymn she sang so often, so often: and then she taught me to sing it with her: it was the first I ever sang. They were always Hebrew hymns she sang; and because I never knew the meaning of the words they seemed full of nothing but our love and happiness" (210).

Mirah's story constructs with uncanny precision that order Lacan speaks of as the Imaginary—the pre-Symbolic order when boundaries between the mother and child are indistinct, when language is unneeded because mother and child are undivided. But Mirah's visionary memory predicts even more closely what Hélène Cixous postulates as the love of "singing" that testifies to woman's freer access to the Imaginary: "The Voice sings from a time before law, before the Symbolic took one's breath away and reappropriated it into language under its authority of separation. The deepest, the oldest, the loveliest Visitation. Within each woman, the first, nameless love is singing."[14] Mirah remembers hearing words she did not "know," and yet she "knew" what they meant. Later she sings this hymn for Daniel and the Meyricks, reconstructing the unknown words from "syllables," and sounds like a childish lisping. Daniel comments, "The lisped syllables are very full of meaning" (374).

Indeed, Mirah's brother Mordecai suggests that both his search for a soulmate to inherit his spiritual quest and that quest itself are constructed in some language that precedes the Symbolic order, or the "spelled" or alphabetic language, and imply the dream of returning to the mother. "You have risen within me like a thought not fully spelled," he tells Daniel. "My soul is shaken before the words are all there" (501). When Daniel replies that he must know more of the "truth" of his own life before he can accept Mordecai's urgent request, Mordecai responds, "I could silence the beliefs which are the mother-tongue of my soul and speak with the rote-learned language of a system, that gives you the spelling of all things, sure of its alphabet covering them all" (502). But what if, he posits, "love lies deeper than any reasons to be found?" Daniel, he later explains, is to him as the "brother that sucked the breasts of my mother" (570), thus uniting them in a common devotion to the "mother" that preceded symbolized, and divided, interests.[15]

Mordecai's prophetic quest, then, also recalls that yearning for the Imaginary Mother inscribed in Mirah's account of her "earliest memory." But Mirah's story strongly suggests a loss that is not only prehistoric, but historic: her story of how her father lured her away by telling her they were going only on "a little journey" sounds suspiciously like that of the little girl Mary Ann Evans being taken away to school by her father.[16] The hermeneutics of Mirah's name confirm this suspicion that her story encodes not only desire for the lost mother, but anger at the presence of the father. Her last name, Lapidoth, identifies her with the Hebrew female poet-prophet tradition, for Deborah the prophetess was the wife of Lapidoth (Judg. 4:4). This name speaks of female anger and vengeance, for Deborah's song celebrates a woman's murder of an enemy general by driving a nail through his head as he sleeps. As Gwendolen tells her mother, "all the great poetic criminals were . . . women" (55). Similarly, the epigraph that prefaces the novel announces an intrapersonal vengeance as its subject: "Let thy chief terror be of thine own soul: / There, 'mid the throng of hurrying desires / That trample o'er the dead to seize their spoil, / Lurks vengeance."

And I suspect Mirah's first name also in this subversive hermeneutics of the author, for the pun constructed by its idiosyncratic spelling suggests a mirror of the author's "dead" self, that undifferentiated self of the little girl still able to recall the face of the mother in her dreams, still able to sing the song of the mother in an unknown language, yet haunted by anger at the father's deception.[17]

Daniel shares with Mirah a history of abrupt, early separation from his mother, although he does not learn of this history until later in the narrative. He notes, however, that "something in his own experience" causes Mirah's search after her mother "to lay hold with peculiar force" on his imagination (205). Perhaps this force seems "peculiar" to Daniel because he has always felt that "his father was to blame" for the "injury" of his birth (279). But what Daniel eventually discovers is that the "injury" lies solely with his mother, who casually gave him up for adoption when he was two years old. "I had not much affection to give you," she tells Daniel. "I did not want affection. I had been stifled with it" (626).

The "peculiar force" of Mirah's search for her mother culminates in Daniel's discovery of maternal power and authority, a discovery abetted by the tradition of matrilineal heritage among the Jews. It is his mother's name that matters to the old man in the synagogue: "What is your parentage—your mother's family—her maiden name?" he demands (368). But it is also the product of Daniel's unconscious quest for the Mother, a quest in which even apparently incidental narrative episodes seem to collude, as when the owner of the pawnbroker's shop calls out "'Mother! Mother!'" when Daniel enters (387). But this all-signifying mother rejects her son emotionally. "Is it not possible that I could be near you often and comfort you?" Daniel pleads. "No, not possible," she answers coldly. She is willing to restore his "inheritance"—his name and history as a Jew—to him but not his bond with the mother. As if acting their parts in a Lacanian allegory of castration, the Name-of-the-Father enters and Daniel is cut off forever from Imaginary union with the Mother, now perceived as lacking the Phallus; that is, as desiring something other than Daniel. Appropriately, the narrator comments that this "cruel" moment made Daniel's life seem "a disappointed pilgrimage to a shrine where there were no longer the symbols of sacredness" (660).

Daniel's mother is only one of several mothers in the narrative whose "love" for their children is thus duplicitous and characterized by violent reversals. Mrs. Arrowpoint too seems quite willing to "cut off" her daughter for reasons of pure self-interest.[18] Although she originally appears as a devoted mother, phallic symbols that fairly bristle with violence invest her from the beginning. As if her married name were not "pointed" enough, we can hardly fail to notice that her maiden name was Miss Cuttler, and that she now lives with her husband and daughter at Quetcham Hall. These indications of a desire to "catch" or "cut" somebody are amply revealed in her exchange with Gwendolen, whom she characterizes as "double and satirical."

But it is her own daughter's intention to marry her Jewish music master that unleashes from the literary mother all manner of violent threats and insinuations, from "horsewhipping" the presumptuous suitor, to comparing his proposal to "poisoning and strangling," to suggesting that her formerly admirable daughter must be mad (246). When both Catherine and Klesmer persist in their stance, Mrs. Arrowpoint declares that Catherine will be disinherited and then orders Klesmer from the house. The Arrowpoints eventually decide to make the best of things and keep the fortune with their clear-headed daughter, even if her name will now be Klesmer. But the incident has produced yet another instance of a mother willing to "cut off" her child in order to serve some interest of her own, a mother whose sudden violence of rejection effects a complete reversal of earlier maternal devotion.

The most catastrophic instance of such rejection is that of Mrs. Glasher's firstborn son. This nameless three-year-old, left behind when his mother eloped with Grandcourt, "happened to die" two years afterward. Mrs. Glasher's passionate devotion to her four children by Grandcourt, we are told, is in part the product of atonement. Like the unexpectedly violent image of the drunkard mother in the epigraph to chapter 18, Mrs. Glasher demonstrates that mothers are "various" in *Daniel Deronda:* the mother who curses Gwendolen for blighting her children's chances of inheritance has herself deserted a child.

But the most globally signifying instance of the maternally rejected child in Daniel Deronda is that of the also nameless Cohen daughter, banished from her family for some "unspeakable" crime. Ezra Cohen's smug eulogy to what God has made woman—"a child-bearing, tender-hearted thing is the woman of our people"—adds to the gothic horror of this embedded story of the banished daughter (575). The biblical associations of the name "Ezra" suggest that this daughter has been "cut off" because of marriage to one of the "uncircumcised," for Ezra the scribe urged the Jews to put away their "strange wives."[19] If the daughter has married a non-Jew, then she has become as one of the uncircumcised herself, for the woman's status derives from her association with the male circumcision, not from any rite proper to the woman. The nameless Cohen daughter, then, figures both circumcision and uncircumcision.

Amidst this crowd of lost or rejecting mothers and "castrated" children, Gwendolen lives in a blissful plenitude of maternal love. In the words of Lacan's theory, she lives in the belief that she herself is the Phallus, for she *is* what her mother desires. This prideful phallic fantasy—this "egoism"—is what the narrative desires to "cut off" from Gwendolen. But the process of this painful cutting always looks back toward the mother. The narrative therefore steals from the discourse on circumcision an erotics of "cutting" that constructs in the daughter's body not only a painful "loss," but a gain—not only a "punishment," but also a ritual signifier of acceptance by the "mother" or creator. The first and most graphic instance of Gwendolen's "circumcision" occurs at the hands of Herr Klesmer in his critique of her musical ability. Let us examine that instance in its revelatory detail.

Before Klesmer's arrival, Gwendolen has reassured herself by the contemplation of her mirrored image, for despite her conviction that "she really felt clever enough for anything," she tends to dread the music master "as part of that unmanageable world which was independent of her wishes" (251). The music master intrudes on Gwendolen's position of privileged security and Imaginary power as her mother's preferred child, a function suggested by his name, Klesmer, which means "instrument of song" or "musical instrument." As in Mirah's names, the name incorporates a doubleness of meaning—as a musical or "poetic" instrument and as an "instrument," a common noun that includes the category of sharp or cutting instruments such as knives.[20] And "cutting" is exactly the function Klesmer performs. Because Gwendolen has always done just as she likes, he informs her, she will never succeed in the life of an artist, in which "praise," like her bread, might be "scanty" or might hardly come at all. In short, he lets her know that it is precisely because of her pride that she is not good enough to be an artist.

The narrative spells out the effect of this devastating revelation in graphic "body language"—the language of circumcision: "The belief that to present herself in public on the stage must produce an effect such as she had been used to feel certain of in private life, was like a bit of her flesh—it was not to be peeled off readily, but must come with blood and pain" (255). As D. A. Miller writes concerning the sensation novel, "the excitement that seizes us here is as direct as the 'fight-or-flight' physiology that renders our reading bodies . . . theaters of neurasthenia."[21] But the project of our "overnice literary criticism" has been to ignore it, to silence the sensations promoted by such language on our "reading bodies." Our "Cartesian" criticism censures such bodily reading, directs our attention away from it to the "meaning" of the text. Yet the narrative of *Daniel Deronda* underlines it, repeats it, insists on the sensation, as here: "Her pride had felt a terrible knife-edge, and the last sentence only made the smart keener" (256).

This is only the first of repeated "cuts" that finally circumcise Gwendolen, the "spoiled child," cutting away her phallic "pride" but ultimately inscribing her with the covenant of acceptance by her "creator." The Protestant discourse on circumcision, elaborated particularly in family bible dictionaries, constructs this narrative ritual, but the narrative also exceeds the intended limits of that discourse, for Gwendolen's punished and disciplined body is not "saved" for the Oedipal plot but prepared for a new one—the still unfinished story of the daughter's return to the mother. In its insistence on writing this eccentric story, the narrative constructs a subversive hermeneutics of circumcision that maps both its pain and its meaning onto the body of the daughter but that divests the Phallus of its status as "privileged signifier."

Reading the Hermeneutics of Circumcision with Lacan, and Lacan with the Hermeneutics of Circumcision

The nineteenth-century Protestant hermeneutic discourse on circumcision documents both the drive to restrain or regulate interpretation and the desire to elaborate the male sexual organ as Phallus: it presents a startlingly explicit example of phallic politics. What was at issue in this discourse was the "modern learning and research" that seriously challenged the traditional interpretation of circumcision as a rite practiced exclusively by the Jews, given to them alone as a sign of the covenant between God and man, and then reinterpreted in Christian theology as the type of

Christian baptism. An examination of a newly popularized genre of religious interpretive literature—family bible dictionaries—will show how "interpretation" directed especially to "the People," while ostensibly welcoming the new research, actually worked to resist that research and conserve traditional readings.

Most significantly in the case of circumcision, nineteenth-century interpretation trained readers to distance themselves from the body. Hermeneutic discourse produced the "meaning" or interpretation—the symbolic value—of circumcision while suppressing the acknowledgment of circumcision as a bodily event. Many dictionary entries, for example, including that in Dr. William Smith's most admired *Dictionary of the Bible* (1860), dispensed with any definition of the word at all, turning the reader off into considerations of its "meaning." Dr. Smith's entry begins, "Circumcision was peculiarly, though not exclusively, a Jewish rite. It was enjoined upon Abraham, the father of the nation, by God, at the institution, and as the token, of the Covenant, which assured to him and his descendants the promise of the Messiah (Gen. xvii.)."[22] One may read to the end of Dr. Smith's dictionary entry without ever having a clue as to what circumcision *is*.[23]

But, as Foucault has taught us, we should be wary of ascribing this discursive distancing from the body to a simple notion of Victorian sexual prudery and our own "emancipation." What was at stake here was not the suppression of sexual discourse but the production of a particular discourse on sexuality at the expense of others. The hermeneutic strategy of Protestant "definitions" of circumcision constructs a historical parallel to Lacan's exposition of the meaning or signification of the Phallus. The Phallus must not be confused with the penis—it is not even to be confused with male sexuality, since, Lacan writes, "It is even less the organ, penis or clitoris, that it symbolizes" (Lacan, "Signification," 285). Lacan pushes constantly toward the meaning of the Phallus, evading or denying its connection with sexual organs of either gender. Yet Muller and Richardson note the emergence of an ambiguity concerning the term in "The Signification of the Phallus" and suggest an "oscillation" between the role of the Phallus as signifier and its role as real or imagined organ.[24]

The Victorian discourse on circumcision similarly produces the penis as Phallus, as signifying organ, while suppressing acknowledgment of it as a small, vulnerable part of the male body that could be painfully wounded or even cut off, despite growing evidence of that perception in the literature on circumcision. Unlike Adam Clarke and other dissenting clergy who wrote bible commentaries, nineteenth-century bible dictionaries do not discuss the womb, even though the word "womb" occurs more often in biblical texts than the word "circumcision."[25]

The discourse on circumcision, then, in a move that precedes and predicts Lacan's, sought to repress the penis but to promote its symbolic significance while maintaining almost total silence on the subject of the female body. But the very project of producing phallic significance through the interpretation of circumcision inevitably forced exegetes into some construction of the physical vulnerability of the penis, though their intention to speak of it as little as possible is clear. I shall briefly describe the "history" of this Victorian discourse as it may have developed among, or informed, the readers of *Daniel Deronda*.

The year began with the reading, and rereading, of circumcision. On January 1 the Anglican Church celebrated the Feast of the Circumcision: this was because, if Christ was born on December 25, he must have been circumcised "on the eighth day," or January 1. The proper lessons for the day were taken from the fourth chapter of Romans, in which Paul asserts that it was Abraham's faith, not his circumcision, that was imputed to him as righteousness, and from the second chapter of Luke, the only account in the gospels of the circumcision of the infant Jesus. On January 2 the Anglican lectionary began the rereading of the bible, starting once again with the first books of the Old and New Testaments and the first epistle of Paul, or the books of Genesis, Matthew, and Romans. Genesis includes the story of the "first" circumcision as well as other, more problematic accounts of the practice, and in Romans Paul considers the topic of "circumcision" and "uncircumcision" obsessively. The readings for the month of January, the first month of the new year, thus continually produced the problem of circumcision.

For it was a problem for Protestant readers—or rather, it was the site of production of several problems. The first of these, as indicated by Paul's discussions, was the meaning of the rite for non-Jewish readers; that is, for nonpracticing readers. Paul's project is both to defend the meaning of circumcision and not to "defend" it as practice. Paul does not simply denounce circumcision but endeavors to retain it as symbolic value.[26] Nineteenth-century exegetes reproduce and extend Paul's treatment. Patrick Fairbairn's exegesis is particularly illuminating for our purposes, for he shows how the meaning of circumcision came to be intrinsic to the defense of symbolic values in general: the ordinances of Judaism, like those of Christianity, he explains, were all of a "symbolical nature, not simply outward or typical," and if this be so, then "the initiatory ordinance of the whole series," circumcision, "was by no means a merely external badge" (Fairbairn, *Hermeneutical Manual,* 147, 149). Indeed, Fairbairn admits that circumcision could hardly have served as a distinguishing "external badge," since not only did certain other peoples practice the rite, but "it is, in fact, one of those customs, the origin of which is lost in a remote antiquity." However, when adopted by God as an "appropriate token and seal," it becomes a symbol of purification, a symbol of "transition from nature's depravity into a spiritual and holy life."

Fairbairn thus produces circumcision as the "initiatory," the very first sign of a transition from "nature's depravity" to a "spiritual and holy" entity. Circumcision therefore is essential to hermeneutics, for it has become the initiatory sign, the originary guarantee of symbolic truth. Circumcision has become, in short, the Phallus. As in Lacan's "The Signification of the Phallus," the connection of circumcision with the bodily phenomenon is downplayed, passed over, while its status as signifier is promoted, made a necessity to all interpretation. But if circumcision is to guarantee hermeneutic Truth, if it is to be the "privileged signifier" of a covenant between Man and his Creator, then it must not be vulnerable to a plurality of meanings, especially to contradictory and less celebratory meanings. Evidence suggesting, for example, that circumcision was not exclusive to the Jews—or even to males—would be profoundly anxiety provoking and would tend to promote counterhermeneutic strategies, such as denial, silencing, or even hysteria.

Such evidence was apparently first presented forcibly to the hermeneutic community in Charles Knight's *Penny Cyclopedia.*[27] A volume published in 1837 contained an article on circumcision to which nearly every bible dictionary published thereafter anxiously refers. This unsigned article begins with the orthodox biblical interpretation of circumcision as a sign of the covenant between Abraham and God, but it continues with a description of variations of the practice, including "the excision of females," among various "savage or imperfectly-civilised races." These accounts are taken mostly from the works of explorers such as Cook and Dampier and document circumcision as a ubiquitous and diverse practice. The article concludes that "the principal distinction" between circumcision as practiced by Jews and by other peoples is that the Jews "always when it is practicable circumcise the child on the eighth day after its birth," whereas other nations usually defer it to a later period (Knight, 196–97).

On this obviously inadequate distinction, the whole hermeneutic house of cards threatened to fall apart. One bible dictionary after another cites the *Penny Cyclopedia* evidence and then attempts to deemphasize it or deny it altogether. Whatever evidence exists for circumcision's practice by other peoples, one writer protests, "it nevertheless distinctly and emphatically characterized the Hebrews till the time of Christ as a peculiar people. They were the circumcision, while all other nations were the uncircumcision."[28] Dr. Smith's solution to the quandary, which I have already quoted, was to distinguish between circumcision as a "peculiarly" but not "exclusively" Jewish rite. Although admitting that "the rite has been found to prevail extensively both in ancient and in modern times," and that in some nations a similar custom is said to be practiced by both sexes, Smith simply asserts that "circumcision certainly belonged to the Jews, as it did to no other people" (Smith, 1:331).

The evidence seems to drive Patrick Fairbairn into male hysteria. Forced to acknowledge the unsavory aspects of circumcision by the "new evidence," Fairbairn turns his revulsion against masculine sexuality. "By the mutilation it [circumcision] practices on the organ of generation, it points to corruption in its source as adhering to the very being and birth of men—propagating itself by the settled constitution of nature, which transmits from parent to child a common impurity. Most appropriately, therefore, might a rite, which consisted in cutting off somewhat of the filth of the flesh of nature's productiveness, be taken as the symbol of a covenant." In a separate entry, Fairbairn names the foreskin "an emblem of corruption."[29]

As the above quotations demonstrate, the attempt to defend circumcision against conflicting interpretations inevitably forced exegetes to construct it as a bodily event. Fairbairn notes that "from the measure of painfulness and mutilation involved in the operation, it could not but be otherwise than repugnant to the natural feelings." Even Dr. Smith mentions the probability of pain during the operation, at least for "grown persons."

Not all nineteenth-century commentators responded to the *Penny Cyclopedia* with such fervent denial or hysteria, however. The most radicalized response appears to be that of F. W. Newman, writing in Kitto's *Cyclopedia*.[30] "The history of Jewish circumcision lies on the surface of the Old Testament," he observes, but the principal object of his article will be to put together what is known of the "extra-Jewish Circumcision," a topic that has been the object of "much research." Newman proceeds to recite increasingly disturbing instances of circumcision among non-Jewish people. Beyond the notices of Asian circumcision collected in the *Penny Cyclopedia,* there are evidences of African tribes who "practised on themselves a yet more shocking mutilation"—and here he lapses into Greek, both concealing and revealing this too-shocking fact by writing it in a language known to exegetes but not generally to the "People." What is more, he continues darkly, there is evidence of that "still more singular and painful process by which a circumcised person was in some sort restored to his natural condition."[31]

As Newman's comments indicate, "modern research" clearly made nineteenth-century male exegetes nervous, and the hermeneutic discourse they produced is a neurotic discourse that writes the Phallus in part as symptom of a difficult repression. What were they repressing? The evidence they manipulated with such quaking pens suggests, from our historically distanced perspective, complex sexual meanings. As Maurice Bloch demonstrates in his study of the circumcision ritual among the Merina people, the meaning of circumcision is historically determined, changing as social and political organization changes. No simple "originary" function can be asserted. But where the practice is both ritualized and made exclusive to males, it seems indisputable that it institutionalizes male bonding, male authority, and male hierarchy, and that it sanctifies the male "generative powers" while devaluing the female.[32] To what extent nineteenth-century British Protestant exegetes unconsciously "read" these meanings in accounts of "extra-Jewish" circumcision I can only speculate, however, as this nervous community preferred to talk about other things.

It is notable that exegesis produced in an earlier and less-threatened era writes all of these possibilities. The texts of two eighteenth-century exegetes, which were reprinted or translated in the nineteenth century and thus circulated in the Victorian discourse on circumcision, also offer an instructive difference from it. The iconoclastic German commentator Johann David Michaelis devoted more than forty pages to the subject of circumcision, considering at length what might have been the "natural reasons" for the practice. Referring to Josephus's account of the Idumacans, Michaelis speculates that "there must have been some special cause that could induce a whole people to submit to this irksome and painful condition for among us, hundreds of thousands would be found determined either to emigrate, or to risk their lives anew . . . were a Mahometan conqueror to issue an order for their circumcision."[33]

Although he considers the most commonly produced rationale (that it was done for "hygienic" purposes), Michaelis also speculates on whether it might have been intended as a deterrent to "manustupration," as his translator spells it. If that were the case, he assures us enthusiastically, every legislator might have reason to enjoin universal male circumcision soon after birth![34] But further consideration convinces him that the practice of "self-pollution" must have been possible "even to circumcised persons, and not so painful, as that the pain . . . could serve as any preservative."

But Michaelis has spoken what Victorian exegetes never did: the possible connection between circumcision and sexual desires. For Michaelis, circumcision is not sacred—it is not the site of production of the Phallus, though it is, he suggests, the site of production of sexual discourse, or of words for the sexual parts. The mere expression "circumcise the prepuce of the parts," he points out, was intelligible to Abraham, yet such a command would not now be understood by many Europeans, for the very term prepuce is known to most people only from the bible. If not for circumcision, Michaelis deduces, "that part of the body would hardly have had a name in common language, because it is not very noticeable, and we have no need to speak of it" (Michaelis, vol. 3, bk. 4, 79).[35]

The eighteenth-century English Dissenter Matthew Henry also

noticed the foreskin's insignificance: circumcision was required by God, he suggested, in part because, prior to Christ's sacrifice, "God would have man enter into covenant by the offering of some part of his own body, and no part could be better spared." The true circumcision, he continued, was of the heart; therefore, God has put an honor on this "uncomely part," the foreskin, by associating it with this "true circumcision." But Henry also did not fail to notice the violence and danger associated with circumcision.[36] Abraham's obedience was extraordinary because he obeyed the command for circumcision, "though circumcision was painful, though to grown men it was shameful; though, while they were sore and unfit for action, their enemies might take advantage against them, as Simeon and Levi did against the Schechemites."

Henry's text, then, produces the penis as a site of pain, shame, and danger but not of particular significance. "No part could be better spared" than the foreskin, and this "uncomely part" of the male body was "honored" by its selection for sacrifice. In Patricia Yaeger's apt phrase, the penis becomes a "dangling signifier" in Henry's commentary, a small, dangling part that signifies male vulnerability and lack of power, as opposed to the privileged Phallus.[37] But Henry's and Michaelis's texts, like the *Penny Cyclopedia* and F. W. Newman's article, testify to their differences from the prevailing mode in the Protestant discourse on circumcision, which repressed the penis, in its frightening vulnerability—and desirability. Resisting the "modern research" and "Biblical science" which they claimed to address, commentators insisted with growing intensity on the "meaning" of circumcision as a covenant between man and his creator. What was left out of this discourse—what did not signify at all—was the female body.

The Circumcision of the Daughter and the "Cutting Off" of the Father

To lose the "effect" she had felt certain of in private life was for Gwendolen, as the narrative spells out for us, like losing "a bit of her flesh—it was not to be peeled off readily, but must come with blood and pain" (255). This is how we "feel" Herr Klesmer's words to her: they "feel" like a circumcision. That is, the words construct an effect that our bodies read in the same way our bodies read some of the accounts of circumcision that I have quoted above. Of course, as twenty-first-century critical readers, as Cartesian critical readers, we did not notice this effect of the text. But now as "Victorian" readers, our conscious (and unconscious) response to the hermeneutics of circumcision gives such language an added "edge." Circumcision was clearly not an abstract or minor issue in Victorian Protestantism: the debate on this "Jewish" rite threatened the foundations of Christian theology and hermeneutics, threatened to unveil the Phallus and disclose the "deification" of the male organ at the very "beginnings" of monotheism. As no-longer innocent readers, let us reexamine circumcision in the text of *Daniel Deronda.*

On January 1, the Feast of the Circumcision, Daniel interprets Gwendolen's marital pain in words that paraphrase the Protestant hermeneutics of circumcision as a type of baptism, its pain a necessary prelude to spiritual vision or light. "Take the present suffering as a painful letting in of light," he suggests. "Turn your fear into a safeguard . . . use it as if it were a faculty, like vision." John Keble's poem for the day demonstrates this conflation of the pain of circumcision with the vision or light of Christianity's new year:

> The year begins with Thee,
>   And Thou beginn'st with woe,
> To let the world of sinners see
>   That blood for sin must flow.
>
> If thou wouldst reap in love,
>   First sow in holy fear:
> So life a winter's morn may prove
>   To a bright endless year.[38]

By taking her "fear" as a safeguard, Gwendolen can turn it into a faculty "like vision": what she sows in "holy fear" she may "reap in love," and what begins as a "winter's morn" may prove the beginning of a "bright endless year." Keble insists on the necessity of pain: "Thine infant cries, O Lord, . . . Are not enough—the legal sword / Must do its stern behest." The blood of the circumcision, "those few precious drops," is "like sacrificial wine." Daniel tells Gwendolen, "I don't think you could have escaped the painful process in some form or other," to which poor Gwendolen replies, "But it is a very cruel form" (452).

Since the interchanges between Daniel and Gwendolen take place as the old year turns into the new, and in the chapters (thirty-five and thirty-six) that mark the precise midpoint of the seventy-chapter narrative structure, the text unites Jew and Christian, past and future, prophecy and history at its formal or poetic center. George Eliot's location of circumcision in the center of her narrative thus constructs a hermeneutic project for her readers that will exploit the traditional interpretation to satisfy a desire for coherence. But as the Victorian discourse on circumcision unwillingly transgressed traditional boundaries, so circumcision in the novel exceeds its "orthodox" hermeneutic project. The erotic attraction of the discourse on circumcision marks everything in the novel as either circumcision or uncircumcision. Circumcision functions not only as a formal "mark" in the textual body, but as the desire that drives it from beginning to end.[39]

Both Gwendolen's and Daniel's stories move toward this signifying date, meet and "cross" on it, and then continue to endings that write the "meaning" of circumcision for each of them. In the "crossing" of their stories, the narrative constructs a subversive erotics of circumcision that transfers meaning from the Jewish to the "extra-Jewish" scene, from the male to the female "member." But as it marks this "crossing over," the narrative sorts itself differently, and what has been two "halves" that we expect the ending to unite instead disperses into three stories that cannot come together. Each of these stories, I will argue, constructs a maternal thematics that threatens phallic authority, for these stories not only return us obsessively to mothers, but expose the father as the "undesirable father," the circumcised "member" that represents only a humiliating reality and a self-serving politics.

What I wish to argue is that the "crossing over" of Daniel's and Gwendolen's stories marked by the sign of circumcision, and their subsequent splintering into three stories, writes a maternal thematics that phallocentric theory can only partially explain. The maternal thematics of Daniel's story, inasmuch as it constructs the pre-Oedipal Mother or the

Mother of the Imaginary register, is complicit with Lacan's theory even as it marks a different emphasis, for the Imaginary Mother is always assumed in the Symbolic register constituted by the entrance of the Name-of-the-Father.[40] The object of Daniel's quest—like Mordecai's and Mirah's—is the "homeland," the "mother tongue," ultimately, the pre-Oedipal Mother. With perfect appropriateness, Daniel's story ends with the male and female signifiers of the Oedipal plot, Mirah and Daniel, wrapped in embrace of the body of the pre-Oedipal plot's prophet, Mordecai. These three Oedipal children, united by a sense of having "sucked the breasts of the same mother," share the pain of Her loss and the visionary goal of returning to Her. Yet even as the meaning of circumcision conforms here to Lacan's notion of castration, we should note the persistence and diversity of its reference to both the Mother and to mothers in the plural, constructing not only the visionary song of the mother and the words "full of meaning" that precede the "spelled" language, but an intensity of interest in mothers' names and histories, in their differences as well as their "difference."

And the "end" of Daniel's story is flanked by two other, nonphallocentric story endings: the story of Gwendolen and her mother, and the story of Mirah and her father. Both of these stories are therefore "the daughter's story," but neither tells the story we expect; that is, the story of the daughter's seduction by the father. What we find in Gwendolen's story is not only the story of the pre-Oedipal romance that surprised Freud with its passion and strength—the attachment of the daughter to the mother—but a different outcome of that romance as constructed by both Freud and Lacan. Instead of consigning Gwendolen to the heroic father figure to whom, in an apparently orthodox Oedipal plot, she seems to have transferred her affection, the narrative returns her to her "insignificant" mother. This is not, however, a return to the Imaginary Mother but an unorthodox story of the daughter learning to love the mother as an other. The meaning of Gwendolen's "circumcision," ultimately, is located in her painful differentiation from her mother and in her final consignment to a community of mothers and daughters. The ritual of circumcision, as "cut" into the daughter's story, thus marks a covenant between women.

Even more radical in its implications than the story of Gwendolen and her mother is the story of Mirah and Mordecai's father, "the father Lapidoth" who makes his first appearance at the end of the narrative only to be "cut off" for good. This story so explicitly deconstructs phallic power and authority as to exceed the radical narrative politics that returns a daughter to an ordinary mother. In this seemingly unnecessary story, the representative of patriarchy figures not as the Phallus, but as that "uncomely" part, the foreskin—the part of which Matthew Henry so devastatingly remarked, "no part could be better spared." These two unexpected narratives disrupt the conventional hermeneutics of both circumcision and the "signification of the Phallus."

Gillian Beer points out that the novel opens with something that is "not quite an encounter between Daniel and Gwendolen," and that Gwendolen's relationship with Daniel thus takes priority over Mirah's for the reader. The reader is much less likely to notice that something that is "not quite an encounter" between Gwendolen and her mother takes place at the beginning of the second chapter, when Gwendolen receives a letter from her mother signed "Fanny Davilow." Not until the fourteenth chapter do we discover that another letter from another mother has preceded this one—the letter from Lydia Glasher urging Gwendolen to meet her at the Whispering Stones, where she appears to Gwendolen as a "ghastly vision saying, 'I am a woman's life'" (152). While Gwendolen's story thus has one beginning, in which she is the object of a male gaze, it has a second "beginning" in a circulation of letters between mother(s) and the daughter. Although this circulation constitutes a second beginning of Gwendolen's story, its "origin" chronologically precedes the first. The male gaze is only a secondary "beginning" in this other story that begins and ends with mothers and daughters.

Indeed, if we attend to the "letter" of the letter, to what it says rather than what it means, we find it inscribed by the mother's reproach of the daughter for leaving her. "I have been expecting to hear from you for a week," it begins. "How could you be so thoughtless as to leave me in uncertainty about your address? I am in the greatest anxiety lest this should not reach you." The repressed intensity of the story of Gwendolen's relationship to her mother in the narrative lays open to question the primacy of the Oedipal plot. It makes possible the supposition that the intervention of Daniel and other "phallic instruments" may be only an "effect" of this other story, the struggle to differentiate from the mother. In the first narrative moment of that struggle, Gwendolen savagely rejects Rex's romantic overtures, then later sobs to her mother, "I shall never love anybody. I can't love people. . . . I can't bear anyone to be very near me but you." At this point Mrs. Davilow also begins to sob, for, as the narrative interprets for us, "this spoiled child had never shown such dependence on her before: and so they clung to each other" (82).

But their clinging together at this moment documents their mutual recognition, in fact, of separation. Gwendolen would not be sobbing if she did not feel her attachment to her mother as a loss. Her profound attachment produces an alternation in her between a sense of identification with her mother and a recurrent sense of guilty responsibility for her, a conviction that her mother is not happy. We may read Gwendolen's obsession with her mother's unhappiness in the terms of object-relations theory as constructing the infantile delusion that the mother demands symbiosis. The infant consequently experiences the drive toward separation as a guilty betrayal of the mother. On her wedding day, for example, Gwendolen is preoccupied with her mother's sadness, telling her, "sorrowing is your sauce" and insisting that she will always love her mother "better than anybody else in the world." When her mother attempts the proper Oedipalization of her daughter's story—"I shall not be jealous if you love your husband better; and he will expect to be first"—Gwendolen brushes it off scornfully as a rather "ridiculous expectation" (356).

In her therapeutic sessions with Daniel after Grandcourt's death, we see Gwendolen attempting to sort out her motives toward her mother, increasingly trying to differentiate between her mother's needs and her own desires. "Perhaps you may not quite know that I really did think a good deal about my mother when I married. I was selfish, but I did love her, and feel about her poverty . . . for I was very precious to my mother—and he took me from her—and he meant—and if she had known" (767). So she tries, with evident difficulty, to separate the "reality" of her marriage from the far less obvious, because less conventional, reality of her relationship with her mother.

The narrative repeatedly resorts to a body language of pain during the long process of Gwendolen's separation from her mother. Living with Grandcourt is like being caught by "a crab or a boa-constrictor which goes on pinching or crushing without alarm at thunder" (423). Lush's speech feels "like a sharp knife-edge drawn across her skin" (600), and Grandcourt's words have "the power of thumbscrews and the cold touch of the rack" (680). Even Daniel's penetrating look has "a keener edge than Klesmer's judgment" for her (330), and we know how keen that earlier "edge" was.

During this painful process of individuation, Gwendolen affirms the benefit of her acquaintance with Daniel three times, as if extracting a ritualized "blessing" from him. On the Feast of the Circumcision, she first insists to Daniel, "it shall be better with me because I have known you" (453). Later, when Daniel first tells her of his engagement to Mirah, she cries out, "I said I should be forsaken." But a few moments later, she gasps out, "I said . . . it should be better . . . better with me . . . for having known you" (805). And she repeats this "blessing" yet a third time at the end of her letter to Daniel on his wedding day: "It is better—it shall be better with me because I have known you" (810).

Gwendolen thus sanctifies her pain by Daniel's acknowledgment of it, but what this pain and blessing accomplish for her is an acceptance into the "covenant" of mothers. In her last words in the narrative, Gwendolen repeats Daniel's promise to her that she will live to be "one of the best of women, who make others glad that they were born" (810). Like the godfather who holds the infant to be circumcised, Daniel's watching her pain transfers to Gwendolen the meaning of circumcision, "blessing" her and accepting her into the community of the shriven. But that privileged community is the community of mothers who have been circumcised in "the foreskin of the heart," who have had the phallic corruption of "pride" cut off. That privileged community in George Eliot's last novel implicitly excludes mothers who have betrayed their children. But the final figure of the traitorous parent is not a mother but a father—"the father Lapidoth."

From the first moment of his appearance on the scene, Mirah's father is named as a figure of betrayal. He is the "unreverend father," the "undesirable father," the "unworthy father" (737, 779, 781). He cannot be trusted. He distorts every story so that it tells a different story. In a move similar to Freud's, he converts the story of his abduction of the daughter into a story of the daughter's fantasy of abduction: "Why did you run away from me, child?" he demands of Mirah. "You know I never made you do anything against your will. . . . What father devoted himself to his daughter more than I did to you?" (737).

Finally, this "father Lapidoth" steals Daniel's father's ring, as he has earlier "stolen" even his name. Mirah remembers that her father called her Lapidoth, saying it was a "name of his forefathers" (215). But as we have seen, "Lapidoth" is really a "dangling signifier," for it acquires significance only in its connection to the prophetic "mother"—to the name of the prophetess Deborah. Similarly the ring that Lapidoth steals—like Grandcourt's ring—acquires its significance only in its circulation through mothers. Perhaps it is not incidental that most nineteenth-century bible dictionaries referred the meaning of circumcision to the Latin *circumcidere,* "to cut around." The "rings" transferred to female "members" in this narrative effect a similar cutting around, but not a cutting off. Painfully, but meaningfully, they circle around mothers and daughters, daughters and their "creators," both in and out of the text. But the father Lapidoth, the "undesirable father," cuts himself off by his theft of the ring Daniel received from his mother. His circumcision then is a fraudulent ring, for it does not speak his covenant with God, but speaks only his own version of the story.

In the writing of that story and others, George Eliot's last novel constructs a female erotics that subverts the phallic monologic of circumcision: the site of many meanings, it may lead us back to that originary loss—the cutting off from the Mother—or it may write a new "ending" to that story in the construction of a bond between women. Then again, it may produce the circumcised penis not as privileged signifier but as the locus of pain and humiliation—as the site of a pleasurable vengeance. The story of the father Lapidoth writes that other story that Victorian exegetes of circumcision wanted to repress: the possibility that the divine authority of circumcision was just a self-serving story, and that the "real" thing afforded no cause for celebration whatever—indeed, that it might be said to exceed the limits of interpretation.

SIX

VICTORIAN SCHEMES
OF THE APOCALYPSE

Profits and Prophecy

"As a traveling speaker for the Campus Crusade for Christ," Hal Lindsey writes in the introduction to his *The Late Great Planet Earth* (1970), "I had the opportunity to give messages on prophecy to thousands of people."[1] Those "messages on prophecy," with the help of the collaborative writer C. C. Carlson, were turned into a book that became the single biggest nonfiction bestseller of the entire decade of the seventies.[2] By 1979, the cover claimed that nine million copies had been sold and a motion picture produced. With constant reference to the "college students" whom Lindsey claims were his particular audience, he prophesies that "Russia will arm and equip a vast confederacy" composed of "Egypt, the Arabic nations, and countries of black Africa" that will lead an attack on a restored Israel (7, 60, 61). Lindsey notes that Asia, which for centuries "has had a tradition of backwardness," will enter the industrial age and become "a great scourge to the Western civilization." In a by-the-way remark, Lindsey mentions that this event had been foreseen in 1864 by "Dr. Cumming," the author of a "fascinating old book, over a hundred years old" (39). To "Dr. Cumming," if we take Lindsey's word for it, goes the credit for employing the Book of Revelation to capitalize on a mass-market print culture by interpreting contemporary military and political events as foreseen in the mystical seals and vials of the Apocalypse, and thereby authorizing an imperialist and racist ideology. Who was the entrepreneurial author of this "fascinating old book"?

On the facing page of an 1855 American edition of John Cumming's

Apocalyptic Sketches: Lectures on the Book of Revelation, first series, we find a description of the author:

> The Rev. John Cumming, D.D. is now the great pulpit orator of London, as Edward Irving was some twenty years since. But very different is the Doctor to that strange, wonderfully eloquent, but erratic man. There could not by possibility be a greater contrast. The one all fire, enthusiasm, and semi-madness; the other a man of chastened energy and convincing calmness. The one like a meteor, flashing across a troubled sky, and then vanishing suddenly in the darkness; the other like a silver star, shining serenely, and illuminating our pathway with its steady ray. He is looked upon as the great champion of Protestantism in its purest form.[3]

The publisher's blurb, for such it is, goes on to state that it is Cumming's "great work on the 'Apocalypse'" on which his "high reputation as a writer rests," and that that work has already reached its fifteenth edition in England. The blurb is placed at the bottom of a list of "The Rev. John Cumming's Works," each of which is priced at seventy-five cents per volume and will be sent by mail, without charge for postage, by the publishers as soon as payment is received. Of the eight titles listed, four deal with "apocalypse" or "prophecy" (Cumming, *Apocalyptic Sketches,* 1st ser., n.p.).

Clearly, the Apocalypse was big business in Victorian times. John Cumming was its "silver star," an apocalyptic seer who could be advertised by his publishers as a "man of chastened energy and convincing calmness," in reassuring contrast with the meteoric Edward Irving, a Scottish preacher whose sermons to his London congregation denounced the world in the awe-inspiring tones of a biblical prophet. Nevertheless, Cumming was himself denounced by the author of an anonymous essay in the October 1855 *Westminster Review,* who charged the "great champion of Protestantism in its purest form" with giving "a charter to hatred." This critic, who later became known as George Eliot, maintained that though Cumming's work "may enjoin charity . . . it fosters all uncharitableness."[4]

Cumming's publications on the Apocalypse were part of a nineteenth-century British consumer culture in "prophecy" that began to grow in the early 1820s and continued into the 1870s.[5] Cumming's acknowledged source for his fund-raising sermons on the Book of Revelation, E. B. Elliott's *Horae Apocalypticae,* first published in 1844, cites a large number of contemporary and preceding apocalyptic expositors of the nineteenth and late eighteenth centuries. Although neither Cumming nor Elliott ever cites a female expositor, women were also attempting to crowd into the apocalyptic marketplace. Robert M. Kachur notes that over thirty commentaries on the Apocalypse were published by British women between 1845 and 1900.[6] He argues that Christina Rossetti and her fellow Tractarian Elizabeth Rundle Charles deploy a subtle critique of male-dominant biblical exegesis in their work, but that Evangelical and dissenting women tend to reproduce a "male" exegesis, which he defines as reinforcing "patriarchal privilege by assigning biblical language fixed meanings dependent on scholarly expertise deemed inappropriate for women to acquire."[7] As example, he cites Mrs. J. C. Martin, who, in her *The Revelation of St. John Briefly Explained* (1851), unveils "her own revelation . . . that the Apocalypse's most pressing message to Victorian readers is to warn against the continuing 'Romish' influence of the Tractarians on the Church of England" (Kachur, "Repositioning the Female Christian Reader," 197). But Mrs. Martin was only one of a number of "commentators," both men and women, who recommodified Elliott's commodification of the Apocalypse by reproducing it in some more popular form. There were a large number of these would-be spin-offs from the commercial success of *Horae Apocalypticae.*[8] At least one other was also by a woman, the anonymous author of *Conversations on the Book of Revelation: Being a Simple Exposition for the Young, According to the Views of the Rev. J. Cumming, and the Rev. E. B. Elliott* (1868).

In the twentieth century, by contrast, a flourishing industry of literary apocalyptics aestheticized the Apocalypse in such a way as to erase the history and politics, much of it violent, of millenarianism. The bulk of these literary apocalyptic studies "disarmed" the Apocalypse, as Steven Goldsmith brilliantly demonstrates in his 1993 work, *Unbuilding Jerusalem: Apocalypse and Romantic Representation.*[9] Not only did this academic consumer culture ignore the enormous contemporary success of Hal Lindsey's 1970 apocalyptic commentary, *The Late Great Planet Earth*—which capitalized on the Apocalypse as divine guarantee of the militarist and imperialist destiny of the United States—it also overlooked the extreme violence of the Book of Apocalypse itself and downplayed, if not ignored, its equally extreme misogyny.

Feminist biblical and theological scholars, however, spotlighted the violence and misogyny of the Christian Book of Apocalypse. Adela Yarbro Collins led the way in her acknowledgment that *power* is a major issue in Revelation: "Christ as lamb is overshadowed by Christ as judge and warrior."[10] Yarbro Collins found herself forced to compare the "symbols" of Revelation—dragon, beasts, and harlot—to "social structures, ideas, and institutional processes" that get out of control like a Frankenstein monster (173). For Yarbro Collins, the aesthetically pleasing and consoling vision of a meaningful End had disintegrated into an abortive assortment of "violent images, symbols, and narratives" (173).

But both Yarbro Collins and the feminist theologian Elisabeth Schüssler Fiorenza repress the vicious misogyny of Apocalypse, choosing in particular to minimize the graphic nature of the burning and eating of the Whore.[11] Not until Tina Pippin's candid statement that the "sexual murder" of the Whore accentuates the hatred of women as much as it does that of imperial power, and that "in terms of an ideology of gender, both women characters in the narrative and women readers are victimized," does a feminist biblical scholar unhesitatingly articulate the gynocidal desires of the text.[12] In her later work, *Apocalyptic Bodies,* Pippin observes, "I see the Apocalypse as a misogynist male fantasy of the end of time," and that she wants "to say 'no' to this text, for ultimately, I do not find the Apocalypse to be a liberating story."[13]

While Pippin and others dissected the Book of Apocalypse to reveal its sexual politics, paranoia, and violence, still other feminist scholars were calling attention to some equally violent apocalyptic strains in the "second wave" feminist movement of the late twentieth century. Catherine Keller critiques Mary Daly's call to "Holy War"—a jihad in effect—against the male trinity and male hierarchy of the Christian, especially the Roman Catholic, Church.[14] Of Monique Wittig's *Les Guérillères,* she exclaims, "This 1969 cult classic, quoted often and ritually among American feminists, announced a purer vision of gender Apocalypse than ever Daly spun: we may call it Gynageddon" (249).

The link between feminist apocalyptic literature and gender violence did not begin with late-twentieth-century, second-wave gender violence, however. Victorian women writers who make explicit appropriations of the Apocalypse similarly engage in apocalyptic "gynageddon," transferring apocalyptic violence to the male body. Two such apocalyptic fictions— Charlotte Brontë's *Jane Eyre* and Elizabeth Barrett Browning's *Aurora Leigh*—also make visible the contemporary forms of commodification of the Apocalypse. They show that it was packaged not only in terms of current events and recent history, but as promotion of British national identity with its religious and racial exclusions. Victorian clerical "schemes of the Apocalypse" were not only schemes for commercial success, but politically motivated strategies as well. We may find the discursive predecessors of the violence, misogyny, and racism of turn-of-the-millennium apocalypticism in the Apocalypse of Victorian consumer culture.

"Protestantism in Its Purest Form"

The "origins" of this enthusiasm for prophecy in nineteenth-century England are far from clear. Ernest R. Sandeen, who documents millenarianism both in the United States and Britain at this time, points first to the French Revolution, which produced a flood of apocalyptic interpretations.[15] But he notes that, while Victorian evangelicals tended to inscribe European political events with apocalyptic meaning, the rise of the Millerite sect in the United States tended to be attributed to the "great revival" of the 1830s.[16] Reform politics in England in the 1820s and 1830s are also cited as possibly instigating an apocalyptic worldview among the British—and indeed, Elliott deals with them at length, and in largely negative terms, in his *Horae Apocalypticae*. Certainly, working-class movements in England invoked apocalyptic authorization. As Barbara Taylor states, "throughout the first half of the nineteenth century, chiliastic cults flourished in many parts of the country. Prophets rose and fell, gathering thousands of disciples one year and losing them the next to another self-proclaimed Messiah."[17] Joanna Southcott, a domestic servant who educated herself almost solely through reading the bible, attracted thousands of followers after hearing voices in the year 1792 that told her she was the

Woman clothed with the Sun [Rev. 12:1]. She produced over sixty volumes of prophetic writings and preached a doctrine of women's spiritual equality, thoroughly shocking more conservative middle-class Christians (Taylor, 162–65).[18] Irving's preaching was similarly perceived as "semimadness," even though he was a university-educated Scottish clergyman who preached to a London congregation.

Even the youthful Mary Ann Evans (later George Eliot) mentioned in an 1838 letter to a friend her own interest in "the study of unfulfilled prophecy," though she hastened to distinguish her beliefs from the "vagaries of the Irvingites and the blasphemies of Joanna Southcote [*sic*]." In 1840 she described her sense of imminent apocalypse in another letter:

> Events are now so momentous, and the elements of society
> in so chemically critical a state that a drop seems enough to
> change its whole form. After expending the imagination in
> questions as to the mode in which the great transmutation of
> the kingdoms of this world into the kingdoms of our Lord will
> be effected we are reduced to the state of pausation in which
> the inhabitants of heaven are described to be held, before the
> outpouring of the Vials.[19]

Evans had plans to publish an "Ecclesiastical Chart" that would in fact have interpreted the scheme of the Apocalypse as a "landscape of time," or map of history, encoded in the mystical symbols and figures of the Book of Revelation.[20] Only the discovery that at least one other such "scheme of prophetic interpretation" had already been published restrained her from becoming an apocalyptic expositor herself.

Just a few years later, in 1844, the Reverend Edward Bishop Elliott published the first edition of his four-volume *Horae Apocalypticae,* later described by Cumming as "one of the ablest productions on the subject," and from which he declared his intention to "beg and borrow" all he could for his lectures on the Apocalypse delivered in London's Exeter Hall (Cumming, *Apocalyptic Sketches,* 1st ser., 2).[21] In his much-admired study, Elliott endeavored to sum up a long line of English Protestant apocalyptic commentary from the Reformation on and to transform it into a single, "continuous" history of the world centered on the Protestant

Reformation—a literary strategy known as "continuous historical exposition" (of the Book of Revelation). In his scheme, and Cumming's later appropriation of it, the Apocalypse figures the whole of Christian history in repeated series of the number seven: seven seals, seven trumpets, and seven vials. The "era" of the French Revolution, interpreted as the beginning of the downfall of popery, is figured under the first six vials of the seventh trumpet, the last of which was seen to be pouring out even as the preacher spoke. Military events—the war against the Turks, the "incorporation" of the city of Rome by the French, the "lessening" of papal power by the German Emperor, and the naval war in which England destroyed the French fleet—all were seen as the work of the destructive angels pouring out the first six vials of the seventh trumpet. Natural events such as "volcanic eruptions in Vesuvius, Iceland and Calabria," and events indicating the spread of contagion through the air—the potato blight, the influenza epidemic, and the cholera epidemic—all indicate that the sixth, and even the seventh, vials were now being poured out, and the Second Coming would surely occur between 1864 and 1867. Despite the daunting size and detail of *Horae Apocalypticae,* it nevertheless went through five editions, continuing into the early 1860s.[22] Meanwhile, Cumming's lectures based on Elliott's work were, as he modestly admitted, so successful that he had been able to use the profits to pay for "everything in the shape of ornament" for the enlarged church being built by his congregation (*Apocalyptic Sketches,* 1st ser., preface).

The success of Cumming's lectures—and Elliott's *Horae Apocalypticae* —was in part based on the fortunate coincidence of the European Revolution of 1848. Cumming's first series of *Apocalyptic Sketches* had been delivered in 1847, and in a second series lecture entitled "1848; or, Prophecy Fulfilled," he declared that what he had announced as "prophecy" in 1847 had become "in 1849 performance."[23] In 1859 the *Times* printed an article, "The School of the Prophets," that describes the popularity of books on prophecy:

> There has arisen during the stirring years which still run their
> course a very widespread attention to the study of unfulfilled
> prophecy. Books on the subject are in great demand, and the
> supply apparently meets the demand. It is not unnatural to

expect this. The last 10 years, dating their beginning at the
great European convulsion of 1848, have, without doubt, witnessed so many national complications, social changes, and individual sufferings—event has so rapidly thundered on event,
and scene flashed on scene—so altered have the face of Europe
and the relations of Cabinets become, and so unsettled is the
European sky at this hour, that intelligent and sober-minded
men, with no spice of fanaticism in their nature, have begun to
conclude that the sublime predictions uttered on the Mount
1800 years ago are being daily translated into modern history.
Students of prophecy allege that they see the apocalyptic "vials"
pouring out, and hear the "seven trumpets" uttering their
voices and pealing in reverberations through Christendom.[24]

Note that the *Times* article comments on the "great demand" for books
on the subject of prophecy; writers rushed in to find a niche in this market. Even Elliott's *Horae Apocalypticae,* despite its voluminous scholarly
notes and often tortuous prose, can be seen to make an appeal to consumers in its inclusion of mystical "charts" and illustrations of exotic
apocalyptic creatures. Beyond the appeal of deciphering mystical codes,
however, Elliott's and Cumming's works vividly demonstrate that these
Victorian "schemes of the Apocalypse" fed imperialist paranoia and corresponding desires for a sense of imperial power and identity. The major
innovation of Elliott's work was to recuperate an earlier "historical" reading of Revelation that identified the rainbow-crowned angel's command
to "prophesy again" as the Reformation (Rev. 10). This reading not only
made Protestantism central to history—as it is roughly "centered" in
Revelation—but located the British (Protestant) Empire as the culmination of the divine plan for history, following the consumption of the
Whore of Babylon, or popery and its earthly domains. In the preface to
the fifth (1862) edition, Elliott attributed the "necessity" for his apocalyptic investigations to "the increasing prevalence among Christian men
in our country of the *futuristic system of Apocalyptic interpretation*—a system
which involved the abandonment of the opinion held by all the chief fathers and doctors of our Church respecting the Roman Popes and Pope-
dom as the great intended anti-Christian power of Scripture prophecy"

(Elliott, 1:v). In other words, Elliott perceived such a threat to his religion and his nation in a "new" system of apocalyptic interpretation that did *not* identify popery as the Antichrist that he felt he had to write an apocalyptic commentary that would disprove that "system." In this work, competing imperial powers—of which France is perceived as the chief—are thoroughly defined and damned as popery or the Antichrist.

But, as in the paranoia of the epistolary section—the seven letters to seven churches—of Revelation, in which mystifying references to the "Satan within," as well as references to the Satan without, are repeated, Elliott's apocalyptics also suspected popery everywhere *within* the British empire and the nation, as well as outside it.[25] In fact, it is probable that the single most important impetus for *Horae Apocalypticae* was the emergence of the Oxford Movement. Elliott reports in a footnote that his work was undertaken in the autumn of 1837, and in the *Horae Apocalypticae* itself he identifies the "False Prophet" of Revelation as "the spirit of the *Oxford Tractarianism,* which in 1833, all so suddenly and influentially, sent forth its voice from the banks of the Isis" (1:i, n.1; 3:516). Certainly for Elliott, Tractarianism was the false prophet; moreover, the *"rapidity and extent of its diffusion* suggests—indeed forces on us—the idea of some *supernatural influence of spirit* . . . the rather as it is a diffusion as well among the laity as the clergy in England, in the country as in the town; and not in England only, but in England's wide-spread colonial possessions; in Canada, Newfoundland, Australia, India" (3:525–26). The "unclean spirits" issuing from the mouth of the false prophet appear to threaten the Church of the British Empire everywhere on the earth, and Elliott accordingly writes an exposition of the Apocalypse that shows the Protestant Reformation to be the center, the turning point, of divine history.

Cumming is at least as paranoiac as Elliott about Tractarianism, which he prefers to call Puseyism. He finds Puseyism everywhere in "the mystery of iniquity": "What we call Puseyism in the nineteenth century, was the predominating religion of the fourth. . . . Almost every element of Popery was in full action, the apostolic church had become to a great extent apostate" (*Apocalyptic Sketches,* 1st ser., 60). In his second series of lectures on Apocalypse, delivered after the Revolution of 1848, Cumming states that the first great "consumption" of the Church of Rome began with the Reformation, and a second "consumption of Babylon" took place at the time of the French Revolution (*Apocalyptic Sketches,* 2nd ser., 480–81). Indeed, almost all of the vials are shown to be related to French imperialism, and Cumming loses no opportunity to speak of Britain's superiority in this respect. For example, following the first vial of the French Revolution, in the second vial France lost all her colonies and her navies were annihilated: "It would occupy too much of your time were I in this syllabus to recount all the brilliant triumphs of our country on the ocean, or the names of that cluster of illustrious admirals who appeared about this time" (*Apocalyptic Sketches,* 1st ser., 492). Cumming identifies the "three unclean spirits" that pervade the world in the time of the sixth vial as Infidelity, Popery, and Tractarianism—which is simply "Popery without a pope; all the venom of the original without its consistency and fulness of development" (*Apocalyptic Sketches,* 1st ser., 495). Because Revelation names the three unclean spirits issuing from the mouth of the false prophet as frogs, Elliott sees a particular activity of the three spirits in France, where "the three frogs, are the old arms of France" (3:533). To clinch his argument, he includes an illustration of ancient French banners on which the "frogs" appear prominently. For Cumming these "unclean spirits" have a subterranean action: even in the deep calm that preceded the Revolution of 1848, "the unclean spirits were acting, working, leavening, undermining deep below the foundations of society" (*Apocalyptic Sketches,* 2nd ser., 457–58). For Cumming these "unclean spirits" are a pollutant of English purity, but he hopes "that our country may not be contaminated to a fatal . . . extent." Though the country may be "scourged for its tampering with Apostasy," he trusts that "old England will not again become, what England once was—the serf of Apostasy" (*Apocalyptic Sketches,* 1st ser., 396).

Cumming's repeated emphasis on the "manhood" of Protestantism, in contrast with the effeminacy of Roman Catholicism and of national cultures associated with it, especially the French, effectively genders British Protestantism. Included among the unclean spirits is infidelity, in which Cumming includes Socialism, especially *French* Socialism (*Apocalyptic Sketches,* 1st ser., 386). The openness and "manhood" of Protestantism is opposed to the underhanded and unclean working of Puseyism, Popery, and Infidelity. Martin Luther, who is identified as the recipient of the rainbow-crowned angel's command to "prophesy again" (Rev. 10:11), is described as shining "in greater lustre than the name of Milton, of Shakspeare [*sic*], or of Newton" (*Apocalyptic Sketches,* 1st ser., 122). Carlyle, whose lectures "On Heroes, Hero-Worship and the Heroic in History" had been delivered in the same hall a few years before, is quoted as having said of Luther that " there was no sham about that man—he was no semblance—that monk was a real man—a true man" (*Apocalyptic Sketches,* 1st ser., 129).[26] And although Luther is, necessarily, not an Englishman, the line of "witnesses" comes down to English ground in the end. The record of witnesses begins with the catalogues of witnesses from the "Magdeburg centuriators [*sic*]" in Germany, but it continues with "that book that ought to be in every Englishman's home, and the records of which ought to be registered in every Briton's memory . . . Fox's Book of Martyrs, composed and published in England" (*Apocalyptic Sketches,* 1st ser., 168).

The events of 1848 conclusively proved that the seventh vial was even then pouring out, and that Britain was the apocalyptic nation.

> All Englishmen, it is said, are escaping from Rome, from Paris, and from the Papal nations of Europe, returning to their own land and their homes, as if Great Britain were destined to be the pillar of the nations, the sheltering asylum in which refugees from the impending judgments upon Babylon shall find peace beneath the overshadowing pinions of a pervading Christianity, and a blessing in communion with our Christian churches. (*Apocalyptic Sketches,* 2nd ser., 491)

Cumming ends his concluding lecture in his second series with his conviction that "chronology has proved, that in the course of less than twenty years more the seventh millennium of the world begins, or the seventh thousand year," and he exhorts his listeners to say "Amen" with him to this glorious event. He concludes the preface to the published series of these lectures with words from the next to last verse of Revelation: "I come quickly. Even so, come, Lord Jesus." What he and other followers of the "continuous historical" school of apocalyptic exposition prayed would come quickly was a millennium for "the people of God"—the Protestant, *English* people of God.

Jane Eyre and the Apocalyptic Nation

"'Surely I come quickly!' and hourly I more eagerly respond,—'Amen; even so come, Lord Jesus!'" So Charlotte Brontë ends her runaway best-selling novel, *Jane Eyre,* published in 1847, and into a second edition before the year was out.[27] It was the same year the Reverend John Cumming was delivering his lectures on Apocalypse to enthusiastic audiences in London's Exeter Hall. It was the year after the second edition of Elliott's *Horae Apocalypticae* had come out, and the year before the great "revolution" that was to convince both Cumming and Elliott that the seventh vial of Apocalypse had now begun to pour out, and that in twenty years or so, the "seventh thousand" year would begin—right there in England.

In a now classic reading of the novel, Gayatri Chakravorty Spivak comments that "it should not be possible to read nineteenth-century British literature without remembering that imperialism, understood as England's social mission, was a crucial part of the cultural representation of England to the English."[28] *Jane Eyre,* however, offers a particularly definitive example of a compelling contemporary technology for representing British imperialism to the English as "England's social mission"—that is, by framing it in reference to the Apocalypse, and thus investing it with prophetic authority. Jane's famous last words suggest that she has positioned herself as the apocalyptic seer and speaks with the authority of the great prophet of the New Testament, creating the impression that her narrative is a feminist apocalypse. But her last words may also be read as enthusiastic agreement with the "continuous historical" interpretation of Apocalypse, and her narrative as yet another commodification of the consumption of the Whore of Babylon.

In her essay, Spivak points out that feminist critics, for whom *Jane Eyre* had become a "cult text," had overlooked Bertha Mason's status as a colonial subject, and thus reproduced the text's imperial racism by treating her as merely a foil for Jane's individualist feminism. Spivak points to Rochester's paean to "Europe" as home of liberty as evidence that the narrative reproduces an imperialist binary of European/Other.[29] Rochester, however, is at this point in the narrative an unreliable narrator, "polluted" by his (sexual) liaisons with feminine representations of the great "Whore"—popery. Brontë's apocalyptic scheme actually under-cuts Rochester's celebration of "Europe," for Europe is the home of pop-ery. Only England can be the true home of liberty, for England is the apocalyptic pillar of the nations in which all Englishmen, fleeing from popery, must take refuge.

Spivak's analysis underlines the hint of a tainting with "black" or African blood in Bertha Mason's status as a "Creole" or person of mixed racial ancestry. But it is probably just as significant for Brontë's scheme that she is tainted with the blood of popery: Rochester describes her as the beauty of "Spanish Town," suggesting that she is also contaminated by her descent from the first imperial conquerors of Jamaica, the Spaniards.[30] Rochester is thus corrupted by his fornication with the Whore of "Span-ish Town" (he makes it clear that Bertha disgusts him not only with her madness, but with her "gross, impure, depraved nature" [302]). Roch-ester's description of his travels about the earth in search of "the An-tipodes of the Creole" in fact take him to all the other great empires of popery: St. Petersburg, Paris, Rome, Naples, Florence. Most telling of all, Rochester has obviously contaminated himself by his activities in France, the particular apocalyptic territory of the three frogs or unclean spirits, of which the visible product is the charming but giddy and in-consequential Adele, child of a French actress with whom Rochester had been involved.

We now see that it is entirely appropriate that Rochester himself should have been partially consumed in the fire set by his "Whore of Babylon," even as she is wholly destroyed as a consequence of her own perversity. We may assume that the fire has transformed Rochester from an "unclean" status to that of a properly purified bridegroom for Jane. It is also appropriate that their apocalyptic union should take place in Fern-dean, that desolate and isolated spot deep in the woods of an obviously still unregenerate England, while St. John Rivers, that "high master-spirit," is dispatched to a heroic martyrdom for Protestantism in India, the British Empire's most important colony. The other members of the Rivers family also continue to serve the apocalyptic empire: one bride-groom is a captain in its divinely authorized navy, the other a clergyman in its true Protestant church.

In her concluding "Amen; even so come, Lord Jesus!" Charlotte

Brontë does not challenge the prevailing British apocalyptic paradigm but marches in its parade, chanting the slogan of its soon-to-be-triumphant Protestant hero. Doubtless excited by European events herself and by her own strong Evangelical faith, she reproduces the "continuous historical" reading of Revelation in which the seer envisions scenes of violence culminating eventually in the apocalyptic marriage of the Lord with his chosen empire. As Carolyn Williams demonstrates, Brontë's apocalyptic last words do not actually represent her own prophecy, but place her in a position of contradiction and double-binding.[31] She says "Amen" only in a final, faithful reading of St. John's articulation of his—and Britain's—apocalyptic mission. And in this not-so-subversive Christian feminism, Brontë extends the violent destruction of the *femme fatale* of the text to the maiming, blinding, and even killing, of its male heroes.

The Whore's Apocalypse: Elizabeth Barrett Browning's *Aurora Leigh*

The vicar preached from "Revelations" (till
The doctor woke), and found me with "the frogs"
On three successive Sundays; ay, and stopped.
To weep a little (for he's getting old)
That such perdition should o'ertake a man
Of such fair acres,—in the parish, too!
He printed his discourses "by request,"
And if your book shall sell as his did, then
Your verses are less good than I suppose.[32]

Before the dissolution of his "vain phalanstery," Romney tells Aurora, the vicar of the local parish preached from the Book of Revelation and on three successive Sundays found him with "the frogs"—the unclean spirits of the sixth vial. The elderly vicar wept a little over Romney's perdition, but his sorrow evidently did not take his mind off the profits to be reaped from the sale of such apocalyptic discourses. The "great bookclub" of the neighborhood "teems / With 'sketches,' 'summaries,' and 'last tracts' but twelve," Romney explains, and the vicar's book sold very well. If Aurora's book should sell as well, then he would think her verses less good than he now supposes (8:899–911).

Romney's account of the vicar's preaching from "Revelations" quite specifically alludes to the interpretation of the apocalyptic frogs—as explicated by Elliott and quoted by Cumming in his *Apocalyptic Sketches,* first series—as "Infidelity," "Popery," and "Priestcraft." Infidelity, according to Elliott, includes all heathenlike infidelity and blasphemy, especially Socialism and Chartism and all other forms of rebelliousness against "proper authority" (*Horae Apocalypticae,* 3:495). In Cumming's account, all three frogs work to undermine English purity, contaminating the apocalyptic nation with infidel French philosophy. Their French origin is proven by the fact that the three frogs are the old arms of France. Romney, whose futile attempts at social reforms in England have been inspired by Fourier, Comte, and Cabet, provides an obvious example of the French origins of these "unclean spirits" (9:868–69).

In comparing Aurora's book with the vicar's best-selling "discourses," Romney places Aurora's work in the context of apocalyptic exposition, suggesting that her book is also an "apocalypse," but not one that will be as popular as the "sketches," "summaries," and "tracts" beloved of book clubs. Yet Barrett Browning's book has placed Romney precisely where Cumming and Elliot would have placed him—with the "frogs" whose "infidelity" acts as a contaminant of English "purity." In the poem's glancing reference to the "continuous historical" apocalyptic exposition of the day, Barrett Browning appears to concur with it: French philosophy is futile, and moreover contaminates England's purity. Romney must be blinded so that he can "see" the folly of his "infidel" (atheist) philosophy. Ultimately, he admits not only that God is essential to any social reform, but that reform inspired by Christianity is the most manly, for "the man most man, with tenderest human hands, / Works best for men,—as God in Nazareth" (9:868–69). How can we determine where Barrett Browning places *herself* in relation to "the Apocalypse" and its relevance for her apocalyptic protagonist?

First, it is useful to know that Barrett Browning's evident interest in the apocalyptic exposition began in her adolescence, when her father began to attend Edward Irving's services in London. According to Margaret Forster,

During his frequent and lengthy absences in London Mr Barrett had taken to visiting the newly built chapel in Regent Square where he greatly enjoyed the preaching of Edward Irving, the Scottish founder of the Catholic Apostolic Church. Irving's writings had been approved Hope End reading ever since 1823 when Elizabeth was given his "For the Oracles of God, Four Orations" by her father. She wrote to Boyd [a blind poet] that although she could not recall "a single word" of it, Irving "as a Preacher" had "affected me more than anyone I ever heard" (though she did not say where she had heard him). Irving affected Mr Barrett even more.[33]

Barrett Browning, then, was exposed to both the "fire, enthusiasm and semi-madness" of Edward Irving—who was later expelled from his congregation for his increasingly "heretical" preaching—and the "silver star, shining serenely, and illuminating our pathway with its steady ray," or Dr. Cumming. Incongruously, Aurora exhibits the characteristics of both, describing herself as "burning through his [Romney's] thread of talk / With a quick flame of emotion" (2:244–45), and yet exhorted by Romney to "'shine, Aurora, on my dark, / Though high and cold and only like a star, / And for this short night only'" (8:317–20). And although Romney obviously satirizes the profitable genre of "continuous historical" apocalyptics in his description of the vicar's discourses, the narrative corroborates his identification with the frogs of the sixth vial. The structure and intent of Barrett Browning's appropriation of nineteenth-century British apocalyptics appear as contradictory as the two varieties (Irvingite and "continuous historical") with which she was apparently familiar.

Irving's *For the Oracles of God, Four Orations. For Judgment to come, An Argument, In Nine Parts* (1823) differs dramatically from "continuous historical" exposition. He rarely quotes scripture at all, and never specifically quotes the Book of Revelation. He makes no predictions of the date of the Second Coming. His work is devoted entirely to persuading men of the judgment to come and of the overwhelming imperative to turn to God, give up sin, and alleviate the ills of their fellow men. But there are nevertheless continuities between his and Cumming's (and Elliott's) work. Like them, he emphasizes "the free and manly spirit" of the English people, indeed of the *excess* of this spirit, since it can be controlled only by the "fear of God," which is almost totally lacking among them (Irving, 229). Like Elliott and Cumming, he warns against the influence of foreign philosophy: "The French and German have their recourse in sentiment, and some classes of our own island have leaned to the same broken reed. But that sentiment to which they have betaken themselves is a spurious bastard, not the true offspring, of the heart" (232). And Irving has even less to say about women—*any* women—than Elliott and Cumming. His argument is addressed exclusively to men, and framed entirely in terms of "the free and manly" English people.

The most radical move of Barrett Browning's apocalyptic epic-novel is that it takes woman as its subject and object, its speaker and spoken-for, its seer and its vision. In Cora Kaplan's introduction to the 1978 Women's Press edition of *Aurora Leigh,* she notes that Barrett Browning's feminist epic is "the fullest and most violent exposition of the 'woman question' in mid-Victorian literature."[34] Marjorie Stone observes that the biblical text most often invoked in *Aurora Leigh* is Revelation, and suggests that *Aurora Leigh* offers "nothing less than a revelation."[35] I will argue that *Aurora Leigh* is both an apocalypse and a parody of apocalypse, that in what Margaret Reynolds calls her "cross-breed" or "bastard verse-novel," Barrett Browning means to write both a feminist prophecy and a feminist critique of that male-identified genre, British apocalyptic exposition.[36] Aurora, as her name suggests, is a shining star, but *Aurora Leigh* is a whore's apocalypse, turning upside-down the misogyny of Revelation and celebrating the female body instead of burning and consuming it. Yet Barrett Browning's apocalyptic scheme still cannot resist retaliatory violence to the male: her hero, Romney Leigh, is also blinded and his ancestral home burned.

Stone points to Aurora's comment that "A dropped star / Makes bitter waters, says a book I've read" (5:917–18) (Stone, 134). The reference is to the great star called Wormwood that flames down from heaven, embittering a third part of the earth's waters (Rev. 8:10–11), but for Aurora it represents something even more destructive: the bitterness of the woman artist who, as Stone suggests, "abandons her vocation for the material security of marriage" (Stone, 134). The covert feminist irony of this interpretation is suggested by a comparison with Cumming's interpretation of Wormwood as Attila—the destructiveness of an embittered woman is equivalent to that of Attila the Hun. But the poem repeatedly plays on the many meanings of "Aurora" associated with light: she is the dawn, the beacon, the "morning-star." And she is both the childhood seer of the tragic female figures glassed on the dead face of her mother—an image that suggests a dark parody of the apocalyptic vision of the elders and the beasts before the "sea of glass" (Rev. 4:4–6)—and the mature seer of the New Jerusalem. The repeated associations with sun and stars also suggest the apocalyptic Woman clothed with the sun, moon, and stars (Rev. 12:1).

Barrett Browning thus plays with apocalyptic imagery and form throughout her novel in verse, alternately satirizing apocalyptic exposition and revisioning the Apocalypse. The poem is in exactly *nine* books, a number consistently associated with satanic forces, especially witches, as it is also associated with that exclusively female period, the nine months of pregnancy. Barrett Browning deliberately renumbers her apocalyptic work, minimizing and ironizing the symbolic import of the apocalyptic number seven, traditionally interpreted as the number of completion, fulfillment, the final "amen." In the seventh book of the poem, Marian finishes the telling of the tale of her rape and subsequent pregnancy to Aurora with a question: "Did God make mothers out of victims, then / And set such pure amens to such hideous deeds?" (7:56–57). By contrast, the entire narrative content of the poem is arranged on either side of the central fifth book in such a way that the books mirror each other. Helen Cooper demonstrates how this arrangement of narrative content can actually be schematized:

England		Abroad
1	Union	9
2	Romney and Aurora, her twentieth birthday	8
3	Marian's story	7
4	Marian's story, the wedding	6
	5 Art	

Herbert F. Tucker speaks of this formal symmetry as a "ring structure," in which the books of the poem "fit firmly into a nested pattern of concentric rings." Tucker explicates this ring structure as one of several "epicizing conventions" in *Aurora Leigh* that allow Barrett Browning to loosen "the realist novel's grip on Victorian narrative as a shaper of women's lives." Tucker suggests this ring structure may derive from an older epic convention linked to Homer, but the Apocalypse's seven seals, seven trumpets, and seven vials had traditionally been represented as a series of concentric rings, making it at least equally likely that Barrett Browning's apocalyptic text is an inversion of that sanctified septenary structure into the "satanic" nine-part structure.[37] The nine books in their nested rings also suggest a formal equivalent of the pregnant woman's body, with its nested womb and fetus. This "nested structure" appropriately represents the epic issue of the work: Marian's violated female body, which gives her the status of both "whore" and "Christ," is the great subject of Aurora's poem.

In various allusions, Barrett Browning draws attention to the number nine, so that the reader can see that this "form" is not an accident. In book 1, Aurora tells us that she lived "nine full years" in Italy after her mother's death (1:204). By making appropriate calculations, the reader can determine that Aurora is twenty-seven years old, or three times nine, at the beginning of book 3, and at the point at which she begins to write in the present. In book 3, the budding poet-prophetess opens nine letters—which should recall the seven letters of the Apocalypse—and as she breaks the red seal of the last, comments, "A ninth seal; / The apocalypse is drawing to a close." Needless to say, no such apocalypse appears at this point in the narrative (3:98–99). In book 6, Aurora speaks of the "Six days' work," on the last day of which God created "MAN" (4:149, 156). But there is no seventh day, or sabbath, on which God concludes that his work is good and rests, in this book. Instead, Aurora rediscovers Marian, who tells her she has been "murdered," meaning raped by man (6:771). And Marian has given birth to an illegitimate male child—thus, man has created a "bastard" man. In book 9, as Stone notes, Aurora declares her love for Romney "three times over" (136), but it is also in this book that, in parody of the premarital bans pronounced on three successive Sundays, the vicar finds Romney with the frogs on three successive Sundays.

It seems no accident that in the central book of her nine-book epic, book 5, Barrett Browning would produce, not the Protestant Reformation, but the Whore's apocalypse. Searching for an image that would "represent the age" (5:202), the poet-prophetess sings exultantly:

> Never flinch,
> But still, unscrupulously epic, catch
> Upon the burning lava of a song
> The full-veined, heaving, double-breasted Age:
> That, when the next shall come, the men of that
> May touch the impress with reverent hand, and say
> "Behold,—behold the paps we all have sucked!
> This bosom seems to beat still, or at least
> It sets ours beating: this is living art,
> Which thus presents and thus records true life." (5:213–22)

Of course, Victorians were shocked by the carnality of the image. The *National Review* critic fumed, "Burning lava and a woman's breast! And concentrated in the latter the fullest ideas of life. It is absolute pain to read it."[38] But no one ever complained about the carnality of the biblical texts actually referred to (Luke 11:27, 23:29), and the grotesque body of the Whore in Revelation was, of course, only a "city," or an empire, or the domain of popery. For Barrett Browning, the Whore has been reformed into an appropriate, "unscrupulously epic" image for the Victorian age: the "Whore" is not a whore, but neither is she an ethereal "angel in the house"—she is a woman whose female body is essential to all human life, but for whom the problems of that body have become central to the age, in the vision of the feminist seer.

The conclusion of that vision, in the final lines of the ninth book, represents this apocalypse as a millennial, rather than a millenarian, vision. "The old world," Romney solemnly tells Aurora, must be renewed, and in that new world "shall grow spontaneously / New churches, new oeconomies, new laws / Admitting freedom, new societies / Excluding falsehood: HE shall make all new" (9:942–49). Churches, economies, and laws must be transformed in the millennium preceding the apocalypse. Yet Romney, whom Aurora now accepts as her bridegroom, is blind. In an

otherwise highly laudatory review, George Eliot protests "the lavish mutilation of heroes' bodies, which has become the habit of novelists."[39]
Barrett Browning defended her narrative against complaints "of the like-
ness to the catastrophe of *Jane Eyre*." She insisted that Romney had not
been blinded *in* the fire that burned down his ancestral home, but that
the sight had caused a "fever, and the eyes, the visual nerve, perished." It
was "necessary," Barrett Browning concluded, "that Romney should be
mulcted in his natural sight."[40] Her remark suggests that to renew the
"old world," men must lose their "natural" vision or undergo a symbolic
castration in order to see with a revolutionary feminist vision.[41] Further,
an examination of Victorian "schemes of the Apocalypse" suggests that
both Charlotte Brontë and Barrett Browning may have conceived of their
newly "Protestant" heroes—no longer associated with popery or the
three frogs of France—as *more* manly, despite or even because of their
war-hero-like wounds. Yet such an intention for the hero's "mutilation"
does not cancel out its violence. Barrett Browning's "apocalypse" could
be seen as the womb for twentieth century second wave feminism's re-
birth of gynageddon—apocalyptic war on the sex/gender system.

Reading the End of History *in* History

"What am *I* doing here, once again, immersing myself in the discourse of
disaster? As I speak of the perversities of apocalypse, am I not also drawn
in by the evil? . . . My previous reading always seems naive and incomplete. How does one gain a balance between finding and facing the apocalyptic horror without giving in to it? I believe all biblical scholarship
gives in to the sublime horror of apocalypse to some extent" (Pippin,
Apocalyptic Bodies, xi).

Tina Pippin eloquently voices the problematic of both scholarly and
literary writing on/through the Apocalypse. Although the realist novel
(or novel in verse) has the capability, as *Aurora Leigh* demonstrates, of cri-
tiquing contemporary commodification of the Apocalypse, it may at the
same moment "give in" to its sublime horror, projecting its violence onto
its male hero(es). Jane Eyre's concluding appropriation of the words of
the apocalyptic text, as well as her appropriation of an apocalyptic tone,

invests her imperialist narrative with prophetic authority. Feminist critics may also buy into the sublimity of apocalyptic violence, imagining gynageddons that reverse the gender politics of the Book of Revelation, but otherwise reinstate its gender violence.

The effects produced by reading a text that has status as part of the canonical Christian Bible are incalculable. Is the secular literary critic, like the biblical scholar, inevitably drawn in by its evil? In this book, I have shown how the Authorized Version, as spoken through the work of multiple commercial commentaries on and illustrations of it, can provide discursive resources for both reactionary and progressive literature—sometimes both in the same work, as in *Aurora Leigh*. In the special case of the Book of Revelation, however, studies of its place in historical consumer cultures can produce quite unexpected revelations. The Apocalypse has veered through extremes of identity, from "the greatest of apocalypses," the divine inspiration of countless readers, to the paranoid text that has impelled racism, misogyny, homophobia, homicide, and suicide. Perhaps even more revelatory, the Apocalypse of Saint John is stripped in such studies of its canonical cover as "sacred text" and disclosed as one of the biggest moneymakers of book history. It is a rough diamond—very rough indeed—available for the taking by eager profiteers who only need to give it a bit of spurious polish from contemporary consumer fads to reap large financial rewards. Studies of how the Apocalypse funds and is funded by historical cultures may provide that necessary position from which we can lever this last and lasting book of the family's bible into a more balanced perspective.

CONCLUSION

PHILOSOPHY AND PHILANTHROPY VERSUS BUYING AND SELLING

Pierre Bourdieu notes that in the history of ideas, "the ordinary effects of derealization and intellectualization are intensified by the representation of philosophical activity as a summit conference between 'great philosophers,'" whereas the "whole philosophical doxa carried along by intellectual rumour—labels of schools, truncated quotations, functioning as slogans in celebration of polemics—by academic routine and perhaps above all by school manuals (an unmentionable reference)" are what actually constitute the "'common sense' of an intellectual generation."[1] The commercial religious genres—such as Family Bibles with notes and illustrations, bible commentaries sold in installments, family bible dictionaries, and "historical" interpretations of the Book of Revelation—provide access to the more concrete debates of the Victorian era that inform the language and structure of literary texts. These for-profit religious genres are "concrete" evidence of what British consumers wanted to buy, of how they saw themselves, or how they wished to see themselves. They elaborate for the student of literature and culture the "common sense" of British families in the eighteenth and nineteenth centuries. If they had not, they would not have sold, and if publishers and editors had not thought they would sell—and sell at a profit—they would not have been produced.

Yet commercial religious literature has been largely ignored in British studies: to put it in the more appropriate fiscal terms, it has been devalued. Scholars have studied the "higher criticism" of the Victorian era—the theology known to have been of interest to intellectuals such as George Eliot—but the commercial enterprise of religious literature that could be marketed to the "middling classes," or those same classes who bought novels in installments or borrowed them from circulating libraries, has been generally thought, ironically, not worth studying. Few libraries collect it: divinity schools in particular tend to "deaccession" such material because it is not the product of "true" religious thinkers. It is only what could be sold for a profit, and it is seen as tainted by that root of all evil, financial motivation.

In contrast to for-profit religious literature, tracts and bibles given out for free or sold at or below cost to encourage consumption have been accurately described as pretty much worthless to the student of Victorian literature and culture. Richard Altick analyzes the production of the "three major religious agencies active in the field throughout the century"—the Religious Tract Society, the British and Foreign Bible Society, and the Society for Promoting Christian Knowledge.[2] As Altick demonstrates, these three agencies and other religious foundations poured out religious tracts for the good of the poor, for the most part distributing them free. Bibles were published by the British and Foreign Bible Society, and distributed either free or as cheaply as possible, as Leslie Howsam's *Cheap Bibles* details. But, as Altick emphasizes, though the amount of religious literature produced and distributed by these agencies is "staggering," the amount actually read is impossible to estimate. Many tracts were pressed into the hands of people who could not read (Altick, 102). They were also produced and tossed out so freely as to resemble paper bills in a society suffering massive inflation. As Altick vividly describes it:

> Religious literature, therefore, was everywhere in nineteenth-
> century England. Tracts were flung from carriage windows;
> they were passed out at railway stations; they turned up in army
> camps and in naval vessels anchored in the roads, and in jails
> and lodging-houses and hospitals and workhouses; they were
> distributed in huge quantities at Sunday and day schools, as re-
> wards for punctuality, diligence, decorum, and deloused heads.
> They were a ubiquitous part of the social landscape. (103)

Simply distributing reading matter so liberally, Altick acknowledges, probably encouraged literacy to some extent (104). But it doubtless had much more negative effects on reading as well. For one thing, "the tract

people made it plain that they were out to substitute good reading matter for bad," so they substituted materials they considered "good" for
those that workers were willing to spend money to buy—such as fiction,
especially sensational fiction (104). These well-intentioned educators could
not seem to resist "using the language of the nursery" in their tracts, and
even semiliterate readers, in Altick's opinion, "knew they were being
talked down to, and reacted accordingly" (105). The free or subsidized religious literature conveyed an air of condescension not only in the language used, but in the "social message the tracts embodied. . . . The
common people, especially those who came under the influence of radical journalists after 1815, were quick to realize that the sugar-coating of religious and moral counsel concealed a massive dose of social sedation"
(105). "Tracts were inseparable from charity, and charity, as practiced in
Victorian times, involved the rubbing in of class distinctions . . . beneath
the veneer of altruism could be seen all too plainly the image of class interest" (107).

Similarly, the distribution of cheap or even free bibles could be handled
in a manner that made said bibles peculiarly unwelcome. "The very methods the societies employed, their indifference to human feelings, often
defeated their own purposes. When a depression struck Paisley in 1837,
throwing thousands of children and adults out of work, bibles were
rushed to the relief of the starving. The British and Foreign Bible Society
prided itself on distributing its bibles and Testaments to the poor in
the city slums 'in anticipation of the visitation of cholera'" (106). Even
installment-plan buying, as Altick demonstrates, was robbed of its attrac-
tions by attempts to make it a lesson in saving rather than spending. "The
Bible Society had a scheme whereby thousands of eager ladies, pencils
and subscription pads in hand, invaded the homes of the poor, trying to
persuade them to pay a penny a week toward the purchase of a family
Bible. Not until the full sum was paid was the book delivered. Thus, the
theory went, the poor could be taught thrift as well as piety" (106). How
much more appealing the commercial Family Bible installment, often
guaranteed to include at least one illustration in each part or number, that
could be taken home to be devoured—pictures, sensational stories, notes
on exotic "Eastern customs" and all—as soon as it was paid for!

Altick presents a powerful case for the utter futility of consulting "religious literature" as a means to discovering the "common sense" of the middling or for that matter the working classes. But the picture is entirely changed when we look at religious literature that was sold for a profit, to willing consumers—the tradesman and the tradesman's wife, the domestic servant, perhaps even the factory worker, either male or female. Commercial religious materials were designed to enhance the consumer's sense of class status, not restrict it. Even in the case of those Family Bibles that might be thought to "talk down" to the consuming family, such as *The Cottager Bible,* the position of one member of that family is talked up—the "Master of the family." Family Bibles thus pit gender hierarchy against class hierarchy, counting on one or the other to produce the "cultural capital" that would make the book worthwhile to buy. Whether the materials were actually read or not was probably not a matter of concern to the publisher—what mattered was simply that they appeal enough to be salable. Accordingly, these commercial religious materials were designed not so much to be *read* as to be looked at. This quality of *to-be-looked-at-ness,* as in Laura Mulvey's classic essay, was achieved by various means: by providing images of sexualized or racialized characters, or by deliberately making a spectacle out of certain "parts" of the Authorized Version, as in bracketing or setting in small print those passages the reader ought to know were not suited for "the family," or by producing an imposingly large, handsomely bound book, such as would advertise the family's sound financial, class, educational, and moral status when displayed in the parlor.[3]

These commercial religious materials, then, can probably tell us more about the "common sense of an intellectual generation"—or of the "middling classes" and their continual mobility—than all the free tracts and cheap bibles, or, for that matter, the "higher criticism," ever can. Even more important to literary studies, they can provide the "concrete debates" behind the often contradictory and confusing references to biblical texts seeded so liberally throughout Victorian literary texts. Charlotte Brontë's decision to name her shockingly revelatory actress figure after a biblical character who refused to "act" as her husband commanded is a case in point: Who would have guessed that the name Vashti is linked to a debate over a woman's right to speak her own language? Or that "flowers," in an era of widespread bible literacy, quite possibly refers to the term used in the Book of Leviticus for that nearly universal aspect of women's bodily experience—menstruation?

This study of the Authorized Version in the marketplace, and of some of the forms in which that Authorized Version was "consumed"—both appropriated by other commercial religious genres and consumed or purchased by readers—has emphasized the construction of sexualities and family values in these varying market forms of Protestantism. The "bracketed" or disciplinary Family Bibles of the nineteenth century graphically illustrate the fact that the Old and New Testaments were recognized as eloquent sources of sexual and racial "knowledge," otherwise known as "Eastern customs." As the mother of the virginal Antonia in Matthew Lewis's scandalous novel *The Monk* (1796) explains, she sees the bible as "little more than a crude sex manual." She tells Ambrosio, "No reading more improper could be permitted a young Woman. . . . Everything is called plainly and roundly by its name; and the annals of a Brothel would scarcely furnish a greater choice of indecent expressions."[1] While free tracts and cheap bibles eliminated or at least minimized the "indecent" aspects of the bible, commercial religious literature played them up, making the most of what was already a best seller and a source of easy profit.

In a time when girls' and even grown women's reading was carefully circumscribed, we should not overlook how much they could learn from that unimpeachable source, "The Bible." We have seen how the subject of menstruation was discussed not only in medical texts, but in bible commentary intended for the family library. That even more taboo subject, male circumcision, was "defined"—more or less—in family bible dictionaries. The "unnatural use" in sexual practices could at least be guessed at, if not fully comprehended, by Family Bible readers. More crucial for students of Victorian culture today is the textual evidence provided by such commercial religious sources for the identification of "unnatural" sex with other races and nationalities, and the corresponding deletion from the British national imagined community of sexual and racial diversity. Yet all of this was based on that strange irony, the identification of a collection of extraordinarily diverse, archaic, and alien texts as the "English Bible," the founding document of the English nation and British empire.

APPENDIX

BRITISH FAMILY BIBLES

Bible editions with "family," "domestic," "cottager,"
and so forth included in formal title.

PRECURSORS TO FAMILY BIBLES (BIBLES WITH COMMENTARY)

1690   *The Holy Bible . . . with Annotations. . . .* By Samuel Clark. London: J. Rawlins.

1708   *The Holy Bible . . . With most profitable annotations . . . Maps . . . The Apocrypha.* [Amsterdam.] (The annotations are the Geneva notes.)

1708–10   *Exposition of the Old and New Testament, 1708–1710.* 5 vols., unfinished. By Matthew Henry.

1720–35   *Bibliotheca Biblica . . . a Commentary. . . .* 5 vols. London: Printed for William and John Innys. *Bibliotheca biblica. Being a commentary upon all the books of the Old and New Testament. Gather'd out of the genuine writings of fathers and ecclesiastical historians, and acts of councils, . . . To which are added, proemial or introductory discourses upon the authors and authentickness of the books, . . .* Edited by Samuel Parker. London: Printed for H. Clements.

FAMILY BIBLES

1735, 1737   *The Compleat History of the Old and New Testament; or, A Family Bible, with . . . annotations, extracted from the writings of the most celebrated authors. Together with maps, cuts, & c. . . .* 2 vols. By S. Smith, D.D. London: Printed by W. Rayner.

1735	(*The Family Companion; or, Annotations upon the Holy Bible. . . .* By S. Smith, D.D. London: Printed by W. Rayner, for J. Wilford.) [Lacks Authorized Version of the text.]
1739	(*The Family Companion; or, Annotations upon the Holy Bible. . . .* By S. Smith, D.D. London: Printed for the author.) [Lacks Authorized Version of the text.]
1739–56	(*The Family Expositor; or, A Paraphrase and Version of the New Testament. . . .* 6 vols. By P. Doddridge, D.D. London: Printed by John Wilson.)[Lacks Authorized Version of NT, preferring Doddridge's own translations and arrangements of text.]
1739	*The Compleat History of the Old and New Testament; or, A Family Bible, with . . . annotations, extracted from the writings of the most celebrated authors. Together with maps, cuts, & c. . . .* 2 vols. By S. Smith, D.D. London: printed for the author.
1752, 1753	*The Compleat History of the Old and New Testament; or, A Family Bible: with large annotations, extracted from the writings of . . . Stackhouse, Calmet, LeClerc, Bishop Patrick, and others. . . .* By S. Smith, D.D. London.
1758, 1759	*The Universal Bible; or, Every Christian Family's Best Treasure. Containing the sacred text . . . illus. With notes and comments. . . .* By S. Nelson, D.D. London: Printed for J. Coote, J. Staples.
1760	*The Holy Bible . . . or, A family Bible, with annotations and parallel scriptures. . . .* By Samuel Clark. London.
1761	*The Universal Bible; or, Every Christian Family's Best Treasure . . . The Second Edition revised and corrected from the Press, By the Rev. Absalom Hurley, A.B.* By S. Nelson, D.D. London: Printed for S. Crowder & Co. and J. Coote.
1761, 1762	*The Compleat Family Bible . . . With notes theological, moral, critical, historical, and explanatory.* 2 vols. By Francis Fawkes, M.A. London: Printed for the author.
1763–67	*The Christian's Family Bible . . . With comments and annotations. . . .* 3 vols. By Rev. W. Rider. London: Printed for the author.
1764, 1766	*The Pulpit and Family Bible. Containing the sacred text . . . and the marginal notes of Mr. John Canne, the parallel scriptures of Mr. Samuel Clarke, and those of Wetsten's Greek New Testament, etc.* 2 vols. Edinburgh.

1765, 1767	*The Elegant Family Bible . . . with notes. . . .* 2 vols. By Rev. Samuel Rogers. London: Printed for S. Bladon.
1765	*The Holy Bible, containing the Old and New Testament; or, A family bible, with annotations and parallel scriptures.* By Samuel Clark. Glasgow: Printed by Joseph Galbraith & Co. for John Orr.
1765	*The New family testament. Containing the sacred text at large. With short and practical notes taken from the best authors. . . .* By an eminent divine of the Church of England. Birmingham: Printed by J. Sketchley, Bookseller.
1767, 1766, 1765	*The Christian's Complete Family Bible . . . Illus. with notes and comments. . . .* 3 vols. By several eminent divines of the Church of England. Manchester: Printed by Joseph Harrop.
1769, 1771	*The Family Bible . . . with annotations . . . from the best commentators. . . .* 2 vols. Aberdeen: J. Bruce and J. Boyle.
1770, 1771	*A New and Complete Family Bible . . . With notes and illus. . . .* 2 vols. By several learned and eminent divines. London: R Baldwin.
1771	*The Complete Family Bible . . . with notes. . . .* By Rev. Samuel Newton. London.
1771, 1773	*A Practical Family Bible . . . with notes . . . from the printed sermons of . . . English divines. . . .* Digested by Hon. and Rev. Francis Willoughby. London.
1773	*The Universal Family Bible; or, Christian's divine library . . . with notes. . . .* By Rev. Henry Southwell. London.
1774	*The Holy Family Bible . . . with . . . notes. . . .* By Rev. Alexander Fortescu. Winchester.
1777	*The New Family Bible; or, Divine library . . . with notes selected from . . . approved commentators.* Shrewsbury.
1777	*The Holy Family Bible. . . .* 2nd ed., 2 vols. By Rev. Alexander Fortescu. Winchester.
[1778]	*Brown's self-interpreting family Bible: Containing the Old and New Testaments; an extensive introduction; marginal references and illustrations; an exact summary of the several books.* By John Brown. Glasgow: James Semple.
[1780?]	*The Bishops Bible; or, A complete family exposition . . . with notes. . . .* London.

1780   *The Protestant's Family Bible . . . notes. . . .* By a society of Protestant divines. London. [With engravings by William B.]

1781, 1785   *The Complete British Family Bible . . . Illustrated with notes. . . .* By Paul Wright. London: Printed for Alex Hogg.

1781, 1785   *The Royal Universal Family Bible; . . . illus. with notes. . . .* 2 vols. By Rev. John Herries, A.M., and others. London: Fielding & Walker.

1782   *The Complete British Family Bible . . . with commentary. . . .* By Paul Wright. London: Printed for Alex. Hogg.

1783   *The Complete family Bible: Containing the Holy Scriptures of the Old and New Testament at large; together with the Apocrypha: With annotations, wherein the objections of infidels are obviated. . . .* Manchester: Printed by Charles Wheeler.

1784   *The universal family Bible, . . . Illustrated with notes and observations. . . .* By James Cookson. London: Printed by the author and sold by W. Nicoll.

1785   *The Complete Family Bible; or, The Christian's Treasury . . . with notes. . . .* By Thomas Sisson. London: Printed for W. Richardson and J. Fielding.

[1790?]   *The Christian's New and Complete Family Bible . . . with notes. . . .* By Rev. Thomas Bankes. London.

[1790?]   *The Complete Family Bible; with notes. . . .* 2 vols. By the Reverend Mr. Ostervald, corrected and revised by several clergymen. Southampton: Printed and sold by T. Skelton and C. Law.

[c. 1790]   *The Christian's New and Complete Universal Family Bible . . . with copious notes. . . .* By Joseph Butler, assisted by several eminent divines. London.

[1793]   *The New Evangelical Family Bible; . . . commentary. . . .* By Rev. T. Priestley. London.

1793, 1795   *The Universal Family Bible . . . with copious notes. . . .* 2 vols. By the late Rev. Benjamin Kennicott, and now considerably improved by a clergyman of this kingdom. Dublin: Printed and published by Zachariah Jackson.

1800   *The family devotional Bible. . . .* By Matthew Henry. London: London Printing and Publishing Company.

[1800?]   *The Grand Imperial Family Bible . . . with commentary. . . .* 3rd ed. By Rev. James Cookson. London.

1804	*The Christian's New and Complete Family Bible. . . .* 2 pts. By Rev. John Bates. Halifax.
1804	*A New Family Bible . . . with notes . . . from . . . exposition of the Rev. Matthew Henry.* 2 vols. [Selected] by Rev. Ezekiel Blomfield. Bungay.
1804	*The New Evangelical Family Bible. . . .* 2 vols. By Rev. Timothy Priestley. London.
1804, 1805	*The Christian's Complete Family Bible . . . Illus. With notes. . . .* Liverpool.
1807	*The Christian's Complete Family Bible. . . .* Liverpool.
1807, 1808	*The Complete Family Bible . . . with notes. . . .* By Rev. Mr. Ostervald. Stourbridge.
1809	*The Holy Bible for the use of families . . . most approved commentators.* 2 vols. London.
1809	*The Christian's Complete Family Bible. . . .* Liverpool.
1809	*A New Family Bible . . . with notes . . . selected . . . the Rev. Matthew Henry. . . .* 2 vols. By Rev. E. Blomfield. Bungay: C. Brightly.
[1810?]	*The Family Bible . . . notes . . . from the Bible of Dr. Dodd.* 2 vols. London.
[1810?]	*The Christian's New and Complete British Family Bible. . . .* By Paul Wright and other eminent divines. London.
1810	*The Christian's Universal Family Bible . . . with choice notes. . . .* By Rev. John Malham. London.
1810, 1811	*The Christian's Family Bible. . . .* Revised and corrected by Rev. James Wood. Liverpool.
1811	*The Devotional Family Bible . . . with notes. . . .* 2 vols. By John Fawcett, D.D. London.
1811, 1814	*The Imperial Family Bible . . . Illus.* [Copious MS notes by Mrs. Piozzi.] Stourbridge.
[1812]	*The Christian's Family Bible. With an evangelical commentary carefully selected. . . .* Stokesley.
1813	*The complete family bible; or, Christian's divine library . . . a copious commentary. . . .* By. Joseph Sutcliffe. Leeds: Printed for Davies & Co. by George Wilson.
[1813]	*The New and Grand Imperial Family Bible . . . Illus. With notes. . . .* By Rev. Henry Moore, D.D. London.

1813	*The Royal Standard Devotional Family Bible . . . compiled from the writings of Gill, Scott, Henry, etc. . . .* 2 vols. By Rev. Samuel Green. Yarmouth.
1814	*The Evangelical Family Bible . . . With notes. . . .* By Rev. Joseph Knight. London.
1814, 1816	*The Christian's Complete Family Bible, with marginal readings. . . .* 2 vols. Dublin.
[1815?]	*The Royal Standard Devotional Family Bible . . . compiled from the writings of Gill, Scott, Henry, etc. . . .* By Rev. Samuel Green. 2 vols. Yarmouth. [Paper cover with title *The Grand Imperial Bible.*]
1815, 1821	*The Evangelical Family Bible . . . Explained. . . .* 2 pts. By Rev. Joseph Knight. London: Thomas Kelly.
[1815, 1816]	*The Impartial Expositor and Family Bible . . . and valuable notes. . . .* 2 vols. By E. Blomfield. Bungay.
1816	*The Family Bible . . . with copious marginal references. . . .* By Rev. William Gurney, M.A. London: W. Lewis & Co.
1817	*The Christian's Complete Family Bible; or, Library of Divine Knowledge . . . compiled from the celebrated commentaries of Henry* [and others]. . . . 2 vols. Berwick-upon-Tweed.
1818	*A new family Bible, and improved version from corrected texts of the originals. . . .* By B. Boothroyd. Pontefract.
1818	*The Royal Standard Devotional Family Bible, etc.* 2 vols. London: Thomas Kelly.
1819	*The Christian's family Bible. Illustrated by notes chiefly extracted from the writings of the most eminent divines.* By J. Rudd and others. London.
1820	*The Holy Bible . . . The Family Guide to the Holy Scriptures. . . .* By the late Beilby Porteus, Bishop of London ("Porteusian Bible"). London: Printed for the Porteusian Bible Society.
1824	*A New Family Bible . . . with notes. . . .* By Rev. B. Boothroyd. 3 vols. Huddersfield: Printed for the author.
[1824?]	*The Family Expositor; or, A short and easy Exposition of the New Testament. For the Use of the Family. . . .* 4 vols. [Mrs. Thompson.] York: A. Barclay.
1825	*The New Family Bible: Containing the Old and New Testaments.* By E. Blomfield. London: J. McGowan.

1825–27	*The Cottage Bible and Family Expositor . . . with . . . notes. . . . 3* vols. By Thomas Williams. London: W. Simpkin & R. Marshall.
1828	*The Cottage Commentator on the Holy Scriptures. . . .* By Ingram Cobbin, A.M. London. [Lacks Authorized Version of the text.]
1828	*The cottage Bible and family expositor. . . .* by Thomas Williams. London.
1833	*The Family Commentary; or, A short and easy exposition of the New Testament, for the use of the Family.* 4 vols. [By Mrs. Thompson.] London.
1835?	*Devotional family Bible: With practical and experimental reflections on each verse of the Old and New Testament; and rich marginal references.* By Rev. Alexander Fletcher. London: G. Virtue.
1836	*The Family Commentary; or, A Short and Easy Exposition of the New Testament, etc., etc. A New Edition. . . .* 2 vols. [By Mrs. Thompson.] London: Hatchard & Son.
1837	*The Condensed Commentary and Family Exposition of the Holy Bible: Containing the most valuable criticisms of the best Biblical writers. . . .* By Rev. Ingraham Cobbin. London: T. Ward & Co.
1838, 1839	*The Illustrated Family Bible . . . with . . . notes . . . of the late Revd. John Brown. . . .* London.
1838, 1841	*The Family Bible; or, Complete commentary and exposition on the sacred texts of the Old and New Testaments . . . by the Rev. Matthew Henry, abridged. . . .* 2 pts. By Rev. Thomas Smith. London: Thomas Kelly.
1839	*The Condensed Commentary and Family Exposition of the Holy Bible. . . .* By Rev. Ingraham Cobbin. London: T. Ward & Co.
1840	*The Illustrated Family Bible . . . with . . . notes . . . of the late Revd. John Brown. . . .* London: Fisher.
[c. 1840]	*The Self-Interpreting Family Bible, with an evangelical commentary by . . . John Brown.* London.
1842	*The family Bible with the self-interpreting and explanatory notes, and marginal references of the late Rev. John Brown.* Edinburgh: T. Nelson.
1844	*The Imperial Family Bible . . . with . . . notes. . . .* Glasgow: Blackie & Son.
[1844 or 1845]	*Devotional family Bible: With practical and experimental reflections*

on each verse of the Old and New Testament; and rich marginal references. 2 vols. By Rev. Alexander Fletcher. London; New York: G. Virtue.

1845, 1847   *Domestic Bible. The Holy Bible . . . with notes. . . .* By Rev. Ingram Cobbin. London.

[1846, 1852]   *The Catholic Family Bible with Notes and Illustrations.* By Rev. Geo. Leo Haydock. Dublin, Edinburgh, and London.

1847   *Domestic Bible. The Holy Bible . . . with notes. . . .* By Rev. Ingram Cobbin. London: Partridge & Oakley.

1850   (*The Oriental Bible. . . .* By Rev. Ingram Cobbin, M.A. London.)

1852   *The Comprehensive Family Bible . . . with . . . notes. . . .* By David Davidson, LL.D. Glasgow: Blackie & Son.

1852   *The Family Devotional Bible . . . With copious notes. . . .* 3 pts. By Rev. Matthew Henry. London and New York: John Tallis & Co.

1853   *The Domestic Commentary on the Old Testament (on the New Testament). . . .* 4 vols. By a Clergyman of the Church of England [R. Shittler]. London: H. Wooldridge.

1853   *The Family Bible; containing the Old and New Testaments with Brief Notes and Instructions.* 2 vols. By Rev. Justin Edwards, D.D. New York and Boston: American Tract Society.

1853   *The Portable Folio Family Bible . . . containing upwards of twenty thousand notes. . . .* [Commentaries by Scott, Henry, Eadie, and standard authors of Europe and America.] Selected by W. McGilvray. Glasgow: W. R. McPhun

1856   *The portable folio family Bible: The Holy Bible.* London: Barrett.

1857   *The Portable Folio Family Bible: The Holy Bible, with . . . Scott and Henry.* Condensed by John Eadie. Glasgow.

1858   *The Presentation Family Bible, etc.* [Edited by John Eadie.] Glasgow: W. R. McPhun.

1858   *The Imperial Family Bible . . . with . . . notes. . . .* London.

1858   *The Pictorial Expository Family Bible . . . Notes. . . .* By John Campbell. Glasgow and London: W. R. McPhun.

1859   *The Comprehensive Family Bible, etc.* Glasgow and London: W. R. McPhun.

1859   *The Self-Explanatory Family Bible . . . with notes. . . .* By Rev. John Brown. Glasgow and London.

[1859–63]   *The Holy Bible: . . . with . . . Notes . . . Cassell's Illustrated Family Bible from the Authorised Version with notes.* London and New York: Cassell, Petter, and Galpin.

1860   *The National Comprehensive Family Bible . . . With . . . Scott and Henry. . . .* Edited by Rev. John Eadie. London and Glasgow: W. R. McPhun.

1860?   *Brown's self-interpreting family Bible.* By J. Brown. Newcastle-on-Tyne.

[1861–65]   *The Holy Bible with a Devotional and Practical Commentary.* By Rev. R. Jamieson, D.D., and Rev. E. H. Bickersteth, A.M. London and New York: J. S. Virtue.

1861   *The family Bible, with brief notes and instructions.* [Begun by J. Edwards, finished and revised by E. P. Barrows, revised again by W. R. Williams.] New York: American Tract Society.

[1862]   *Payne's Illustrated Family Bible . . . notes . . . from the best Biblical authors.* By Joseph Temple, Esq., and Rev. W. Hickman Smith. London and Reudnitz: James Hagger.

1862   *The Self-Interpreting Family Bible. . . .* By John Brown.

1862–68   *The Royal Family Bible . . . with . . . notes. . . .* By Rev. John Stoughton. London and New York.

[1863]   *The Illustrated Family Bible . . . with . . . notes . . . of the late Rev. John Brown.* Edinburgh: A. Fullarton & Co.

1863   *The Condensed Commentary and Family Exposition of the Holy Bible. . . .* By Rev. Ingram Cobbin. London: W. Tegg.

[186-?]   *The devotional family Bible containing the Old and New Testaments, according to the most approved copies of the authorized version, with rich marginal references and readings.* By Rev. Alexander Fletcher. New York: Virtue, Yorston, & Co. [Library of Congress dates this Family Bible as 1864.]

1864   *The Holy Bible, containing the Old and New Testaments, . . . with the marginal readings . . . and commentaries of Henry and Scott, condensed by the Rev. John M'Farlane.* [Secondary title: *Pictorial Family Bible.*] Glasgow: William Collins.

1864   *The Royal Family Bible . . . with . . . notes. . . .* By Rev. John Stoughton. London.

1864   *The Self-Explanatory Family Bible. . . .* 2 pts. London and Glasgow.

1867	*The Holy Bible: Containing the Old and New Testaments . . . with marginal readings, and original and selected parallel references, printed at length.* [Secondary title: *The self-explanatory family Bible.*] Toronto: James Campbell & Son.
[1868]	*Cassell's Illustrated Family Bible.* London.
1868	*The Illustrated Family Bible . . . with . . . notes . . . of the late Rev. John Brown.* Edinburgh.
[187-?]	*The devotional family Bible.* New York: Virtue & Yorston.
[c. 1870?]	*Brown's Self-Interpreting family Bible.* Bath: Green & Marsh.
1870	*Holy Bible, containing the Old and New Testaments.* [Secondary title: *The Self- explanatory family Bible.*] Glasgow: W. Collins.
[1870?]	*The National Comprehensive Family Bible.* . . . Edited by Rev. John Eadie. London.
1870	*The Royal Family Bible . . . with . . . notes.* . . . By Rev. John Stoughton. London.
[1871–72]	*Cobbin's Illustrated Family Bible and People's Commentary.* . . . By Rev. Ingram Cobbin. London: Ward, Lock, & Co.
[1871–76]	*The Illustrated Family Bible . . . with . . . notes.* . . . By John Kitto. . . . London.
[c. 1873]	*The complete domestic Bible, containing the Old and New Testaments, together with . . . valuable aids and elegant embellishments.* Guelph, Ontario: J. W. Lyon.
[1873–75]	*The Graphic Family Bible . . . With notes.* . . . By Joseph Temple and Rev. Hickman Smith. London.
[1876]	*The Illustrated Family Bible.* . . . By Rev. John Brown. . . . London: A. Fullarton & Co.
[1876]	*The Universal Family Bible . . . with . . . notes.* . . . Southampton.
[c. 1880]	*Brown's Self-Interpreting Family Bible . . . notes.* . . . By the late Rev. John Brown. London: John G. Murdoch.
[1883–86]	*The Churchman's Family Bible . . . commentary by various authors.* . . . London.
[c. 1885]	*Brown's Self-Interpreting Family Bible . . . notes.* . . . By the late Rev. John Brown. Glasgow: James Semple.

NOTES

INTRODUCTION

1. No North American library known to me has a representative collection of British Family Bibles. Most North American research collections, whether large or small, have a few of these commercial bibles, as do some older public libraries. But only the British Library possesses a reasonably comprehensive collection of them, and even this is not complete, as editions scattered in other British libraries reveal.

2. The commercial genre of Family Bibles is capitalized throughout my text in order to distinguish it from "family bible" used as a common noun form to refer to bibles owned and used by families and, more specifically, to bibles in which a family genealogy has been inscribed by some member of the family.

3. On the American Family Bible, see Paul C. Gutjahr, *An American Bible: A History of the Good Book in the United States, 1777–1880* (Stanford: Stanford University Press, 1999); and Colleen McDannell, *Material Christianity: Religion and Popular Culture in America* (New Haven: Yale University Press, 1995), chap. 3, "The Bible in the Victorian Home."

4. Elizabeth Langland, *Nobody's Angels: Middle-Class Women and Domestic Ideology in Victorian Culture* (Ithaca: Cornell University Press, 1995).

5. Elizabeth Kowaleski-Wallace, *Consuming Subjects: Women, Shopping, and Business in the Eighteenth Century* (New York: Columbia University Press, 1997).

6. McDannell, *Material Christianity,* 4.

7. Leslie Howsam, *Cheap Bibles: Nineteenth-Century Publishing and the British and Foreign Bible Society* (Cambridge: Cambridge University Press, 1991).

8. Gutjahr provides a very interesting discussion of the similarly motivated marketing practices of the American Bible Society (which modeled itself on the British and Foreign Bible Society), noting, for example, that the society began to bind bibles as well as print them in order to prevent customers from binding "extra material" such as notes or the apocrypha into them (*American Bible,* 31).

9. George P. Landow, *Victorian Types, Victorian Shadows: Biblical Typology in Victorian Literature, Art, and Thought* (Boston: Routledge & Kegan Paul, 1980); and Herbert Sussman, *Fact into Figure: Typology in Carlyle, Ruskin, and the Pre-Raphaelite Brotherhood* (Columbus: Ohio State University Press, 1979).

10. Michel Foucault, *The History of Sexuality,* vol. 1 (New York: Random House, 1978).

11. McDannell similarly comments that "practically nothing has been written on the meaning of the body in American Christianity" (*Material Christianity,* 14). Richard Rambuss, while welcoming the seminal work in the pre- and early modern fields on "the body's place in the sphere of religious devotion," is troubled by "the ways in which the pioneering and still prevailing scholarship on devotion has too readily circumscribed both the libidinal and the transgressive potentialities of the sacred body" (*Closet Devotions,* Durham, N.C.: Duke University Press, 1998), 2, 3.

12. Ellis Hanson, *Decadence and Catholicism* (Cambridge: Harvard University Press, 1997).

13. Kathryn Bond Stockton, *God between Their Lips: Desire between Women in Irigaray, Brontë, and Eliot* (Stanford: Stanford University Press, 1994); Irene Tayler, *Holy Ghosts: The Male Muses of Emily and Charlotte Brontë* (New York: Columbia University Press, 1990).

14. I thank Kathryn Bond Stockton for this irresistibly appropriate pun.

15. Ruth Perry, "De-familiarizing the Family: Or, Writing Family History from Literary Sources," *Eighteenth-Century Literary History: An MLQ Reader,* edited by Marshall Brown (Durham, N.C.: Duke University Press, 1999), 164.

16. Reina Lewis, *Gendering Orientalism: Race, Femininity and Representation* (New York: Routledge, 1996), 3.

CHAPTER 1

1. Jefferys Taylor, *The Family Bible Newly Opened: With Uncle Goodwin's Account of It* (London: 1853), 16. The preface is signed by Isaac Taylor, October 1, 1852. In it Isaac explains that his brother, who has frequently "addressed himself to young readers," has been disabled by a stroke. The account of the bible discovery is found in chapter 1, "An Ancient Heritage . . . The Family Bible Produced—the Pedigree."

2. M. H. Black, "The Printed Bible," in *The Cambridge History of the Bible* (Cambridge: Cambridge University Press, 1963–70), 463.

3. S. Smith, *The Compleat History of the Old and New Testament; or, A Family Bible . . .* (London: 1735, 1737), n.p. Rayner's allusion to the bible as "property" documents the location of the *Compleat History* in the early modern discourse on the definition of literary property and the proper limits of copyright law. See John Brewer and Susan Staves, eds., *Early Modern Conceptions of Property* (New York: Routledge, 1995), especially Laura J. Rosenthal, "(Re)Writing Lear," 323–38; and also Mark Rose, "The Author as Proprietor: *Donaldson v. Becket* and the Genealogy of Modern Authorship," *Representations* 23 (summer 1988): 51–85, on the development of the concept of "literary property" in early modern England.

4. Neil McKendrick, John Brewer, and J. H. Plumb, in *The Birth of a Consumer Society: The Commercialization of Eighteenth-Century England* (London: Europa Publications, 1982), present the case for the interpretation of eighteenth-century England as the first consumer society in Western history. Jean-Christophe Agnew, in "Coming Up for Air: Consumer Culture in Historical Perspective," summarizes and critiques the arguments against this interpretation, as do John Brewer and Roy Porter in their introduction to the volume in which Agnew's essay appears, *Consumption and the World of Goods* (New York: Routledge, 1993). Black, in "The Printed Bible," and G. E. Bentley Jr., in "Images of the Word: Separately Published English Bible Illustrations, 1539–1830" (*Studies in Bibliography* 47 (1994): 103–28), discuss publication of the bible in the vernacular, sometimes in parts, in various European cities, and publication of illustrations for the English Bible separately from the text, respectively.

5. Michael McKeon, "Historicizing Patriarchy: The Emergence of Gender Difference in England, 1660–1760," *Eighteenth-Century Studies* 28, no. 3 (1995): 295–322.

6. Eve Tavor Bannet, "The Marriage Act of 1753: 'A Most Cruel Law for the Fair Sex,'" *Eighteenth-Century Studies* 30 no. 3 (1997): 233–54.

7. Thomas Laqueur, *Making Sex: Body and Gender from the Greeks to Freud* (Cambridge: Harvard University Press, 1990).

8. Eve Kosofsky Sedgwick, *Between Men: English Literature and Male Homosocial Desire* (New York: Columbia University Press, 1985), 83–96.

9. Dror Wahrman, "Gender in Translation: How the English Wrote Their Juvenal, 1644–1815," *Representations* 65 (winter 1999): 1–41.

10. Foucault, *History of Sexuality,* 1:43.

11. Todd C. Parker writes, "We move, in other words, from a plurality of sexual practices legitimated by class and social rank to a dominant representation of sexuality in which male and female bodies naturally and inevitably invoke each other," referring to the period from the Restoration to 1750. See *Sexing the Text: The Rhetoric of Sexual Difference in British Literature, 1700–1750* (Albany: State University of New York Press, 2000), 4.

12. Leonore Davidoff and Catherine Hall, *Family Fortunes: Men and Women of the English Middle Class, 1780–1850* (Chicago: University of Chicago Press, 1987).

13. Mary Poovey, *Uneven Developments: The Ideological Work of Gender in Mid-Victorian England* (Chicago: University of Chicago Press, 1988).

14. Susan Kingsley Kent, *Gender and Power in Britain, 1640–1990* (New York: Routledge, 1999).

15. Langland, *Nobody's Angels,* 24–61.

16. Raphael Samuel, *Island Stories: Unravelling Britain.* Vol. 2 of *Theatres of Memory,* ed. Alison Light with Sally Alexander and Gareth Stedman Jones (New York: Verso, 1998), 17.

17. Leslie Howsam notes, "Most publishers and editors have been men; the majority of writers of scholarly, legal, theological and political works were men; printing trade workers at all levels were almost always men" *SHARP News* 7, no. 4, (autumn 1998): 1.

18. The *Nineteenth-Century Short Title Catalog* lists the 1833 edition in the Bodleian collection.

19. Christine L. Krueger documents the difficulty Methodist women preachers experienced in actually publishing what they were, for a limited time at least, able to preach. As she notes, the realm of Methodist publishing was "solidly male-controlled," and this appears to have been even more the case with publishing in the realm of the state, or Anglican, religion. See *The Reader's Repentance: Women Preachers, Women Writers, and Nineteenth-Century Social Discourse* (Chicago: University of Chicago Press, 1992), especially chapter 5, "Publishing the Word," 69–82.

20. Linda K. Hughes and Michael Lund suggest that the identification of the novel with both readers and writers of the feminine gender was particularly associated with the serialized form of the novel. See "Textual/Sexual Pleasure and Serial Publication," in *Literature in the Marketplace: Nineteenth-Century British Publishing and Reading Practices*, ed. John O. Jordan and Robert L. Patten (Cambridge: Cambridge University Press, 1995).

21. Smith, *Compleat History,* preface, n.p.

22. Black gives 1720 as the date of the first bible with notes, but he is apparently referring to the *Bibliotheca biblica. Being a commentary upon all the books of the Old and New Testament.* . . . I do not include this work in my account of Family Bibles, not only because it does not include the word "family" in the title, but because the preface indicates it was supported by a patron rather than by sale in parts. The work appears to have been published in five bound volumes, and covers only the five books of the Pentateuch, despite the title.

23. S. Smith, *The Family Companion; or, Annotations upon the Holy Bible* (London: 1735). This is not a Family Bible, as it consists of a narrativized version of the texts of the Old and New Testaments, or a sort of running narrative and commentary combined, with frequent insertion of "dissertations" between the more biblical texts. Whether S. Smith actually existed or, if he did, had anything to do with Rayner's publications, is also speculative: S. A. Alibone, in *A Critical Dictionary of English Literature and British American Authors,* lists a contemporary minister named Samuel

Smith, but does not include among his publications either *The Family Companion* or *The Compleat History*.

24. Kent, *Gender and Power,* 26, 33.

25. Mary Beth Norton, *Founding Mothers and Fathers: Gendered Power and the Forming of American Society* (New York: Vintage Books, 1996), 59, 17. Sara Maza, in "Only Connect: Family Values in the Age of Sentiment: Introduction" (*Eighteenth-Century Studies* 30, no. 3 [1997]), articulates the opposition between theories of the "egalitarian" family in early modern Europe and feminist critiques of the "complacency underlying such arguments" (207–12). Bannet, in "The Marriage Act of 1753," also argues for the hierarchical and patriarchal order of the family.

26. John Brewer, *Pleasures of the Imagination: English Culture in the Eighteenth Century* (New York: Farrar Straus Giroux, 1997), xviii.

27. Black, "The Printed Bible," 457–59. F. F. Bruce comments that the Authorized Version may have been authorized by an "Order in Council," which might have been destroyed in a fire at Whitehall on 12 January 1618. He notes that King James is known to have taken a leading part in organizing the work of the translation, and that the translators' dedication to "the most high and mighty prince James" indicates his approval of the finished product (*History of the Bible in English,* New York: Oxford University Press, 1978, 99–100). But Bruce does not contest Black's statement that there is no documented record that James I gave his official seal of approval to the translation.

28. Paul Wright, *The Complete British Family Bible* (London: 1782), n.p.

29. Sir Leslie Stephen and Sir Sidney Lee, eds., *The Dictionary of National Biography* 6 (Oxford: Oxford University Press, 1921–22 . . . 1967–68), 1128–29.

30. Timothy Priestley, *A Funeral Sermon, Occasioned by the Death of the Late Rev. Joseph Priestley* (London: 1804), vi.

31. Rev. Ingraham Cobbin, *The Condensed Commentary and Family Exposition of the Holy Bible . . .* (London: 1837), iv–v.

32. John Eadie, *The Portable Folio Family Bible* (Glasgow: 1857), "Publisher's Preface," iii–iv.

33. Colleen McDannell reproduces a version of this print and comments, "This Noah's Ark was originally published in Diderot's *Encyclopédie.*" She continues, "Its order, balance and symmetry were appropriate both for the Age of enlightenment of the *philosophes* and the readers of the 1822 *Complete Family Bible*" (*Material Christianity,* illustration note 57, 92). However, Diderot's *Encyclopédie* was first published in 1751–52, so the print's appearance in the *Compleat History* (1735) predates the *Encyclopédie* by more than fifteen years.

34. Foucault posits, "The sodomite had been a temporary aberration; the homosexual was now [in the late nineteenth century] a species" (*History of Sexuality,* 1:43).

35. Alan Bray, *Homosexuality in Renaissance England* (New York: Columbia University Press, 1995), 13.

36. Alan Sinfield, *The Wilde Century: Effeminacy, Oscar Wilde, and the Queer Movement* (London: Cassell, 1994), 38. Randolph Trumbach, "Sodomitical Subcultures, Sodomitical Roles, and Sex Gender Revolution of the Eighteenth Century: The Recent Historiography," in *'Tis Nature's Fault: Unauthorized Sexuality During the Enlightenment,* ed. Robert Purks Maccubbin (Cambridge: Cambridge University Press, 1987).

37. Linda Dowling, *Hellenism and Homosexuality in Victorian Oxford* (Ithaca: Cornell University Press, 1994), xv.

38. Smith, *Compleat History* (1735, 1752), n.p.

39. S. Nelson, *The Universal Bible; or, Every Christian Family's Best Treasure* (London: 1758, 1759), n.p.

40. Francis Fawkes, *The Compleat Family Bible . . .* (London: 1761, 1762), n.p.

41. The Latin noun *scortum,* literally meaning a "skin" or "hide," is used a number of times in Plautus, Cicero, Livy, and Petronius to refer to a male prostitute. I am indebted to Dr. Ross Kilpatrick, Queen's University, for this reference.

42. Rev. W. Rider, *The Christian's Family Bible,* 3 vols. (London: 1763–67), n.p.

43. Rev. John Herries, *The Royal Universal Family Bible,* 2 vols. (London: 1781, 1785), n.p.

44. *A New and Complete Family Bible,* 2 vols. (London: 1770, 1771), n.p.

45. Rev. Henry Southwell, *The Universal Family Bible; or, Christian's divine library* (London: 1773), n.p.

46. Rev. John Bates, *The Christian's New and Complete Family Bible* (Halifax: 1804), n.p.

47. John Fawcett, *The Devotional Family Bible,* 2 vols. (London: 1811), n.p.

48. Samuel Clark, *The Holy Bible . . . or, A family Bible* (London: 1760), n.p.

49. Mark A. Noll, *A History of Christianity in the United States and Canada* (London: SPCK, 1992), 91, 93. On Whitefield's genius for publicity, see Harry S. Stout, *The Divine Dramatist: George Whitefield and the Rise of Modern Evangelism* (Grand Rapids, Mich.: W. B. Eerdmans, c. 1991), and Frank Lambert, "Pedlar in Divinity," *Journal of American History* 77, no. 3 (December 1990): 812–37.

50. Susan O'Brien details the spread of the Great Awakening through transatlantic publishing networks in "Eighteenth-Century Publishing Networks in the First Years of Transatlantic Evangelicalism," in *Evangelicalism: Comparative Studies of Popular Protestantism in North America, the British Isles, and Beyond, 1700–1990,* ed. Mark A. Noll et al. (New York: Oxford, 1994).

51. According to G. M. Bentley Jr. and Martin K. Nurmi, William Blake did an engraving of "Judith giving the Head of Holofernes to her Maid" for *The Royal Universal Family Bible* (1780), along with four other plates (*A Blake Bibliography,* Minneapolis: Minnesota University Press, 1964, 92–93). However, the copy of *The Royal Universal Family Bible* I examined at the British Library was dated 1781, 1785, and it did not contain a plate of Judith with the head of Holofernes. Bentley and Nurmi note that Blake is known to have engraved plates for *The Protestants [sic] Family Bible* [1781?] as well, and that "Family Bibles were obviously extremely profitable in the late eighteenth century" (91, 93).

52. Dianne Dugaw, *Warrior Women and Popular Balladry, 1650–1850* (Cambridge: Cambridge University Press, 1989), 162.

53. Joy Wiltenburg, *Disorderly Women and Female Power in the Street Literature of Early Modern England and Germany* (Charlottesville: University Press of Virginia, 1992), 7.

54. Anne Lister, *No Priest But Love: The Journals of Anne Lister from 1824–1826,* ed. Helena Whitbread (New York: New York University Press, 1992), 33.

55. P. Doddridge, *The Family Expositor: Or, a Paraphrase and Version of the New Testament,* 6 vols. (London: 1739–56), 4:223.

56. Terry Castle, *The Apparitional Lesbian: Female Homosexuality and Modern Culture* (New York: Columbia University Press, 1993), 1–20.

57. Emma Donoghue documents the use of terms such as "tribade," "Sapphist," and "Tommy" in *Passions between Women: British Lesbian Culture, 1668–1801* (London: Scarlet Press, 1993).

58. Martha Vicinus, "'They Wonder to Which Sex I Belong': The Historical Roots of the Modern Lesbian Identity," in *The Lesbian and Gay Studies Reader,* ed. Henry Abelove et al. (New York: Routledge, 1993), 436–37.

59. Kent, *Gender and Power,* 103–4.

60. Ibid., 42. Again, Lister's diary provides a corollary for this interpretation in her references to the "use of phalli" between women. See *No Priest but Love,* 32. Later, Lister and her friend Mrs. Barlow view a collection of "Egyptian antiquities" and Lister points out two phalli (42).

61. Kent, *Gender and Power,* 120.

CHAPTER 2

1. Rev. B. Boothroyd, *A New Family Bible . . . with notes* (Huddersfield: 1824), Preface signed "THE AUTHOR. Pontefract, October, 1818" (n.p.). Boothroyd was both a Dissenting minister and a bookseller and printer. He had previously published a Hebrew Bible, *Biblia Hebraica,* in 1810 and a Family Bible in 1818 (S. A. Alibone, *A Critical Dictionary of English Literature and British and American Authors, from Earliest Accounts to Mid-Nineteenth-Century* [London, 1859–71]).

2. Thomas Williams, *The Cottage Bible and Family Expositor . . . with . . . notes. . . .* 3 vols. (London, 1825–27), vii.

3. Ingram Cobbin, *The Cottage Commentator on the Holy Scriptures. . . .* (London, 1828), n.p.

4. The British Library has only the first volume of this commentary, which covers Genesis through 1 Samuel. A note on the paper cover indicates that the commentary may have been discontinued.

5. Cobbin also points out his "improved readings," which "sometimes include a better rendering than is given in our received translation, and in all cases where vulgar and obsolete words are retained, the ready substitution of better will be found a benefit . . ." (v–vi). His title still claims, as usual, to be *The Holy Bible, Containing the Old and New Testaments, According to the Authorized Version. . . .*

6. Paul Rabinow, introduction to *Michel Foucault: Ethics, Subjectivity and Truth,* ed. Rabinow, trans. Robert Hurley and others (New York: New Press, 1997), xiii–xiv.

7. Beilby Porteus, *The Holy Bible . . . The Family Guide to the Holy Scriptures. . . .* (London, 1820), vii.

8. Michel Foucault, *The Birth of the Clinic: An Archaeology of Medical Perception,* trans. A. M. Sheridan Smith (New York: Vintage Books, 1994), xii.

9. Eve Kosofsky Sedgwick, *Epistemology of the Closet* (Berkeley: University of California Press, 1990), 11.

10. Foucault, *History of Sexuality,* 1:59–63.

11. Samuel Slater, *A Discourse of the Closet (or secret) prayer* (London, 1691), 91, 92, as quoted in Marta Straznicky, "Privacy, Playreading, and Early Modern Women's Closet Drama" (unpublished manuscript).

12. Richard Rambuss, *Closet Devotions* (Durham, N.C.: Duke University Press, 1998), 109. Rambuss protests the critical and historical accounts that posit the disappearance of "sacred eroticism" in the mid- or late seventeenth century (133). Both the material circumstances and subjective effects of Victorian "closet devotions" have yet to be examined.

13. Andrew Elfenbein, "Stricken Deer: Secrecy, Homophobia, and the Rise of the Suburban Man," *Genders* 27 (1998), par. 6, as cited on http://www.genders.org.

14. Howard Eilberg-Schwartz, "The Problem of the Body for the People of the Book," in *Reading Bibles, Writing Bodies,* ed. Timothy K. Beal and David M. Gunn (New York: Routledge, 1997), 38, 40.

15. Linda Colley, *Britons: Forging the Nation, 1707–1837* (New Haven: Yale University Press, 1992), 286.

16. Louis Crompton, *Byron and Greek Love: Homophobia in Nineteenth-Century England* (Berkeley: University of California Press, c. 1985).

17. Edward Said, *Orientalism* (New York: Vintage Books, 1979), 42.

18. Randolph Trumbach, "The Birth of the Queen: Sodomy and the Emergence of Gender Equality in Modern Culture, 1660–1750," in *Hidden from History: Reclaiming the Gay and Lesbian Past,* ed. Martin Duberman, Martha Vicinus, and George Chauncey Jr. (New York: Meridian, 1989), 129.

19. It seems the height of irony that, as Patrick Brantlinger notes in *The Reading Lesson: The Threat of Mass Literacy in Nineteenth-Century British Fiction* (Bloomington: Indiana University Press, 1998), objections to novel reading by the newly literate "masses" were often religious (2). Obviously, the bracketed Family Bibles attest to fear about what might happen if the masses *really* read the bible.

20. Juliet Barker, *The Brontës* (New York: St. Martin's Griffin, 1994), 11.

21. Howsam, *Cheap Bibles,* 79–81. Gutjahr, in *An American Bible,* documents how stereotyping similarly revolutionized bible publishing in the United States, where the American Bible Society adopted the British and Foreign Bible Society as its model (29–30).

22. *The Christian's Complete Family Bible. . . ,* 2 vols. (Dublin: 1814, 1816), preface, n.p.

23. Thomas Smith, *The Family Bible . . . by the Rev. Matthew Henry, abridged* (London: 1838, 1841), preface, n.p.

24. Linda K. Hughes and Michael Lund, *The Victorian Serial* (Charlottesville: University Press of Virginia, 1991), 3.

25. As the Bible and Culture Collective states, "[T]here is no innocent reading of the Bible, no reading that is not already ideological" (*The Postmodern Bible,* New Haven: Yale University Press, 1995), 4. I must include my own statement here as such an "already ideological" reading, yet point out that historical biblical scholarship typically acknowledges the diversity of this collection of texts. Even Robert Alter and Frank Kermode, who exclude Marxist, psychoanalytic, deconstructionist, and feminist criticism, or any sort of criticism that uses "the text as a springboard for cultural or metaphysical ruminations," nevertheless describe the bible as "a miscellany of documents" (*The Literary Guide to the Bible* [Cambridge, Mass.: Belknap Press, 1987], 6, 1).

26. The partitioning of the Family Bible for "cottagers" and others of the working classes, marking passages to be omitted from family reading, may have been a peculiarly British device. In an 1834 American edition of Williams's *Cottage Bible and Family Expositor,* the editor comments,

> In the London edition, some words in the text, "esteemed objectionable," were "exchanged for others more suitable to the present state of our language and of society." These, though they were carefully pointed out in the Notes, have been rejected, and the language of the authorized version retained. A new division of the chapters into paragraphs was also introduced "for the convenience of family reading"; these have been rejected, and the usual divisions followed. Considerable portions of the text were printed in smaller type, to denote, that they were "unsuitable for reading in families": Upon these, the Author furnished no exposition. In the present edition, the type of the text is uniform throughout, and with the exception of the books of Chronicles, an Exposition has been supplied, by selections from the judicious commentary of Thomas Scott. (n.p.)

One hesitates to assume that this change was made for purely democratic reasons, however. In the antebellum United States, the privilege of unrestricted bible reading was determined on the basis of *racial,* rather than class or gender, status.

27. Elizabeth Langland, *Nobody's Angels,* 54.

28. Raphael Samuel, *Island Stories,* 4.

29. Samuel Burder, *The Scripture Expositor* (London: 1809).

30. William Dodd (1729–77) was a popular preacher in the established Church who published a commentary on the bible in monthly parts from 1765 to 1770. The commentary, based on manuscripts attributed to Locke, was collected in three volumes folio in 1770. Dodd later forged a bond in Lord Chesterfield's name, for which he was tried, convicted and hung, despite intervention from Samuel Johnson, among others. See *Dictionary of National Biography,* 5:1060–62.

31. Rev. R Jamieson and Rev. E. H. Bickersteth, *The Holy Bible with a Devotional and Practical Commentary* (London and New York, [1861–65]), 242.

32. Joseph Temple . . . and the Rev. Hickman Smith, *The Graphic Family Bible* (London, [1873–75]), 166.

33. Rev. John Eadie proclaims, "Our Scriptures are the legacy of the Reformation; and we feel a peculiar joy in knowing that, in consequence of Anglo-Saxon Protestantism and enterprise, the sun never sets on the English Bible" (preface to *National Comprehensive Family Bible,* ed. John Eadie, London, [1870?], v).

CHAPTER 3

1. *The Imperial Family Bible.* . . . Stourbridge, 1811, 1814 [copious MS notes by Mrs. Piozzi].

2. Langland, *Nobody's Angels,* 26.

3. Kowaleski-Wallace demonstrates the importance of women as "consuming subjects" in eighteenth-century consumer culture, well before the advent of nineteenth-century mass market print technology (*Consuming Subjects*). But the evidence of Family Bibles strongly suggests that *publishers* did not begin to catch on to women's importance as consumers of this central icon of patriarchal religion until some time in the 1830s.

4. Davidoff and Hall, *Family Fortunes,* 30.

5. Rev. John Eadie, ed., *The National Comprehensive Family Bible* (London and Glasgow: 1860), v. The preface is signed, "John Eadie, Glasgow, July 1851," indicating that it first appeared in a Family Bible published in 1851.

6. Anne McClintock, *Imperial Leather: Race, Gender and Sexuality in the Colonial Contest* (New York: Routledge, 1995), 209.

7. Joseph Temple, Esq., and the Rev. W. Hickman Smith, *Payne's Illustrated Family Bible* (London and Reudnitz, [1862]), 132.

8. John Kitto, *The Illustrated Family Bible.* . . . (London, [1871–76]), 174–75.

9. Jamieson and Bickersteth, *Holy Bible.*

10. *The Illustrated Family Bible* (London, 1838, 1839), n.p.

11. Margaret Linley notes that "publishers began defining the women's market in the 1820s and the juvenile market at the end of the decade through gift books and annuals. From the appearance of Rudolph Ackermann's *Forget-Me-Not, A Christmas and New Year's Present* in 1823 to the thirtieth and final issue of the *Keepsake* in 1857, the annual market was fiercely competitive, with sixty-three gift books making an appearance in 1832 and more than two hundred by the end of the decade" ("A Centre that Would Not Hold," in *Nineteenth-Century Media and the Construction of Identities,* ed. Laurel Brake, Bill Bell, and David Finkelstein [New York: Palgrave, 2000]).

12. McDannell notes that after the Civil War in the United States, such additional features as photo albums, temperance pledges, wedding certificates, and family record pages began to be included in American family bibles, but British publishers evidently introduced these features earlier in the nineteenth century (*Material Christianity,* 89).

13. David Davidson, *The Comprehensive Family Bible* (Glasgow: Blackie & Son, 1852), n.p.

14. Ibid., commentary on the Song of Solomon, 1:701.

15. Meredith Veldman impressively documents, in over two hundred nineteenth-century British

children's books, the increasing feminization of Jesus, such that Jesus became "in fact, the Perfect Daughter, the ideal of feminine passivity and self-abnegation" ("Dutiful Daughter versus All-Boy: Jesus, Gender, and the Secularization of Victorian Society," *Nineteenth Century Studies* 11 [1997]: 4).

16. Lynda Nead, *Myths of Sexuality: Representations of Women in Victorian Britain* (Oxford: Basil Blackwell, 1988), 15.

17. *Edinburgh Witness* (as qtd in *Imperial Family Bible,* n.p.).

18. Kitto, *Illustrated Family Bible,* 1–2.

19. See Jan Marsh, *Christina Rossetti: A Writer's Life* (New York: Viking, 1994), 433–35, for a discussion of Rossetti's active interest in the cause of antivivisection.

20. See appendix for the cessation of publication of bibles with the word "family" in the formal title. McDannell notes that a steady decline in *all* new editions of the bible in the United States began in 1870 (*Material Christianity,* 100). However, Gutjahr argues that although the number of editions declined, the number of bibles actually published "remained strong up through 1880 and beyond" (*American Bible,* 182).

21. Martyn J. Lee, *Consumer Culture Reborn: The Cultural Politics of Consumption* (New York: Routledge, 1993).

22. Ann Bermingham, introduction to *The Culture of Consumption, 1600–1800,* ed. Ann Bermingham and John Brewer (New York: Routledge, 1995), 9, 14.

23. Lyn Pykett, "The Cause of Women and the Course of Fiction: The Case of Mona Caird," in *Gender Roles and Sexuality in Victorian Literature,* ed. Christopher Parker (Aldershot, U.K.: Scolar Press, 1995), 128.

24. Linda K. Hughes and Michael Lund, *The Victorian Serial* (Charlottesville: University of Virginia Press, 1991), 230.

CHAPTER 4

1. Miriam Allott, ed., *The Brontës, the Critical Heritage* (Boston: Routledge & Kegan Paul, 1974), 206.

2. Charlotte Brontë, *Villette,* ed. Margaret Smith and Herbert Rosengarten, with an introduction and notes by Tim Dolin (Oxford: Oxford University Press, 2000). All further references in my text are to this edition and will be indicated parenthetically.

3. Keith A. Jenkins, "Charlotte Brontë's New Bible," in *Approaches to Teaching Brontë's* Jane Eyre, ed. Diane Long Hoeveler and Beth Lau (New York: Modern Language Association of America, 1993).

4. Stockton, *God between Their Lips,* 246.

5. Tayler, *Holy Ghosts,* 283.

6. Christina Crosby, *The Ends of History: Victorians and "the Woman Question"* (New York: Routledge, 1991), 113. Barry Qualls also speaks of Brontë's constant use of biblical language in *Villette,* but is chiefly interested in reading the novel as "an allegory very much in the tradition of *Pilgrim's Progress* and *Sartor Resartus*" (*The Secular Pilgrims of Victorian Fiction: The Novel as Book of Life* [Cambridge: Cambridge University Press, 1982], 75).

7. Keith A. Jenkins, "The Influence of Anxiety: *Bricolage* Brontë Style" (Ph.D. diss., Rice University, Texas, 1993), 8.

8. Crosby, *Ends of History,* 136. Jenkins also comments on the "radically altered form in which the action and imagery of the sacred text find their place" in *Jane Eyre* ("Charlotte Brontë's New

Bible," 69), while Maggie Berg notes that this novel "implicitly challenges all aspects of the status quo subsumed under the Christian tradition . . ." (*Jane Eyre: Portrait of a Life* [Boston, Twayne Publishers, 1987], 112).

9. Marianne Thormälen remarks on the fact that "[f]rom their early youth, the children of Haworth Parsonage ridiculed Methodists and Baptists, and the portrayals of Dissenters in the Brontë novels are consistently uncomplimentary" (*The Brontës and Religion* [Cambridge: Cambridge University Press, 1999], 13). Indeed, Lucy Snowe comments condescendingly on a "little book" that reminds her of "certain Wesleyan Methodist tracts" she had read as a child, flavored with "the same seasoning of excitation to fanaticism" (*Villette*, 413). But Lucy's attitude should not be taken as identical to that of her creator, nor even to that of the authorial Lucy, writing from a mature perspective not available to the younger self whose story she tells. Juliette Barker also comments that although it was the Methodists at whom the Brontë children aimed most of their sarcasm, this sect had in fact always been among Patrick's most reliable allies, and notes that not only the children's aunt, but their mother, had been raised Methodist (*The Brontës*, 251). Stockton reports that because Patrick Brontë was "sympathetic to Wesleyan Nonconformity . . . the parish of Haworth . . . had acquired note as a frequent spot on the Wesley brothers' preaching circuit" (*God between Their Lips*, 115).

10. Christina Crosby, "Charlotte Brontë's Haunted Text," *Studies in English Literature* 24 (1984): 703.

11. Patricia Yaeger, *Honey-Mad Women: Emancipatory Strategies in Women's Writing* (New York: Columbia University Press, 1988), 69.

12. Joseph Litvak, *Caught in the Act: Theatricality in the Nineteenth-Century English Novel* (Berkeley: University of California Press, 1992), 81.

13. Peter Melville Logan, *Nerves, and Narratives: A Cultural History of Hysteria in Nineteenth-Century British Prose* (Berkeley: University of California Press, 1997), 16.

14. Sally Shuttleworth, *Charlotte Brontë and Victorian Psychology* (Cambridge: Cambridge University Press, 1996), 1.

15. Ann Digby, "Women's Biological Straitjacket," in *Sexuality and Subordination: Interdisciplinary Studies of Gender,* ed. Susan Mendus and Jane Rendall (New York: Routledge, 1989), 198.

16. Dr. J. G. Millingen's 1848 work, *The Passions; or, Mind and Matter,* states that woman "is less under the influence of the brain than the uterine system, the plexi of abdominal nerves, and irritation of the spinal cord; in her, a hysteric predisposition is incessantly predominating from the dawn of puberty" (as quoted in Shuttleworth, *Charlotte Brontë and Victorian Psychology,* 76). Adam Clarke, *The Holy Bible . . . with a critical commentary and notes,* 5 vols. (London: 1825).

17. See Margaret Smith, ed., *Letters of Charlotte Brontë: With a Selection of Letters by Friends* (Oxford: Clarendon Press, 1995), 2:648, 652, and 717. Critics have extensively documented the identity of the actress called Vashti in *Villette* as that of the French actress Rachel, whose performance Brontë had seen in London in 1851. See John Stokes, "Rachel's 'Terrible Beauty': An Actress Among the Novelists," *ELH* 51 (1984): 771–93; Rachel M. Brownstein, "Representing the Self: Arnold and Brontë on Rachel," *Browning Institute Studies* 13 (1985): 1–23; Sandra M. Gilbert and Susan Gubar, *The Madwoman in the Attic* (New Haven: Yale University Press, 1979), 421–25; Litvak, *Caught in the Act,* 75–107; Lisa Surridge, "Representing the 'Latent Vashti': Theatricality in Charlotte Brontë's *Villette*," *Victorian Newsletter* 87 (spring 1995): 4–14; Joseph A. Boone, "Depolicing *Villette*: Surveillance, Invisibility and the Female Erotics of 'Heretic Narrative,'" *Novel* 26 (1992): 20–42; Jill Matus, *Unstable Bodies: Victorian Representations of Sexuality and Maternity* (Manchester: Manchester University Press, 1995), 131–48; Reina Lewis, *Gendering Orientalism: Race, Femininity and Representation* (London and New York: Routledge, 1996), 35–43.

18. Sedgwick insightfully interprets Esther's act as comparable to that of the homosexual's "coming out" in *Epistemology of the Closet,* 75–82.

19. Simon Patrick, *Commentary Upon the Historical Books of the Old Testament,* 2 vols. (London: 1809). Bishop Simon Patrick (1626–1707) originally published his commentary in 1707, but it was reprinted throughout the eighteenth and nineteenth centuries, and was incorporated into numerous commercial Family Bibles.

20. Ann Laura Stoler's discussion of the colonial society of the Dutch East Indies, in which European men secured property through marriage to colonial wives, may be relevant here. By the mid-nineteenth century, she notes, Dutch colonial authorities "saw these strong mestizo and creole connections, produced out of interracial unions, threatening the metropolitan hold on colonial authority and sought specific cultural measures to remedy the situation. . . . Most notable were attempts to enforce spoken Dutch in newly established private schools for European children" (*Race and the Education of Desire: Foucault's* History of Sexuality *and the Colonial Order of Things* [Durham, N.C.: Duke University Press, 1995], 43). British authors of bible commentary, steeped in missionary concerns, may have echoed the urgency of maintaining linguistic authority in the British colonies.

21. Rev. Justin Edwards, *The Family Bible. . . ,* 2 vols. (New York and Boston: American Tract Society, 1853).

22. Clarke, *Holy Bible,* n.p.

23. James Eadie observes of the popularity and financial success of Scott's commentary:

> Few books have commanded so large and constant a sale as Scott's Commentary. The first edition, which was begun in 1788, and was published in numbers, consisted of five thousand copies; the second edition, in 1805, was one of two thousand; an edition of similar size was published in 1810; a fourth, of three thousand copies, in 1812; and another was stereotyped in 1822, the revision of which was the last and cherished work of the author, and he had four times engaged in a similar service. Many issues have been made since his death, and thousands of copies have also been sold in the United States of America. During the author's lifetime, the sales amounted to nearly £200,000. Scott's Commentary thus continues to "praise him in the gates." The first edition was written to the demands of the press, "in weakness and in fear, and in much trembling," and amidst the external discomfort of a limited income and a growing family. The publication led him, moreover, into pecuniary embarrassment; but the popularity of the work at length relieved him of all such anxiety. (*Presentation Family Bible* [Glasgow: 1858], xv)

24. In Judg. 4, Deborah the prophetess tells Barak the Lord will deliver Sisera into his hand, indeed that "the Lord shall sell Sisera into the hand of a woman" (4:9). Barak destroys all of Sisera's host, "and there was not a man left," but Sisera escapes (4:16). He seeks refuge in the tent of Jael, where he feels safe because Jael is the wife of Heber the Kenite, who is allied with the Israelites' enemy. However, Jael tricks and kills him, for reasons not explained, and in the next chapter, Deborah and Barak sing a song of praise. Jael is thus a figure for feminine ambiguity, as well as feminine violence.

25. Matus points out that the physician Elizabeth Garrett Anderson argued that "menstruation is the body's way of getting rid of what it has in excess, that surplus nutritive material is disposed of rather than a deficit being incurred," and that there was no reason why a woman's system should be considered depleted or overtaxed by menstruation (*Unstable Bodies,* 27). Anderson's argument was occasioned by Henry Maudsley's 1874 essay, "Sex in Mind and Education," which presented

the dominant Victorian medical view that intellectual development could overtax the female reproductive system. Anderson's progressive argument that menstruation simply represents surplus nutritive material dates back, however, to classical medical views. Laqueur explains that menstrual blood was seen as "a plethora or leftover of nutrition," and that pregnant women were thought to transform "superfluous food into nourishment for the fetus" (*Making Sex*, 36). Isidore of Seville, a seventh-century encyclopedist, wrote that "after birth . . . whatever blood has not yet been spent in the nourishing of the womb flows by natural passage to the breasts, and whitening . . . by their virtue, receives the quality of milk" (qtd in *Making Sex*, 36). Elaine and English Showalter in fact state, "In the first half of the [nineteenth] century it was generally believed that the menstrual flow came from an excess of nutrient in the female . . ." ("Victorian Women and Menstruation," in *Suffer and Be Still*, ed. Martha Vicinus [Bloomington: Indiana University Press, 1973], 38). Shuttleworth and others, however, emphasize the pathologization of menstruation throughout the nineteenth century, and Adam Clarke's emphasis on the "superabundance" of the female body seems remarkably unconventional and even feminist for the time (*Charlotte Brontë and Victorian Psychology*).

26. See, for example, David Sandner's "The Little Puzzle: The Two Shipwrecks in Charlotte Brontë's *Villette*," (*English Language Notes* 36 [March 1999]), in which he states that the first shipwreck is "simply metaphor that describes in the brief space of two paragraphs Lucy's loss—over an eight-year period—of her family and home" (67). Later, however, Sandner states, "The reader receives no picture at all of Lucy Snowe's family, happy or not. The metaphor of the ship stands in its place, obscuring vision of the family itself" (70). Sandner concludes that "the book asks the reader to puzzle over the problem of Lucy Snowe's tempest-tossed life" (74).

27. Ellen Moers sensitively describes the "female landscape" representing female genitalia found in many women writers' works, such as the chapter "In the Red Deeps" in George Eliot's *The Mill on the Floss* (*Literary Women* [Garden City, N.Y.: Doubleday, 1976], 254).

28. Susan Bernstein, *Confessional Subjects: Revelations of Gender and Power in Victorian Literature and Culture* (Chapel Hill: University of North Carolina Press, 1997), 64.

29. Stockton, *God between Their Lips*, 148. Both Stockton and Tayler comment on the similarly sexual nature of the description that begins the chapter on Vashti: "Conceive a dell, deep-hollowed in forest secrecy; it lies in dimness and mist: its turf dank, its herbage pale and humid" (Stockton, *God between Their Lips*, n. 148; Tayler, *Holy Ghosts*, 260–64; Brontë, *Villette*, 253). Tayler links this passage to Brontë's construction of the female sexual symbols of similar "forest dells," such as Nunnwood in *Shirley* and Lowood in *Jane Eyre* as female sexual symbols—but she reads these in *Villette* as images of Lucy's desire for a "fetal retreat" (262).

30. Shuttleworth notes that the speculum was coming into increasing use in the 1840s, and that Brontë's fiction, "with its emphasis on the unveiling of inner secrets, and its assertion of the sexuality of its heroines, participates within and contributes to Victorian discourses on the body" (Shuttleworth, *Charlotte Brontë and Victorian Psychology*, 96).

31. Mary Jane Lupton, *Menstruation and Psychoanalysis* (Urbana: University of Illinois Press, 1993), 62.

32. Erhard S. Gerstenberger notes that the Levitical proscriptions concerning "discharges" have no specific terms even for "penis" or "vagina," sometimes referring to the former euphemistically as "the feet." Similarly, "the expression 'mucous flow' . . . is applied in several variations also to menstruation, even though a specific term is available (v. 33: *dawâ*; cf. Lev. 20.18)." The "'impurity' of a woman's discharge is designated by the peculiar word (*niddâ*), whose meaning fluctuates between 'something abhorrent' and 'menstruation' . . ." (*Leviticus: A Commentary* [Louisville, Ky.: Westminster/John Knox Press, 1996], 198, 203). Gerstenberger comments that the Levitical taboos

suggest that "menstrual blood is particularly powerful. . . . It is clear that the woman is indirectly pushed to the periphery within the orthodox Jewish cult (and far beyond the Jewish cult, also—unconsciously or with hypocritical discretion—in Christian churches) because she is the regular bearer of what from the male perspective is an uncanny, antidivine power. . . . Menstruation appears to be the real reason for the exclusion of women from priestly service" (207).

33. Lupton also points out that nineteenth-century bible dictionaries commonly defined "flowers" as menstruation (*Menstruation and Psychoanalysis*, 60).

34. On Lev. 15:24, quoted above, Adam Clarke warns that "the common sense of all mankind has led them to avoid the gross impropriety referred to in this verse; and it has been a general opinion, that offspring obtained in this way, has been infected with leprous, scrophulous [*sic*], and other deeply radicated diseases, from which they and their posterity have been scarcely ever freed" (*Holy Bible*, n.p.).

35. See Elaine Showalter on the menarcheal implications of the red room scene in *Jane Eyre* (*A Literature of Their Own: British Women Novelists from Brontë to Lessing* [Princeton: Princeton University Press, 1977], 114–15).

36. Showalter, *Literature of Their Own*, 15.

37. Interestingly, Bernstein notes that an 1851 article in *The Christian Observer* "contemplates reforming the practice of confession so that women penitents confess to 'some discreet and pious female—a wife, a sister, or else some kind and experienced Christian woman'" (*Confessional Subjects*, 51). In this context, Paulina's confession to another woman conforms to anti-Catholic sentiment. It provides a vehicle for contradictory impulses to articulate woman's most potent sexuality and simultaneously to subordinate that desire to conservative religious ideology.

38. The notes to the Oxford edition locate this as a quote from Matt. 25:13, where Jesus warns, "ye know neither the day nor the hour wherein the Son of man cometh" (Brontë, *Villette*, 521). However, phrasing as similar occurs in so many New Testament texts that it becomes almost a cliché. In Rev. 3:3, the text reads, "I will come on thee as a thief, and thou shalt not know what hour I will come upon thee." The intercolumnar notes relate this text to Luke 12:39, "And this know, that if the goodman of the house had known what hour the thief would come, he would have watched, and not have suffered his house to be broken through. Be ye therefore ready also: for the Son of man cometh at an hour when ye think not." The intercolumnar notes of the Authorized Version refer the reader to a number of other related passages.

CHAPTER 5

1. George Eliot, *Daniel Deronda*, ed. Terence Cave (London: Penguin Books, 1995), 73. All further references in my text are to this edition and will be cited parenthetically. Readers who have commented on George Eliot's punitive language include Sedgwick, *Between Men*; Neil Hertz, "George Eliot's Remainderman" (paper delivered at the MLA session "Psychoanalysis and Critical Theory," Chicago, Ill., 18 December 1985); Dianne F. Sadoff, *Monsters of Affection: Dickens, Eliot, and Brontë on Fatherhood* (Baltimore: Johns Hopkins University Press, 1982); and Gilbert and Gubar, *Madwoman in the Attic*.

2. Laura Mulvey, "Visual Pleasure and Narrative Cinema," in *Feminisms: An Anthology of Literary Theory and Criticism*, ed. Robyn R. Warhol and Diane Price Herndl (New Brunswick, N.J.: Rutgers University Press, 1993). All further references to this essay in my text are to this edition.

3. Mulvey notes that "we are still separated by a great gap from important issues for the female unconscious," but that psychoanalytic theory "can at least advance our understanding of the status quo, of the patriarchal order in which we are caught" ("Visual Pleasure and Narrative Cinema," 439). My concern, however, is to read a historical discourse that does not conform to the "status quo" of History, thus using it as a lever to overturn *both* the traditionalist interpretation of history and Lacan's reading of this traditionalist interpretation back into a universalization of psychic development. I am here suggesting not an "alternative out of the blue," but that we can begin to make a break not only by examining patriarchy with the tools that psychoanalysis provides, but by examining psychoanalysis with the tools that "patriarchy" (i.e., a reading of now discarded patriarchal discourses) unwillingly provides.

4. Jacqueline Rose develops such a Lacanian reading of the novel in "George Eliot and the Spectacle of the Woman," making the interesting proposal that George Eliot *masquerades* as the male spectator whose gaze hystericizes woman (*Sexuality in the Field of Vision* [London: Verso, 1986], 105–22). Catherine Belsey, in "Re-Reading the Great Tradition," also discusses Gwendolen as "spectacle of woman" but suggests that the narrative constantly undermines this imaginary transcendence and constructs an "impossible resistance" to the patriarchal order (in *Re-Reading English*, ed. Peter Widdowson [London: Methuen, 1982], 121–35).

5. Jacques Lacan, "Signification of the Phallus," in *Ecrits: A Selection,* trans. Alan Sheridan (New York, c. 1977), 289. Jacqueline Rose explains that "castration means first of all this—that the child's desire for the mother does not refer to her but *beyond* her, to an object, the phallus, whose status is first imaginary (the object presumed to satisfy her desire) and then symbolic (recognition that desire cannot be satisfied). The place of the phallus in the account, therefore, follows from Lacan's return to the position and law of the father, but this concept has been reformulated in relation to that of desire"(introduction 2 to *Feminine Sexuality: Jacques Lacan and the Ecole Freudienne,* ed. Juliet Mitchell and Jacqueline Rose, trans. Jacqueline Rose [New York: W. W. Norton & Co., 1982], 38). The concept of castration has been "reformulated" in relation to that of a male concept of male desire. This circular formulation proposes that desire can have only a single, universal structure, and an uncritical reiteration of it leads to the reification of women's writing as always already structured by phallic desire. We can begin to undo this double oppression, however, by placing Lacan's theories in historical perspective, or by doing to them as Marianne Krüll proposes concerning Freud's theories, namely, testing them "carefully with a view to determining which of them merely served Freud to disguise important problems that impinged on Jacob's [his father's] taboo" (*Freud and His Father,* trans. Arnold J. Pomerans [New York: W. W. Norton & Co., 1986], 212).

6. In his introduction to the 1995 Penguin edition of *Daniel Deronda,* Terence Cave points out that a contemporary critic, James Picciotto, writing in the November 1876 issue of the *Gentlemen's Magazine,* noted that it was "singular" that Deronda "should never have suspected his origin, which ought to have left visible traces" (xvi). Writing in the twentieth century, Stephen Marcus notes that the "invisibility" of Deronda's circumcised penis demonstrated the unworkability of George Eliot's plot, since in order not to have known he was a Jew, he must never have "looked down"; and in Cynthia Chase's reading of the deconstruction of history and causality in the novel, the narrative "goes aground" on this "rock" (Marcus, *Representations: Essays on Literature and Society* [New York: Random House, 1976], 212; Chase, "The Decomposition of Elephants: Double-Reading *Daniel Deronda,*" *PMLA* 93 [March 1978]: 222). In "Daniel Deronda and Circumcision," however, K. M. Newton points out that circumcision—without anesthetic—was sometimes recommended in the nineteenth century as an "effective" deterrent to masturbation, when such other measures as the application of "blistering fluid" to the penis and the thighs had failed. Newton concludes that circumcision was an

"ambiguous sign" and that it promotes the "realism" of Deronda's quest to determine his own origin, since it suggests but does not prove that he may be a Jew—among other possibilities. However, Saleel Nurbhai and K. M. Newton's recent book, *George Eliot, Judaism, and the Novels: Jewish Myth and Mysticism* (New York: Palgrave, 2002), which posits George Eliot's long-term interest in Jewish mythology and history extending as far back as her first novel, *Adam Bede,* makes it seem more likely that she would have considered circumcision primarily in its Jewish context.

7. Mary Wilson Carpenter, "The Apocalypse of the Old Testament: *Daniel Deronda* and the Interpretation of Interpretation," *PMLA* 99 (January 1984): 56–71.

8. Patrick Fairbairn speaks of circumcision as "the initiatory ordinance" of all "symbolical" rites (*Hermeneutical Manual,* 2nd ed. [Philadelphia, 1859], 149). In describing circumcision as a rite practiced "between men," my emphasis derives from Sedgwick's revelatory analysis of the spectrum of homosocial relations between men constructed in English literary texts in *Between Men.*

9. Nancy Chodorow, *The Reproduction of Mothering: Psychoanalysis and the Sociology of Gender* (Berkeley: University of California Press, 1978).

10. Gordon Haight, *George Eliot, A Biography* (Oxford: Oxford University Press, 1968), 6.

11. Ruby Redinger, *George Eliot: The Emergent Self* (New York: Knopf, 1975). Rosemary Ashton suggests more simply that Mrs. Evans "is scarcely mentioned in George Eliot's surviving letters and journals, and when she does make an appearance there, we learn nothing of what she was like" (*George Eliot, A Life* [New York: Penguin Books, 1996], 17). Ashton does note that Mrs. Evans died of breast cancer, and that Mary Ann went home at Christmas, 1835, and was there when her mother died (18, 22).

12. Haight notes that twin sons were born to Mrs. Evans on 16 March 1821, when Mary Ann was less than a year and a half old. These twins lived only ten days, and their birth and death might be expected to have produced depression in the mother and traumatic repression in the little Mary Ann (*George Eliot, A Biography,* 3).

13. Both Haight and Redinger speak of the "night terrors" suffered by Mary Ann Evans after she was sent away to boarding school, and Redinger specifically links these to Gwendolen Harleth's terror (Haight, *George Eliot, A Biography,* 6; Redinger, *George Eliot, A Life,* 41–44, 64).

14. Hélène Cixous, *The Newly Born Woman,* trans. Betsy Wing, foreword by Sandra M. Gilbert (Minneapolis: University of Minnesota Press, 1986), 93.

15. Dianne Sadoff interprets "familial desire" in *Daniel Deronda* as a yearning for "filial ties," and "feelings of exile" as signaling a search for patrimony (*Monsters of Affection,* 103–4). I suggest here a very different emphasis. We may read Mordecai's vision of recovering a Jewish homeland instead as a poeticization of the desire for the lost mother, for, according to Freud, "'Love is homesickness'; and whenever a man dreams of a place or a country and says to himself, while he is still dreaming: 'this place is familiar to me, I've been here before,' we may interpret the place as being his mother's genital or her body" ("The Uncanny," in *The Standard Edition of the Complete Psychological Works of Sigmund Freud,* translated by James Strachey in collaboration with Anna Freud, assisted by Alix Strachey and Alan Tyson [London: Hogarth Press and the Institute of Psycho-Analysis, 1955], 17:245). Jane Gallop elaborates here: "Freud says of homesickness that it can be understood psychoanalytically as a longing to return to the womb, that the lost homeland is the mother's womb" (*Reading Lacan* [Ithaca: Cornell University Press, 1985], 148).

16. It was Mary Ann Evans's father who took her away to school, as it was her father who later brought her home for occasional weekends (Haight, *George Eliot, A Biography,* 6).

17. Mirah's first name may testify as well to a "double-edged" female history, for it appears to be a made-up name composed of the first three letters of Miriam—the only other female prophet

in the Old Testament, and one whose song also celebrates murder and vengeance (Exod. 15:21)—and the last two letters of Deborah. The idiosyncratic spelling of the name with an "i" suggests the Hebrew name Mira, a short form of Miriam, rather than the English name Myra.

18. It is interesting to note that in this story of maternal rejection by an artist mother, feminism is located on the daughter's side: the narrator comments that Catherine Arrowpoint's declaration of her intention to marry the man of her choice results from "Nature's" mistake in first making an only child a daughter and then in endowing that "misplaced daughter with a clear head and a strong will," such that she refuses to "consider herself an appendage to her fortune" (279). Catherine is thus a counterpart to Daniel's mother, yet we find the narrative in support of this feminist artistry, so long as it is located in the daughter rather than the mother.

19. See the Book of Ezra, especially chapters 9 and 10, in which Ezra prevails upon the Jews to separate themselves from the "strange wives of the people of the land" with whom they have intermarried.

20. Debra Cash, "Klezmer Music Makes a Comeback," *Boston Globe Magazine,* 28 February 1982, 13–25. We see here that Klesmer is actually a very compatible name for the Arrowpoint daughter.

21. David A. Miller, *"Cage aux Folles:* Sensation and Gender in Wilkie Collins's *The Woman in White," Representations* 14 (spring 1986): 107.

22. William Smith, *A Dictionary of the Bible, Comprising its Antiquities, Biography, Geography and Natural History,* 2 vols. (Boston, 1860; vol. 3 published 1863), 1:330. An edition was published simultaneously by J. Murray in London. Smith (1813–93) was a self-educated classicist who later obtained a degree from University College. The bible dictionary is considered his greatest work, and it certainly attained an unprecedented degree of popularity. The National Union Catalog lists sixty-one editions, and this is an incomplete list. Smith was eventually knighted for his efforts.

23. Even when a dictionary entry supplied some such definition as "the cutting off of the foreskin," the reader was likely to be stymied by the absence of a definition of "foreskin."

24. John P. Muller and William J. Richardson, *Lacan and Language: A Reader's Guide to Ecrits* (New York: International Universities Press, 1982), 337. Jane Gallop goes further, pointing to Lacan's apparent slip in speaking of the "real phallus," as if there might be such a thing, and to a still more (apparently) unconscious slip in characterizing the castration complex as a "knot," since the French word for knot is "a well-known crude term for 'penis'" (Lacan, "Signification," 289; Gallop, *Reading Lacan,* 156). Kaja Silverman states: "the inevitable conclusion to which Lacan's argument pushes us is that the phallus somehow mirrors or resembles the penis. The fundamental symmetry between the penis and the phallus within the Lacanian scheme is nowhere more startling evidently than in his seminars on Hamlet, where he remarks that 'Claudius's real phallus is always somewhere in the picture' (50)" (*The Subject of Semiotics* [Oxford: Oxford University Press, 1983], 187). Malcolm Bowie bluntly calls the Phallus the "male genital, transcendentalized" in *Lacan* (Cambridge: Harvard University Press, 1991), 142–43.

25. For example, *Cruden's Concordance* (first published in 1737 but reprinted throughout the nineteenth century), lists some forty references for "womb" but fewer than thirty for "circumcision" or "of circumcision."

26. Paul repeatedly insists in his epistles that "neither circumcision availeth any thing, nor uncircumcision" (Gal. 5:6), and he confronted Peter—to whom the "gospel of the circumcision" was said to be committed—on the issue, evidently countering Peter's attempt to impose this and other aspects of the Mosaic law on converts (Gal. 2). Acts 15 recounts a movement to require circumcision "after the manner of Moses" among new converts to Christianity. Paul and Barnabas disputed this idea, and a compromise was reached that new converts be required only to "abstain from pol-

lutions of idols, and from fornication, and from things strangled, and from blood" (15:20). Nevertheless, to satisfy the demands of some, Paul himself circumcised Timothy, a disciple whose mother was Jewish but whose father was Greek (Acts 16:3). References to the "meaning" of circumcision occur in Philippians, Colossians, Romans, and Ephesians, and the debate on circumcision appears to be the overriding concern of the Epistle to the Galatians.

27. Charles Knight, *The Penny Cyclopedia,* vol. 7 (London, 1837).

28. John Lawson and John M. Wilson, *Cyclopedia of Biblical Geography, Biography, Natural History, and General Knowledge,* 2 vols. (Edinburgh, London, and Dublin, 1866), 604.

29. Patrick Fairbairn, *Imperial Bible-dictionary, historical, biographical, geographical and doctrinal* (London, 1867), 1:332–35, 600.

30. John Kitto, ed., *The Cyclopedia of Biblical Literature,* 10th ed., 2 vols. (New York, 1851), 1:439–42.

31. Many bible dictionaries allude to this practice, especially as described in the apocryphal work, 1 Maccabees, in which certain Jews in the time of Antiochus Epiphanes are said to have built a gymnasium in Jerusalem and "made themselves uncircumcised, and forsook the holy covenant and joined themselves to the heathen, and were sold to do mischief" (1 Macc. 1:15). Paul urged new converts not to "become uncircumcised" (1 Cor. 7:18). William Lindsay Alexander's edition of *Kitto's Cyclopedia* suggests that there were two methods: "Sometimes this was done by a surgical operation, such as Celsus describes . . . sometimes by other means" (*Kitto's Cyclopedia,* 4th ed., 2 vols., under the direction of C. Taylor [London, 1845], "Circumcision," נ פ) *Calmet's Dictionary of the Bible* suggests that "many Jews used art to enlarge their foreskin," for "Jerom and others have affirmed that the mark of circumcision was indelible." On the other hand, the writer continues, "Epiphanius speaks of the instruments used by physicians, and the means practised by them for this purpose. The celebrated physician, Carniolus Celsus, has a whole chapter on this subject" (*Calmet's Dictionary of the Bible, as published by the late Charles Taylor.* . . . [Boston, 1832]).

32. Maurice Bloch suggests that the complex circumcision ritual among the Merina people of Madagascar involves not only the positive blessing of a line of descent—the power to obtain wealth, strength, and progeny—but the strong devaluation of entities associated with birth and female reproduction such as the house and warmth. The male child must be exited from the house, symbolizing birth "by violence"—that is, with the violence of circumcision, performed among this people when the boy is one or two years old. After the violence of the operation the excised foreskin is consumed by a male observer and the child is then handed back into the house to his mother through a window, thus enacting a "re-entry into the tamed feminine world." Circumcision is therefore both "a fertility ritual and an antibirth ritual." Although women are humiliated in the ritual, Bloch suggests they are willing to participate because it secures the blessing of descent for both men and women, whereas birth seems to belong to women alone. Although Bloch feels strongly that "gender antagonism" is not the main focus of the ceremony, he summarizes its central meanings as follows: "Circumcision is the demonstration that blessing is the true transcendental source of eternal life through descent. This is established by the denial of the value of sexuality, birth, women and nature; however, this refined solution although suitable for the ancestors is not suitable for the living. In this world women, sex, birth and nature cannot be finally expelled: they have to be reintroduced if life is to be life, but violently conquered" (Bloch, *From Blessing to Violence: History and Ideology in the Circumcision Ritual of the Merina of Madagascar* [Cambridge: Cambridge University Press, 1986], 84–104).

33. Johann David Michaelis, *Commentaries on the Laws of Moses,* trans. from the German by Alexander Smith (London: 1814), vol. 3, bk. 4, 61.

34. *The Oxford English Dictionary* notes that "manustupration" is an etymologizing alteration of "masturbation." The earliest reference given for it is a medical dictionary published in 1832: James Copland, *Dictionary of Practical Medicine.*

35. It's interesting that the word Alexander Smith chooses for his translation, "prepuce," probably would not have been known to most (nonmedical) English readers, for the word used in the Authorized Version is "foreskin."

36. Circumcision was "a bloody ordinance," he wrote, suggesting an allusion to the words of Moses' wife, Zipporah, when she cut off the foreskin of her son with a sharp stone, cast it at the feet of her husband, and said, "A bloody husband thou art, because of the circumcision" (Exod. 4:25–26) (Matthew Henry, *An Exposition of the Old and New Testament,* ed. George Burder and Joseph Hughes, 1st American ed. [Philadelphia, 1830], 107–8).

37. Patricia Yaeger, "The Case of the Dangling Signifier: Phallic Imagery in Eudora Welty's 'Moon Lake,'" *Twentieth Century Literature* 28 (winter 1982): 431–52.

38. John Keble, *The Christian Year* (Boston, 1867), 35, 37.

39. Jacques Derrida speaks of the date as like a circumcision in that it may be considered as a "cut" or "incision" that the poem (literary text) bears in its "body" like a memory, or like several memories. The date marks both a "one-and-only-time" and a "spectral return," for the date would be unreadable if it did not "recur" in our reading of it (Derrida, "Shibboleth," in *Midrash and Literature,* ed. Geoffrey H. Hartman and Sanford Budick [New Haven: Yale University Press, 1986], 341). But Derrida follows other exegetes in his failure to comment on the gender implications of circumcision in the Western theological tradition.

40. As Jane Gallop states, "the institution of motherhood is a cornerstone of patriarchy. . . . The early mother may appear to be outside patriarchy, but that very idea of the mother (and the woman) as outside of culture, society, and politics is an essential ideological component of patriarchy" ("Reading the Mother Tongue: Psychoanalytic Feminist Criticism," *Critical Inquiry* 13 [winter, 1987]: 322.

CHAPTER 6

1. Hal Lindsey, *The Late Great Planet Earth* (Grand Rapids, Mich.: Zondervan Publishing House, 1970), vii.

2. According to Peter Steinfels, by 1990 *The Late Great Planet Earth* had sold twenty-eight million copies ("Bible's Last Book was Key to Cult," *New York Times,* 25 April 1993, 32).

3. Rev. John Cumming, *Apocalyptic Sketches,* 1st ser. (Philadelphia: Lindsay and Blakiston, 1855), n.p.

4. George Eliot, "Evangelical Teaching: Dr. Cumming," in *George Eliot: Selected Critical Writings,* ed. Rosemary Ashton (Oxford: Oxford University Press, 1992), 159.

5. *The Christian Observer* (in which Mary Ann Evans published her first poem, in 1840) printed two sequential review articles on recent English works on prophecy, suggesting that a surge in publications on this topic took place in the early 1820s (July 1825, 422–34; August 1825, 489–520).

6. Robert M. Kachur, "Repositioning the Female Christian Reader: Christina Rossetti as Tractarian Hermeneut in *The Face of the Deep,*" *Victorian Poetry* 35, no. 2 (summer 1997), 196.

7. Robert M. Kachur, "Getting the Last Word: Women and the Authoritative Apocalyptic Voice in British Literature, 1845–1900" (Ph.D. diss., University of Wisconsin, Madison, 1996), 7; Kachur, "Repositioning the Female Christian Reader," 194; 212, n. 5.

8. An electronic search of the British Library catalogue retrieved eight such explicit recommodifications, as well as many more "replies" to or disputes with the work. This search did not include such recommodifications as Cumming's, which does not refer to Elliott's work in its title.

9. Steven Goldsmith, *Unbuilding Jerusalem: Apocalypse and Romantic Representation* (Ithaca: Cornell University Press, 1993).

10. Adela Yarbro Collins, *Crisis and Catharsis: The Power of the Apocalypse* (Philadephia: Westminster Press, 1984), 173.

11. Yarbro Collins, *Crisis and Catharsis*, 121. Elisabeth Schüssler Fiorenza, *The Book of Revelation: Justice and Judgement* (Philadelphia: Fortress Press, 1985), 24, 199.

12. Tina Pippin, *Death and Desire: The Rhetoric of Gender in the Apocalypse of John* (Louisville, Ky.: Westminster/John Knox Press, 1992), 58.

13. Tina Pippin, *Apocalyptic Bodies: The Biblical End of the World in Text and Image* (New York: Routledge, 1999), 117.

14. Catherine Keller, *Apocalypse Now and Then: A Feminist Guide to the End of the World* (Boston: Beacon Press, 1996), 248.

15. Ernest R. Sandeen, *The Roots of Fundamentalism: British and American Millenarianism, 1800–1930* (Chicago: University of Chicago Press, 1970), 5.

16. Interestingly, Mark A. Knoll notes that "Miller's message was promoted in ways that were also typical of the period. Joseph V. Himes (1805–95), his main publicist, was a communications genius who popularized Miller's views in something over five million pieces of literature." It was in response to this "media barrage," according to Knoll, that "thousands (perhaps tens of thousands) waited expectantly for the Lord's return on March 21, 1843, and, when nothing happened then, on a second predicted date, October 22, 1844." (*A History of Christianity*, 193).

17. Barbara Taylor, *Eve and the New Jerusalem: Socialism and Feminism in the Nineteenth Century* (London: Virago Press, 1983), 123.

18. On Joanna Southcott and the millenarian tradition in nineteenth-century Britain, see also J. F. C. Harrison, *The Second Coming: Popular Millennarianism, 1780–1850* (New Brunswick, N.J.: Rutgers University Press, 1979).

19. George Eliot, *The George Eliot Letters,* ed. Gordon Haight (New Haven: Yale University Press, 1954), 1:11–12.

20. Mary Wilson Carpenter, *George Eliot and The Landscape of Time: Narrative Form and Protestant Apocalyptic History* (Chapel Hill: The University of North Carolina Press, 1986), 5–11.

21. Rev. Edward Bishop Elliott, *Horae Apocalypticae; or, A Commentary on the Apocalypse, Critical and Historical; Including also an Examination of the Chief Prophecies of Daniel. Illustrated by an Apocalyptic Chart, and Engravings from Medals and Other Extant Monuments of Antiquity. With Appendices; containing, besides other matter, A Sketch of the History of Apocalyptic Interpretation, Critical Reviews of the Chief Apocalyptic Counter-Schemes, and Indices,* 5th ed., 4 vols. (London: Seeley, Jackson, & Halliday, 1862).

22. *Horae Apocalypticae* appeared in a three-volume edition in 1844, and four-volume editions in 1846, 1847, 1851, and 1862.

23. Rev. John Cumming, *Apocalyptic Sketches,* 2nd ser. (Philadelphia: Lindsay and Blakiston, 1854), 456.

24. *The Times,* 9 November 1859, n.p.

25. The speaker in the opening letters to the seven churches repeatedly claims to "have a few things against thee," implying the listener's secret guilt and likely punishment. See Mary Wilson Carpenter, "Representing Apocalypse: Sexual Politics and the Violence of Revelation," in *Postmod-*

ern Apocalypse: Theory and Cultural Practice at the End, ed. Richard Dellamora (Philadelphia: University of Pennsylvania Press, 1995), 114–15.

26. Carlyle presented his lectures in Exeter Hall in 1840 and published them in book form the year after.

27. Charlotte Brontë, *Jane Eyre,* ed. Beth Newman (Boston: Bedford Books, 1996), 441. All further references in my text are to this edition and will be made parenthetically.

28. Gayatri Chakravorty Spivak, "Three Women's Texts and a Critique of *Imperialism,*" as reprinted in *Feminisms,* 798.

29. See *Jane Eyre,* 304, for Rochester's contrast between the hell of West India and the "glorious liberty" of Europe. Spivak reads this as a key passage in the construction of "Europe and its not-yet-human Other, of soul making" ("Three Women's Texts," in *Feminisms,* 802).

30. After years of conquests and counterconquests, the Spanish ceded Jamaica to the British in 1671.

31. Carolyn Williams, "Closing the Book: The Intertextual End of *Jane Eyre,*" in *Victorian Connections,* ed. Jerome J. McGann (Charlottesville: University Press of Virginia, 1989).

32. Elizabeth Barrett Browning, *Aurora Leigh,* Norton Critical Edition, ed. Margaret Reynolds (New York: W. W. Norton & Co., 1996), 8:903–11. All further references in my text are to this edition and will be referred to parenthetically.

33. Margaret Forster, *Elizabeth Barrett Browning: A Biography* (London: Chatto and Windus, 1988), 49.

34. Cora Kaplan, introduction to *Aurora Leigh,* by Elizabeth Barrett Browning, ed. Cora Kaplan (London: The Women's Press, 1978), 5.

35. Marjorie Stone, *Elizabeth Barrett Browning* (London: Macmillan, 1995), 134, 137.

36. Margaret Reynolds, "[Allusion in the Verse-Novel: Experimental Bricolage]," in *Aurora Leigh,* ed. Reynolds, 553, 555. Marjorie Stone, in her thorough and discerning study of Barrett Browning's mythopoesis, "Juno's Cream: *Aurora Leigh* and Victorian Sage Discourse," notes that "Aurora is repeatedly affiliated with Biblical, classical, and even Muslim prophets and figures of wisdom, at times in a spirit of parody, at times in complete seriousness" (Stone, *Elizabeth Barrett Browning,* 145).

37. Helen Cooper details this symmetrical structure in *Elizabeth Barrett Browning, Woman and Artist* (Chapel Hill: University of North Carolina Press, c. 1988), 153–55. Also see Herbert F. Tucker, "*Aurora Leigh:* Epic Solutions to Novel Ends," in *Famous Last Words: Changes in Gender and Narrative Closure,* ed. Alison Booth (Charlottesville: University Press of Virginia, 1993), 64, 62.

38. As quoted in Kaplan's introduction, *Aurora Leigh,* ed. Kaplan, 13.

39. *Westminster Review* (January 1857). As quoted in *Aurora Leigh,* ed. Reynolds, 408.

40. Letter to Anna Jameson, 26 December 1856. As quoted in *Aurora Leigh,* ed. Reynolds, 340.

41. See Angela Leighton, *Victorian Women Poets: Writing against the Heart* (London: Harvester Wheatsheaf, 1992), 87–93, for her reading that in blinding Romney, Barrett Browning "attacks the whole sexually appreciating voyeurism of the literature she inherits." Gilbert and Gubar, in *Madwoman in the Attic,* 575–80, read the blinding of Romney and Aurora's willingness to see for him as "Barrett Browning's compromise aesthetic of service," but note that this conceals, but does not obliterate, "*Aurora Leigh*'s revolutionary impulses."

CONCLUSION

1. Pierre Bourdieu, *The Field of Cultural Production: Essays on Art and Literature,* edited and introduced by Randall Johnson (New York: Columbia University Press, 1993), 32.

2. Richard Altick, *The English Common Reader: A Social History of the Mass Reading Public, 1800–1900* (Chicago: University of Chicago Press, 1957), 100.

3. Mulvey, "Visual Pleasure and Narrative Cinema."

4. As quoted in Emily Eakin, "In Those Days, Too, Blood and Sex Could Make a Best Seller," *New York Times,* 31 August 2002, A17.

BIBLIOGRAPHY

Abelove, Henry, Michèle Aina Barale, and David M. Halperin, eds. *The Lesbian and Gay Studies Reader.* New York: Routledge, 1993.

Abrams, M. H. *Natural Supernaturalism: Tradition and Revolution in Romantic Literature.* New York: W. W. Norton & Co., 1971.

Agnew, Jean-Christophe. "Coming Up for Air: Consumer Culture in Historical Perspective." In *Consumption and the World of Goods,* edited by John Brewer and Roy Porter. New York: Routledge, 1993.

Alexander, William Lindsay, ed., under the direction of C. Taylor. *Kitto's Cyclopedia,* 4th ed. 2 vols. London, 1823, vol. 1, "Circumcision."

Allibone, S. A. *A Critical Dictionary of English Literature, and British and American Authors, Living and Deceased, from Earliest Accounts to the Middle of the Nineteenth Century.* 3 vols. Philadelphia: J. Lippincott, 1858–71.

Allott, Miriam, ed. *The Brontës: The Critical Heritage.* Boston: Routledge & Kegan Paul, 1974.

Alter, Robert, and Frank Kermode, eds. *The Literary Guide to the Bible.* Cambridge, Mass.: Belknap Press, 1987.

Altick, Richard. *The English Common Reader: A Social History of the Mass Reading Public, 1800–1900.* Chicago: University of Chicago Press, 1957.

Armstrong, Nancy. *Desire and Domestic Fiction: A Political History of the Novel.* Oxford: Oxford University Press, 1987.

Ashton, Rosemary. *George Eliot, A Life.* New York: Penguin Books, 1996.

Bannet, Eve Tavor. "The Marriage Act of 1753: 'A Most Cruel Law for the Fair Sex.'" *Eighteenth-Century Studies* 30, no. 3 (1997): 233–54.

Barker, Juliet. *The Brontës.* New York: St. Martin's Griffin, 1994.

Beal, Timothy K., and David M. Gunn, eds. *Reading Bibles, Writing Bodies.* New York: Routledge, 1997.

Belsey, Catherine. "Re-Reading the Great Tradition." In *Re-Reading English,* edited by Peter Widdowson. London: Methuen, 1982.

Bentley, G. E., Jr. "Images of the Word: Separately Published English Bible Illustrations, 1539–1830." *Studies in Bibliography* 47 (1994): 103–28.

Bentley, G. M., Jr., and Martin K. Nurmi. *A Blake Bibliography: Annotated Lists of Works, Studies, and Blakeana.* Minneapolis: Minnesota University Press, 1964.

Berg, Maggie. *Jane Eyre: Portrait of a Life.* Boston: Twayne Publishers, 1987.

Bermingham, Ann. Introduction to *The Culture of Consumption 1600–1800: Image, Object, Text,* edited by Ann Bermingham and John Brewer. New York: Routledge, 1995.

Bermingham, Ann, and John Brewer, eds. *The Culture of Consumption 1600–1800: Image, Object, Text.* New York: Routledge, 1995.

Bernheimer, Charles. *Figures of Ill Repute: Representing Prostitution in Nineteenth-Century France.* Cambridge: Harvard University Press, 1989.

Bernstein, Susan. *Confessional Subjects: Revelations of Gender and Power in Victorian Literature and Culture.* Chapel Hill: University of North Carolina Press, 1997.

Bible and Culture Collective, The. *The Postmodern Bible.* New Haven: Yale University Press, 1995.

Black, M. H. "The Printed Bible." In *The Cambridge History of the Bible.* Vol. 3, *The West, from the Reformation to the Present Day,* edited by S. L. Greenslack. Cambridge: Cambridge University Press, 1963.

Bloch, Maurice. *From Blessing to Violence: History and Ideology in the Circumcision Ritual of the Merina of Madagascar.* Cambridge: Cambridge University Press, 1986 (all quotations taken from chapter 5, "The Symbolism of Circumcision," 84–104).

Bloom, Harold. *The Anxiety of Influence: A Theory of Poetry.* New York: Oxford University Press, 1973.

Boone, Joseph A. "Depolicing *Villette:* Surveillance, Invisibility, and the Female Erotics of 'Heretic Narrative.'" *Novel* 26 (1992): 20–42.

Booth, Alison, ed. *Famous Last Words: Changes in Gender and Narrative Closure.* With an afterword by U. C. Knoepflmacher. Charlottesville: University Press of Virginia, 1993.

Bourdieu, Pierre. *The Field of Cultural Production: Essays on Art and Literature.* Edited with an introduction by Randall Johnson. New York: Columbia University Press, 1993.

Bowie, Malcolm. *Lacan.* Cambridge: Harvard University Press, 1991.

Brake, Laurel, Bill Bell, and David Finkelstein, eds. *Nineteenth-Century Media and the Construction of Identities.* New York: Palgrave, 2000.

Brantlinger, Patrick. *The Reading Lesson: The Threat of Mass Literacy in Nineteenth-Century British Fiction.* Bloomington: Indiana University Press, 1998.

Bray, Alan. *Homosexuality in Renaissance England.* With a new afterword by Alan Bray. New York: Columbia University Press, 1995.

Brewer, John. *Pleasures of the Imagination: English Culture in the Eighteenth Century.* New York: Farrar Straus Giroux, 1997.

Brewer, John, and Roy Porter, eds. *Consumption and the World of Goods.* New York: Routledge, 1993.

Brewer, John, and Susan Staves, eds. *Early Modern Conceptions of Property.* New York: Routledge, 1995.

Brontë, Charlotte. *Jane Eyre.* Edited by Beth Newman. Boston: Bedford Books, 1996.

———. *Villette.* Edited by Margaret Smith and Herbert Rosengarten, with an introduction and notes by Tim Dolin. Oxford: Oxford University Press, 2000.

Brown, John (1715–66). *Estimate of the Manners and Principles of the Times.* London, 1757.

Brown, John (1722–87). *The Self-Interpreting Bible.* Edinburgh, 1778.

Brown, Marshall, ed. *Eighteenth-Century Literary History: An MLQ Reader.* Durham, N.C.: Duke University Press, 1999.

Browning, Elizabeth Barrett. *Aurora Leigh.* Edited by Cora Kaplan. London: The Women's Press, 1978.

———. *Aurora Leigh,* Norton Critical Edition. Edited by Margaret Reynolds. W. W. Norton & Co., 1996.

Brownstein, Rachel M. *Becoming a Heroine: Reading about Women in Novels.* New York: The Viking Press, 1982.

———. "Representing the Self: Arnold and Brontë on Rachel." *Browning Institute Studies* 13 (1985): 1–23.

Bruce, F. F. *History of the Bible in English.* New York: Oxford University Press, 1978.

Burder, Samuel. *The Scripture Expositor.* London, 1809.

Calmet's Dictionary of the Holy Bible, as published by the late Charles Taylor . . . Boston, 1832.

Carpenter, Mary Wilson. "'A Bit of Her Flesh': Circumcision and 'The Significance of the Phallus' in *Daniel Deronda.*"*Genders* 1 (spring 1988): 1–23.

————"The Apocalypse of the Old Testament: *Daniel Deronda* and the Interpretation of Interpretation." *PMLA* 99 (January 1984): 56–71.

————. *George Eliott and the Landscape of Time: Narrative Form and Protestant Apocalyptic History.* Chapel Hill: University of North Carolina Press, 1986.

————. "Representing Apocalypse: Sexual Politics and the Violence of Revelation." In *Postmodern Apocalypse: Theory and Cultural Practice at the End,* edited by Richard Dellamora. Philadelphia: University of Pennsylvania Press, 1995.

————. "The Trouble with Romola." In *Victorian Sages and Cultural Discourse: Renegotiating Gender and Power,* edited by Thaïs E. Morgan. New Brunswick, N.J.: Rutgers University Press, 1990.

Castle, Terry. *The Apparitional Lesbian: Female Homosexuality and Modern Culture.* New York: Columbia University Press, 1993.

————. *Masquerade and Civilization: The Carnivalesque in Eighteenth-Century English Culture and Fiction.* Palo Alto: Stanford University Press, 1986.

Chase, Cynthia. "The Decomposition of the Elephants· Double-Reading *Daniel Deronda.*" *PMLA* 93 (March 1978): 215–27.

Chodorow, Nancy. *The Reproduction of Mothering: Psychoanalysis and the Sociology of Gender.* Berkeley: University of California Press, 1978.

Cixous, Hélène. *The Newly Born Woman.* Translated by Betsy Wing, foreword by Sandra M. Gilbert. Minneapolis: University of Minnesota Press, 1986.

Clarke, Adam. *The Holy Bible . . . with a critical commentary and notes.* 5 vols. London, 1825.

Cobbin, Ingraham. *Cottage Commentator on the Holy Scriptures.* London, 1928.

————. *The Oriental Bible.* London, 1850.

Colley, Linda. *Britons: Forging the Nation, 1707–1837.* New Haven: Yale University Press, 1992.

Collins, Adela Yarbro. *Crisis and Catharsis: The Power of the Apocalypse.* Philadelphia: Westminster Press, 1984.

————. "Persecution and Vengeance in the Book of Revelation." In *Apocalypticism in the Mediterranean World and the Near East: Proceedings of the International Colloquium on Apocalypticism, Uppsala, August 12–17, 1979,* edited by D. Hellholm. Tübingen, Germany: Mohr, 1983.

Collins, J. J. *Apocalypticism in the Dead Sea Scrolls.* New York: Routledge, 1997.

Collins, J. J., Bernard McGinn, and Stephen J. Stein. General introduction to *The Encyclopedia of Apocalypticism.* 3 vols. New York: Continuum, 1998.

Cooper, Helen. *Elizabeth Barrett Browning, Woman and Artist.* Chapel Hill: University of North Carolina Press, c. 1988.

Crompton, Louis. *Byron and Greek Love: Homophobia in Nineteenth-Century England.* Berkeley: University of California Press, c. 1985.

Crosby, Christina. "Charlotte Brontë's Haunted Text." *Studies in English Literature* 24 (1984): 701–15.

————. *The Ends of History: Victorians and "the Woman Question."* New York: Routledge, 1991.

Cruden's Concordance. East Northfield, Mass., n.d. (first published 1737).

Cumming, Rev. John. *Apocalyptic Sketches: Lectures on the Book of Revelation,* 1st ser. Philadelphia: Lindsay and Blakiston, 1855.

———. *Apocalyptic Sketches: Lectures on the Book of Revelation,* 2d ser. Philadelphia: Lindsay and Blakiston, 1854.

Davidoff, Leonore, and Catherine Hall. *Family Fortunes: Men and Women of the English Middle Class, 1780–1850.* Chicago: University of Chicago Press, 1987.

Dellamora, Richard. *Apocalyptic Overtures: The Sense of an Ending.* New Brunswick, N.J.: Rutgers University Press, 1994.

———, ed. *Postmodern Apocalypse: Theory and Cultural Practice at the End.* Philadelphia: University of Pennsylvania Press, 1995.

Derrida, Jacques. "Shibboleth." In *Midrash and Literature,* edited by Geoffrey H. Hartman and Sanford Budick. New Haven: Yale University Press, 1986.

Dictionary of National Biography, The. Edited by Sir Leslie Stephen and Sir Sidney Lee. Oxford: Oxford University Press, 1921–22 . . . 1967–68.

Digby, Anne. "Women's Biological Straitjacket." In *Sexuality and Subordination: Interdisciplinary Studies of Gender in the Nineteenth Century,* edited by Susan Mendus and Jane Rendall. New York: Routledge, 1989.

Donoghue, Emma. *Passions between Women: British Lesbian Culture, 1668–1801.* London: Scarlet Press, 1993.

Douglas, Mary. *Purity and Danger: An Analysis of Concepts of Pollution and Taboo.* C. 1966. Reprint, Boston: Ark Paperbacks, 1984.

Dowling, Linda. *Hellenism and Homosexuality in Victorian Oxford.* Ithaca: Cornell University Press, 1994.

Duberman, Martin, Martha Vicinus, and George Chauncey Jr., eds. *Hidden from History: Reclaiming the Gay and Lesbian Past.* New York: Meridian, 1989.

Dugaw, Dianne. *Warrior Women and Popular Balladry, 1650–1850.* Cambridge: Cambridge University Press, 1989.

Eilberg-Schwartz, Howard. "The Problem of the Body for the People of the Book." In *Reading Bibles, Writing Bodies,* edited by Timothy K. Beal and David M. Gunn. New York: Routledge, 1997.

Elfenbein, Andrew. "Stricken Deer: Secrecy, Homophobia, and the Rise of the Suburban Man." *Genders* 27 (1998), par. 6, as cited on http://www.genders.org.

Eliot, George. *Daniel Deronda.* Edited by Terence Cave. London: Penguin Books, 1995.

———. "Evangelical Teaching: Dr. Cumming." In *George Eliot: Selected Critical Writings,* edited by Rosemary Ashton. Oxford: Oxford University Press, 1992.

———. *The George Eliot Letters,* 9 vols. Edited by Gordon Haight. New Haven: Yale University Press, 1954.

Elliott, Rev. Edward Bishop. *Horae Apocalypticae; or, A Commentary on the Apocalypse, Critical and Historical; Including also an Examination of the Chief Prophecies of Daniel. Illustrated by an Apocalyptic Chart, and Engravings from Medals and Other Extant Monuments of Antiquity. With Appendices; containing, besides other matter, A Sketch of the History of Apocalyptic Interpretation, Critical Reviews of the Chief Apocalyptic Counter-Schemes, and Indices.* 5th ed., 4 vols. London, 1862.

Fairbairn, Patrick. *Hermeneutical Manual.* 2d ed. Philadelphia, 1859.

———. *Imperial Bible-dictionary, historical, biographical, geographical and doctrinal.* London, 1867.

———. *In Memory of Her: A Feminist Theological Reconstruction of Christian Origins.* New York: Crossroad, 1984.

Forster, Margaret. *Elizabeth Barrett Browning: A Biography.* London: Chatto and Windus, 1988.

Foucault, Michel. *The Birth of the Clinic: An Archaeology of Medical Perception.* Translated by A. M. Sheridan Smith. New York: Vintage Books, 1994.

———. *The History of Sexuality.* 1st American ed., vol. 1. Translated by Robert Hurley. New York: Random House, 1978.

———. "Nietzsche, Genealogy, History." In *Language, Counter-Memory, Practice,* edited with an introduction by Donald F. Bouchard. Translated from the French by Donald F. Bouchard and Sherry Simon. Ithaca: Cornell University Press, 1977.

———. "The Punitive Society." In *Michel Foucault: Ethics, Subjectivity, and Truth,* edited by Paul Rabinow, translated by Robert Hurley and others. New York: The New Press, 1997.

Freud, Sigmund. "Fetishism." In *The Standard Edition of the Complete Psychological Works of Sigmund Freud,* James Strachey, gen. ed. Vol. 21. London: Hogarth Press and the Institute of Psycho-Analysis, 1961.

———. "The Uncanny." In *The Standard Edition of the Complete Psychological Works of Sigmund Freud,* James Strachey, gen. ed. Vol. 17. London: Hogarth Press and the Institute of Psycho-Analysis, 1955.

Frye, Northrop. *Anatomy of Criticism: Four Essays.* Princeton: Princeton University Press, 1957.

———. *Fearful Symmetry: A Study of William Blake.* 1949. Reprint, Princeton: Princeton University Press, 1969.

Gallagher, Susan VanZanten. "*Jane Eyre* and Christianity." In *Approaches to Teaching Brontë's* Jane Eyre, edited by Diane Long Hoeveler and Beth Lau. New York: Modern Language Association of America, 1993.

Gallop, Jane. *Reading Lacan.* Ithaca: Cornell University Press, 1985.

———. "Reading the Mother Tongue: Psychoanalytic Feminist Criticism." *Critical Inquiry* 13 (winter 1987): 314–29.

———. *Thinking through the Body.* New York: Columbia University Press, 1988.

Gates, Henry Louis Jr., ed. *"Race," Writing, and Difference.* Chicago: University of Chicago Press, 1985.

Gerstenberger, Erhard S. *Leviticus: A Commentary.* Louisville, Ky.: Westminster/John Knox Press, 1996.

Gilbert, Sandra M., and Susan Gubar. *The Madwoman in the Attic.* New Haven: Yale University Press, 1979.

Gilman, Sander. "Black Bodies, White Bodies: Toward an Iconography of Female Sexuality in Late Nineteenth-Century Art, Medicine, and Literature." In *"Race," Writing, and Difference,* edited by Henry Louis Gates Jr. Chicago: University of Chicago Press, 1985.

Gissing, George. *The Odd Women.* New York: W. W. Norton & Co., c. 1977.

Goldsmith, Steven. *Unbuilding Jerusalem: Apocalypse and Romantic Representation.* Ithaca: Cornell University Press, 1993.

Greenslade, S. L., ed. *The West, from the Reformation to the Present Day.* Vol. 3 of *The Cambridge History of the Bible.* Cambridge: Cambridge University Press, 1963.

Gutjahr, Paul C. *An American Bible: A History of the Good Book in the United States, 1777–1880.* Palo Alto: Stanford University Press, 1999.

Haight, Gordon. *George Eliot, A Biography.* Oxford: Oxford University Press, 1968.

Hanson, Ellis. *Decadence and Catholicism.* Cambridge: Harvard University Press, 1997.

Hanson, Paul. *The Dawn of Apocalyptic.* Philadelphia: Fortress Press, 1975.

Harrison, J. F. C. *The Second Coming: Popular Millenarianism, 1780–1850.* New Brunswick, N.J.: Rutgers University Press, 1979.

Hartman, Geoffrey H., and Sanford Budick, eds. *Midrash and Literature.* New Haven: Yale University Press, 1986.

Hellholm, D., ed. *Apocalypticism in the Mediterranean World and the Near East: Proceedings of the International Colloquium on Apocalypticism, Uppsala, August 12–17, 1979.* Tübingen, Germany: Mohr, 1983.

Henry, Matthew. *An Exposition of the Old and New Testament.* 1st American ed. Edited by George Burder and Joseph Hughes. Philadelphia, 1830.

Hertz, Neil. "George Eliot's Remainderman." Paper delivered at MLA session, "Psychoanalysis and Critical Theory," Chicago, Ill., 18 December 1985.

Hoeveler, Diane Long, and Beth Lau, eds. *Approaches to Teaching Brontë's* Jane Eyre. New York: Modern Language Association of America, 1993.

Houghton, Walter. "Victorian Periodical Literature and the Articulate Classes." *Victorian Studies* 22, no. 4 (summer 1979): 389–412.

Howsam, Leslie. *Cheap Bibles: Nineteenth-Century Publishing and the British and Foreign Bible Society.* Cambridge: Cambridge University Press, 1991.

———. *SHARP News* 7, no. 4 (autumn 1998): 1.

Hughes, Linda K., and Michael Lund. "Textual/Sexual Pleasure and Serial Publication." In *Literature in the Marketplace: Nineteenth-Century British Publishing and Reading Practices,* edited by John O. Jordan and Robert L. Patten. Cambridge: Cambridge University Press, 1995.

———. *The Victorian Serial.* Charlottesville: University of Virginia Press, 1991.

Jenkins, Keith A. "Charlotte Brontë's New Bible." In *Approaches to Teaching Brontë's* Jane Eyre, edited by Diane Long Hoeveler and Beth Lau. New York: Modern Language Association of America, 1993.

———. "The Influence of Anxiety: *Bricolage* Brontë Style." Ph.D. diss., Rice University, Texas, 1993.

Jordan, John O., and Robert L. Patten, eds. *Literature in the Marketplace: Nineteenth-Century British Publishing and Reading Practices.* Cambridge: Cambridge University Press, 1995.

Kachur, Robert M. "Getting the Last Word: Women and the Authoritative Apocalyptic Voice in British Literature, 1845–1900." Ph.D. diss., University of Wisconsin, Madison, 1996.

———. "Repositioning the Female Christian Reader: Christina Rossetti as Tractarian Hermeneut in *The Face of the Deep,*" *Victorian Poetry* 35, no. 2 (summer 1997): 193–214.

Keble, John. *The Christian Year.* Boston, 1867.

Keller, Catherine. *Apocalypse Now and Then: A Feminist Guide to the End of the World.* Boston: Beacon Press, 1996.

Kent, Susan Kingsley. *Gender and Power in Britain, 1640–1990*. New York: Routledge, 1999.

Kitto, John, ed., *The Cyclopedia of Biblical Literature*. 10th ed., 2 vols. New York, 1851.

Knight, Charles. *The Penny Cyclopedia*. Vol. 7. London, 1837.

Knoepflmacher, U. C. "Avenging Alice: Christina Rossetti and Lewis Carroll." *Nineteenth Century Literature* 41, no. 3 (December 1986): 299–328.

Knoll, Mark A. *A History of Christianity in the United States and Canada*. London: SPCK, 1992.

———, et al., eds. *Evangelicalism: Comparative Studies of Popular Protestantism in North America, the British Isles, and Beyond, 1700–1990*. New York: Oxford, 1994.

Kowaleski-Wallace, Elizabeth. *Consuming Subjects: Women, Shopping, and Business in the Eighteenth Century*. New York: Columbia University Press, 1997.

Krueger, Christine L. *The Reader's Repentance: Women Preachers, Women Writers, and Nineteenth-Century Social Discourse*. Chicago: University of Chicago Press, 1992.

Krüll, Marianne. *Freud and His Father*. Translated by Arnold J. Pomerans. New York: W. W. Norton & Co., 1986.

Lacan, Jacques. *Ecrits: A Selection*. Translated by Alan Sheridan. New York: Norton, c. 1977.

———. *Feminine Sexuality: Jacques Lacan and the Ecole Freudienne*. Edited by Juliet Mitchell and Jacqueline Rose. Translated by Jacqueline Rose. New York: W. W. Norton & Co., 1982.

———. "The Mirror Stage as Formative of the Function of the I as Revealed in Psychoanalytic Experience." In *Ecrits: A Selection,* translated by Alan Sheridan. New York: Norton, c. 1977.

———. "The Signification of the Phallus." In *Ecrits: A Selection,* translated by Alan Sheridan. New York: Norton, c. 1977.

Lambert, Frank. "Pedlar in Divinity." *Journal of American History* 77, no. 3 (December 1990): 812–37.

Landow, George P. *Victorian Types, Victorian Shadows: Biblical Typology in Victorian Literature, Art, and Thought*. Boston: Routledge & Kegan Paul, 1980.

Langland, Elizabeth. *Nobody's Angels: Middle-Class Women and Domestic Ideology in Victorian Culture*. Ithaca: Cornell University Press, 1995.

Laqueur, Thomas. *Making Sex: Body and Gender from the Greeks to Freud*. Cambridge: Harvard University Press, 1990.

Lawson, John, and John M. Wilson. *Cyclopedia of Biblical Geography, Biography, Natural History and General Knowledge*. 2 vols. Edinburgh, London, and Dublin, 1866.

Lee, Martyn J. *Consumer Culture Reborn: The Cultural Politics of Consumption*. New York: Routledge, 1993.

Leighton, Angela. *Victorian Women Poets: Writing against the Heart*. London: Harvester Wheatsheaf, 1992.

Lewis, Reina. *Gendering Orientalism: Race, Femininity, and Representation*. London and New York: Routledge, 1996.

Lindsey, Hal. *The Late Great Planet Earth*. Grand Rapids, Mich.: Zondervan Publishing House, 1970.

Linley, Margaret. "A Centre that Would Not Hold: Annuals and Cultural Democracy." In *Nineteenth-Century Media and the Construction of Identities,* edited by Laurel Brake, Bill Bell, and David Finkelstein. New York: Palgrave, 2000.

Lister, Anne. *I Know My Own Heart: The Diaries of Anne Lister, 1791–1840.* Edited by Helena Whitbread. London: Virago, 1988.

————. *No Priest but Love: The Journals of Anne Lister from 1824–1826.* Edited by Helena Whitbread. New York: New York University Press, 1992.

Litvak, Joseph. *Caught in the Act: Theatricality in the Nineteenth-Century English Novel.* Berkeley: University of California Press, 1992.

Logan, Peter Melville. *Nerves and Narratives: A Cultural History of Hysteria in Nineteenth-Century British Prose.* Berkeley: University of California Press, 1997.

London, Bette. "The Pleasures of Submission: *Jane Eyre* and the Production of the Text." *ELH* 58 (1991): 196–213.

Lovell, Terry. "Subjective Powers? Consumption, the Reading Public, and Domestic Woman in Early Eighteenth-Century England." In *The Culture of Consumption, 1600–1800: Image, Object, Text,* edited by Ann Bermingham and John Brewer. New York: Routledge, 1995.

Lupton, Mary Jane. *Menstruation and Psychoanalysis.* Urbana: University of Illinois Press, 1993.

Maccubbin, Robert Purks. *'Tis Nature's Fault: Unauthorized Sexuality during the Enlightenment.* Cambridge: Cambridge University Press, 1987.

Marcus, Stephen. *Representations: Essays on Literature and Society.* New York: Random, 1976.

Marsh, Jan. *Christina Rossetti: A Writer's Life.* New York: Viking, 1994.

Matus, Jill. *Unstable Bodies: Victorian Representations of Sexuality and Maternity.* Manchester: Manchester University Press, 1995.

Maza, Sara. "Only Connect: Family Values in the Age of Sentiment: Introduction." *Eighteenth-Century Studies* 30, no. 3 (1997): 207–12.

McClintock, Anne. *Imperial Leather: Race, Gender, and Sexuality in the Colonial Contest.* New York: Routledge, 1995.

McDannell, Colleen. *Material Christianity: Religion and Popular Culture in America.* New Haven: Yale University Press, 1995.

McGann, Jerome J., ed. *Victorian Connections.* Charlottesville: University Press of Virginia, 1989.

McGinn, Bernard. "Early Apocalypticism: The Ongoing Debate." In *The Apocalypse in English Renaissance Thought and Literature,* edited by C. A. Patrides and Joseph Wittreich. Manchester: Manchester University Press, 1984.

McKendrick, Neil, John Brewer, and J. H. Plumb. *The Birth of a Consumer Society: The Commercialization of Eighteenth-Century England.* London: Europa Publications, 1982.

McKeon, Michael. "Historicizing Patriarchy: The Emergence of Gender Difference in England, 1660–1760." *Eighteenth-Century Studies* 28, no. 3 (1995): 295–322.

Mendus, Susan, and Jane Rendall, eds. *Sexuality and Subordination: Interdisciplinary Studies of Gender in the Nineteenth Century.* New York: Routledge, 1989.

Mermin, Dorothy. "Heroic Sisterhood in *Goblin Market.*" *Victorian Poetry* 21, no. 2 (summer 1983): 107–18.

Michaelis, Johann David. *Commentaries on the Laws of Moses.* Translated from the German by Alexander Smith. London, 1814.

Miller, David A. *"Cage aux folles:* Sensation and Gender in Wilkie Collins's *The Woman in White." Representations* 14 (spring 1986): 107–36.

Mitchell, Juliet, and Jacqueline Rose, eds. *Feminine Sexuality: Jacques Lacan and the Ecole Freudienne*. New York: W. W. Norton & Co., 1982

Moers, Ellen. *Literary Women*. Garden City, N.Y.: Doubleday, 1976.

Morgan, Thaïs E., ed. *Victorian Sages and Cultural Discourse: Renegotiating Gender and Power*. New Brunswick, N.J.: Rutgers University Press, 1990.

Muller, John P., and William J. Richardson. *Lacan and Language: A Reader's Guide to Ecrits*. New York: International Universities Press, 1982.

Mulvey, Laura. "Visual Pleasure and Narrative Cinema." In *Feminisms: An Anthology of Literary Theory and Criticism,* edited by Robyn R. Warhol and Diane Price Herndl. New Brunswick, N.J.: Rutgers University Press, 1993.

Nead, Lynda. *Myths of Sexuality: Representations of Women in Victorian Britain*. Oxford: Basil Blackwell, 1988.

Newton, K. M. "*Daniel Deronda* and Circumcision." *Essays in Criticism* 31 (1981): 313–27.

Noll, Mark A. *A History of Christianity in the United States and Canada*. London: SPCK, 1992.

Norton, Mary Beth. *Founding Mothers and Fathers: Gendered Power and the Forming of American Society*. New York: Vintage Books, 1996.

Nurbhai, Saleel, and K. M. Newton. *George Eliot, Judaism, and the Novels: Jewish Myth and Mysticism*. New York: Palgrave, 2002.

Nussbaum, Felicity A. *Torrid Zones: Maternity, Sexuality, and Empire in Eighteenth-Century English Narratives*. Baltimore: Johns Hopkins University Press, 1995.

O'Brien, Susan. "Eighteenth-Century Publishing Networks in the First Years of Transatlantic Evangelicalism." In *Evangelicalism: Comparative Studies of Popular Protestantism in North America, the British Isles, and Beyond, 1700–1990,* edited by Mark A. Noll, et al. New York: Oxford, 1994.

O'Leary, Stephen D. "Apocalypticism in American Popular Culture: From the Dawn of the Nuclear Age to the End of the American Century." In *Apocalypticism in the Modern Period and the Contemporary Age,* edited by J. J. Collins, Bernard McGinn, and Stephen J. Stein. Vol. 3 of *The Encyclopedia of Apocalypticism,* New York: Continuum, 1998.

Parker, Christopher, ed. *Gender Roles and Sexuality in Victorian Literature*. Aldershot, U.K.: Scolar Press, 1995.

Parker, Todd C. *Sexing the Text: The Rhetoric of Sexual Difference in British Literature, 1700–1750*. Albany: State University of New York Press, 2000.

Patrick, Simon. *Commentary upon the Historical Books of the Old Testament*. 2 vols. London, 1809.

Patrides, C. A., and Joseph Wittreich, eds. *The Apocalypse in English Renaissance Thought and Literature*. Manchester: Manchester University Press, 1984.

Penley, Constance, ed. *Feminism and Film Theory*. New York: Routledge, 1988.

Perry, Ruth. "De-familiarizing the Family; or, Writing Family History from Literary Sources." In *Eighteenth-Century Literary History: An MLQ Reader,* edited by Marshall Brown. Durham, N.C.: Duke University Press, 1999.

Pippin, Tina. *Apocalyptic Bodies: The Biblical End of the World in Text and Image*. New York: Routledge, 1999.

———. *Death and Desire: The Rhetoric of Gender in the Apocalypse of John*. Louisville, Ky.: Westminster/John Knox Press, 1992.

Poovey, Mary. *The Proper Lady and the Woman Writer: Ideology as Style in the Works of Mary Wollstonecraft, Mary Shelley, and Jane Austen.* Chicago: University of Chicago Press, 1984.

———. *Uneven Developments: The Ideological Work of Gender in Mid-Victorian England.* Chicago: University of Chicago Press, 1988.

Priestley, Timothy. *A Funeral Sermon, Occasioned by the Death of the Late Rev. Joseph Priestley.* London, 1804.

Pykett, Lyn. "The Cause of Women and the Course of Fiction: The Case of Mona Caird." In *Gender Roles and Sexuality in Victorian Literature,* edited by Christopher Parker. Aldershot, U.K.: Scolar Press, 1995.

Qualls, Barry. *The Secular Pilgrims of Victorian Fiction: The Novel as Book of Life.* Cambridge: Cambridge University Press, 1982.

Rabinow, Paul. Introduction to *Michel Foucault: Ethics, Subjectivity, and Truth.* Edited by Paul Rabinow. Translated by Robert Hurley and others. New York: The New Press, 1997.

Rambuss, Richard. *Closet Devotions.* Durham, N.C.: Duke University Press, 1998.

Redinger, Ruby. *George Eliot: The Emergent Self.* New York: Knopf, 1975.

Rich, Adrienne. "Compulsory Heterosexuality and Lesbian Existence." In *Powers of Desire: The Politics of Sexuality,* edited by Ann Snitow, Christine Stansell, and Sharon Thompson. New York: Monthly Review Press, 1983.

Rose, Jacqueline. Introduction 2 to *Feminine Sexuality: Jacques Lacan and the Ecole Freudienne,* edited by Juliet Mitchell and Jacqueline Rose, translated by Jacqueline Rose. New York: W. W. Norton & Co., 1982.

———. *Sexuality in the Field of Vision.* London: Verso, 1986.

Rose, Mark. "The Author as Proprietor: *Donaldson v. Becket* and the Genealogy of Modern Authorship." *Representations* 23 (summer 1988): 51–85.

Rosenthal, Laura J. "(Re)Writing Lear: Literary Property and Dramatic Authorship." In *Early Modern Conceptions of Property,* edited by John Brewer and Susan Staves. New York: Routledge, 1995.

Rossetti, Christina. *The Face of the Deep: A Devotional Commentary.* London, 1892.

Sadoff, Dianne F. *Monsters of Affection: Dickens, Eliot, and Brontë on Fatherhood.* Baltimore: Johns Hopkins University Press, 1982.

Said, Edward. *Orientalism.* New York: Vintage Books, 1979.

Samuel, Raphael. *Island Stories: Unravelling Britain.* Vol. 2 of *Theatres of Memory,* edited by Alison Light with Sally Alexander and Gareth Stedman Jones. London and New York: Verso, 1998.

Sandeen, Ernest R. *The Roots of Fundamentalism: British and American Millenarianism, 1800–1930.* Chicago: University of Chicago Press, 1970.

Sandner, David. "The Little Puzzle: The Two Shipwrecks in Charlotte Brontë's *Villette*." *English Language Notes* 36 (March 1999): 67–75.

Schüssler Fiorenza, Elisabeth. *The Book of Revelation: Justice and Judgement.* Philadelphia: Fortress Press, 1985.

Scott, Thomas. *The Holy Bible . . . with original notes . . . by Thomas Scott.* London, 1788–92.

Sedgwick, Eve Kosofsky. *Between Men: English Literature and Male Homosocial Desire.* New York: Columbia University Press, 1985.

———. *Epistemology of the Closet.* Berkeley: University of California Press, 1990.

Showalter, Elaine. *A Literature of Their Own: British Women Novelists from Brontë to Lessing.* Princeton: Princeton University Press, 1977.

Showalter, Elaine, and English Showalter. "Victorian Women and Menstruation." In *Suffer and Be Still: Women in the Victorian Age,* edited by Martha Vicinus. Bloomington: Indiana University Press, 1973.

Shuttleworth, Sally. *Charlotte Brontë and Victorian Psychology.* Cambridge: Cambridge University Press, 1996.

Silverman, Kaja. *The Subject of Semiotics.* New York: Oxford University Press, 1983.

Sinfield, Alan. *The Wilde Century: Effeminacy, Oscar Wilde, and the Queer Movement.* London: Cassell, 1994.

Slater, Samuel. *A Discourse of the Closet (or Secret) Prayer.* London, 1691.

Smith, Margaret, ed. *Letters of Charlotte Brontë: With a Selection of Letters by Family and Friends.* Oxford: Clarendon Press, 1995.

Smith, William. *A Dictionary of the Bible, Comprising Its Antiquities, Biography, Geography, and Natural History.* 3 vols. Boston, 1860–63.

Smith-Rosenberg, Carroll. *Disorderly Conduct: Visions of Gender in Victorian America.* New York: A. A. Knopf, 1985.

Snitow, Ann, Christine Stansell, and Sharon Thompson, eds. *Powers of Desire: The Politics of Sexuality.* New York: Monthly Review Press, 1983.

Spivak, Gayatri Chakravorty. "Three Women's Texts and a Critique of *Imperialism.*" In *Feminisms: An Anthology of Literary Theory and Criticism,* edited by Robyn R. Warhol and Diane Price Herndl. New Brunswick, N.J.: Rutgers University Press, 1993.

Stanton, Elizabeth Cady, and the Revising Committee. *The Woman's Bible.* 1898. Reprint, Seattle: Coalition on Women and Religion, 1984.

Stein, Stephen J., ed. *Apocalypticism in the Modern Period and the Contemporary Age,* vol. 3 of *The Encyclopedia of Apocalypticism,* edited by J. J. Collins, Bernard McGinn, and Stephen J. Stein. New York: Continuum, 1998.

Stockton, Kathryn Bond. *God between Their Lips: Desire between Women in Irigaray, Brontë, and Eliot.* Palo Alto: Stanford University Press, 1994.

Stokes, John. "Rachel's 'Terrible Beauty': An Actress among the Novelists." *ELH* 51 (1984): 771–93.

Stoler, Ann Laura. *Race and the Education of Desire: Foucault's History of Sexuality and the Colonial Order of Things.* Durham: Duke University Press, 1995.

Stone, Marjorie. *Elizabeth Barrett Browning.* London: Macmillan, 1995.

Stout, Harry S. *The Divine Dramatist: George Whitefield and the Rise of Modern Evangelism.* Grand Rapids, Mich.: W. B. Eerdmans, c. 1991.

Straznicky, Marta. "Privacy, Playreading, and Early Modern Women's Closet Drama." Unpublished manuscript.

Surridge, Lisa. "Representing the 'Latent Vashti': Theatricality in Charlotte Brontë's *Villette.*" *Victorian Newsletter* 87 (spring 1995): 4–14.

Sussman, Herbert. *Fact into Figure: Typology in Carlyle, Ruskin, and the Pre-Raphaelite Brotherhood.* Columbus: Ohio State University Press, 1979.

Tayler, Irene. *Holy Ghosts: The Male Muses of Emily and Charlotte Brontë.* New York: Columbia University Press, 1990.

Taylor, Barbara. *Eve and the New Jerusalem: Socialism and Feminism in the Nineteenth Century.* London: Virago Press, 1983.

Taylor, Jefferys. *The Family Bible Newly Opened: With Uncle Goodwin's Account of It.* London, 1853.

Thompson, Leonard. *The Book of Revelation: Apocalypse and Empire.* New York: Oxford University Press, 1990.

Thompson, Mrs. *The Family Commentary; or, A Short and Easy Exposition of the New Testament, etc., etc. A New Edition.* 2 vols. London and York, 1836.

———. *The Family Expositor; or, A short and easy Exposition of the New Testament for the Use of the Family; or, The Private Reading of such persons as have neither leisure to read, nor the means of purchasing, books of larger comment.* 4 vols. York, London, Edinburgh, and Dublin, 1824.

Thormälen, Marianne. *The Brontës and Religion.* Cambridge: Cambridge University Press, 1999.

Trumbach, Randolph. "The Birth of the Queen: Sodomy and the Emergence of Gender Equality in Modern Culture, 1660–1750." In *Hidden from History: Reclaiming the Gay and Lesbian Past,* edited by Martin Duberman, Martha Vicinus, and George Chauncey Jr. New York: Meridian, 1989.

Tucker, Herbert F. "*Aurora Leigh:* Epic Solutions to Novel Ends." In *Famous Last Words: Changes in Gender and Narrative Closure,* edited by Alison Booth. Charlottesville: University Press of Virginia, 1993.

Veldman, Meredith. "Dutiful Daughter versus All-Boy: Jesus, Gender, and the Secularization of Victorian Society." *Nineteenth Century Studies* 11 (1997): 1–24.

Vicinus, Martha. *Independent Women: Work and Community for Single Women, 1850–1920.* Chicago: University of Chicago Press, 1985.

———. "'They Wonder to Which Sex I Belong': The Historical Roots of the Modern Lesbian Identity." In *The Lesbian and Gay Studies Reader,* edited by Henry Abelove et al. New York: Routledge, 1993.

———, ed. *Suffer and Be Still: Women in the Victorian Age.* Bloomington: Indiana University Press, 1973.

Wahrman, Dror. "Gender in Translation: How the English Wrote Their Juvenal, 1644–1815." *Representations* 65 (winter 1999): 1–41.

Walkowitz, Judith R. *Prostitution and Victorian Society: Women, Class, and the State.* Cambridge: Cambridge University Press, 1980.

Warhol, Robyn R., and Diane Price Herndl, eds. *Feminisms: An Anthology of Literary Theory and Criticism.* New Brunswick, N.J.: Rutgers University Press, 1993.

Widdowson, Peter, ed. *Re-Reading English.* London: Methuen, 1982.

Williams, Carolyn. "Closing the Book: The Intertextual End of *Jane Eyre.*" In *Victorian Connections,* edited by Jerome McGann. Charlottesville: University Press of Virginia, 1989.

Wiltenburg, Joy. *Disorderly Women and Female Power in the Street Literature of Early Modern England and Germany.* Charlottesville and London: University Press of Virginia, 1992.

Yaeger, Patricia. "The Case of the Dangling Signifier: Phallic Imagery in Eudora Welty's 'Moon Lake.'" *Twentieth Century Literature* 28 (winter 1982): 431–52.

———. *Honey-Mad Women: Emancipatory Strategies in Women's Writing.* New York: Columbia University Press, 1988.

INDEX

Note: Page numbers appearing in *italic type* refer to illustrations.

Index

Perry, Ruth, xx
Peterloo Massacre, 42
phalli, 169 n. 60
Phallus, 102, 110, 111, 112, 119, 180 n. 24; circumcision as, 114; penis as, 112–13; phallic instruments, 122–23; and power, 122; as signifier, 103
Pickwick Papers, The (Dickens), 43
Piozzi, Hester Thrale, 49–50
Pippin, Tina, 130, 147
plagiarism, 8–9, 80
playing: with biblical allusions, 71; and language, 84–85
Plumb, J. H., 166 n. 4
Poovey, Mary, 7
popery, 139
"Porteusian Bible" (1820), 36, 42
portrait albums, 56
Postmodern Bible, The (Bible and Culture Collective, 1995), 171 n. 25
power: in Book of Revelation, 130, and knowledge, 35–36; maternal, 108, 120–21; and Phallus, 122
pregnancy, 87–88
prepuce. *See* foreskin
property: bible as, 166 n. 3; and marriage, 175 n. 20
prophecy: popularity of, 133–34; publications on, 182 n. 5
Protestantism, 134, 136–37; and circumcision, 119; Reformation, 132–33, 134
Protestant's Family Bible, The (1780), 169 n. 51
psychoanalytic theory, xxii, 73, 177–78 n. 3
psychology, Victorian, 73–74
publishers: A. Fullarton & Company, 63; American, xvi, 66, 171 n. 21; Blackie & Son, 56–58, 64; of cheap bibles, 42–43; of Family Bibles, 5; restrictions against, xvi, 5; serials, 5, 65, 80
Puseyism. *See* Tractarianism
Pykett, Lyn, 65–66

Qualls, Barry, 173 n. 6

Rabinow, Paul, 35
Rachel (actress), 76, 174 n. 17
Rambuss, Richard, xix, 38–39, 165 n. 11, 170 n. 12
rape, 54, 144–45
Rayner, W., 5, 166 n. 3
reading: and bible, 171 n. 25; of bibles, 41; and language, 96; and the masses, 171 n. 26; surveillance and, 45; in *Villette*, 82
Redinger, Ruby, 105, 179 n. 13
Reform politics, 131
Religious Tract Society, 150
Revelation, 127, 133; in *Aurora Leigh*, 141; end

of, 137; epistolary section, 135; unclean spirits, 136; witnesses, 137; *see also under* biblical references
Revelation of St. John Briefly Explained, The (1851), 129
Richardson, William J., 112
Rider, W., 23
Roman Catholic Church, 136
Rose, Jacqueline, 178 n. 5
Rose, Mark, 166 n. 3
Rosenthal, Laura J., 166 n. 3
Rossetti, Christina, 9, 58, 64, 129, 173 n. 19
Royal Family Bible (1862–68), 54
Royal Universal Family Bible, The (1781), 9, 23, 169 n. 51
Rudd, Susanna, 49
Ruth, 52; in illustrations, 58, 61, 64

sadism, 101, 105
Sadoff, Dianne, 179 n. 15
Said, Edward, 40
Samuel, Raphael, 9, 45
Sandeen, Ernest R., 131
Sandner, David, 176 n. 26
Satan, 135
scorta mascula, 22, 23, 169 n. 41
scortum, 169 n. 41
Scott, Thomas, 80, 175 n. 23
Scott, William Bell, 64
Scripture Expositor, The (1809), 45–46
Sedgwick, Eve Kosofsky, 6, 38, 39, 175 n. 18, 177 n. 1
Self-Interpreting Bible, The (1778), 80, 81
separate spheres, 7
seven vials, 145
Seven Years' War (1756–63), 40
sexuality: and circumcision, 117; and difference, 167 n. 11; and Eastern customs, 46; and language, 97; and menstruation, 74–75; metaphors, 99–100; and Song of Solomon, 98; studies in Victorian, 6; unnatural, 37–38; women and, 90–91; women's cycle of, 94–95
Shittler, Robert, 51, 53
Showalter, Elaine, 94, 176 n. 25
Showalter, English, 176 n. 25
Shuttleworth, Sally, 73–74, 176 n. 30
Sinfield, Alan, 20
Sisera, 85, 91, 175 n. 24
"Sisters of Bethany, The," 59
Smith, William, 112, 115, 180 n. 22
social control, 44–45
social status, 152; and bible publication, 44; and education, 53; and Family Bibles, 44–45; lower classes, 44, 63; middle classes, 149–50, 152; and reading, 9,

205